PRISONS & PRISONERS
SOME PERSONAL EXPERIENCES
By CONSTANCE LYTTON and
JANE WARTON, Spinster

with a new introduction
by Midge Mackenzie

Published by VIRAGO PRESS Limited 1988
20–23 Mandela Street, London NW1 0HQ

First published by William Heinemann, London, 1914
Introduction copyright © Midge Mackenzie 1988

British Library Cataloguing in Publication Data

A CIP catalogue record for this book
is available from the British Library

Printed in Great Britain by Cox & Wyman Ltd
of Reading, Berkshire

CONTENTS

INTRODUCTION TO NEW EDITION

Prisons and Prisoners, Some Personal Experiences by Constance Lytton and Jane Warton, spinster, published in 1914, remains a unique document: the story of one woman's awakening to dedication and courage. A social reformer, with a discreet and genteel vision suitable to her aristocratic class, Lady Constance Lytton joined the ranks of the militant suffragists in 1909 and engaged in controversial and dangerous acts of political activism. This journal documents her personal journey of political transformation.

It is within a world of aristocratic tradition, as a member of the nobility, that Constance Lytton grew up, her childhood friends members of the Royal Family, her parents intimates of Queen Victoria. The third child of Robert, First Earl of Lytton, diplomat and poet, and Edith Villiers, she spent her childhood in Vienna, Paris and Lisbon, where her father was in the diplomatic service, and in India where, as Viceroy, he proclaimed Victoria Empress of India in 1877. On her father's death, the family experienced unexpected financial losses; as a result, Edith Villiers accepted the post of Lady-in-Waiting to Queen Victoria. It was not until 1905, when Constance Lytton was thirty-six, that she and her mother left the court and moved back to the family home, Knebworth in Hertfordshire. A chronic invalid since infancy, suffering from a weak heart and rheumatism, she lived quietly in the country.

Constance Lytton had an interest in music, and when, in 1906, she received a small inheritance from her godmother, Lady Bloomfield, she brought members of the Esperance Girls Club to her village to teach traditional folk dances to the villagers as a lively revival of "joy giving native arts". It was through this contact with the Esperance Girls Club that, quite uncharacteristically, she left her home and travelled to the Green Lady Hostel, a summer home for working girls from the city. Here, a chance meeting in the summer of 1908 with militant suffrage leaders Emmeline Pethick Lawrence and Annie Kenney caused Lady Constance to realise

at once that I was face to face with women of strong personality – a force greater than their own seemed behind them. Their remarkable individual powers seemed illumined and enhanced by a light that was apart from them as are the colours and patterns of a stained-glass window by the sun shining through it. I had never before come across this kind of spirituality. I have since found it a characteristic of all the leaders in the militant section of the women's movement, and many of the rank and file.

Emmeline Pethick Lawrence

met all my arguments, all my prejudices and false deductions with counter-arguments, and above all, facts of which, until then, I had no conception. I became a member of the Women's Social and Political Union on the twenty-eighth of January 1909. I wrote to Mrs Pethick Lawrence offering myself for the deputation. I did not tell anybody but her of my decision. On the thirtieth I received her answer, accepting my offer . . .

Arrested while a member of this deputation to the House of Commons, Constance Lytton appeared at Bow Street Court on 25 February. Sentenced to one month in prison, refusing to be bound over to keep the peace, she stated, "I have been more proud to stand by my friends in their trouble than I have ever been of anything in my life before." The deep and passionate spirituality that had been inward turning, contemplative, quiescent, and silent, was transformed to action. And within that action she discovered the joy of shared purpose and friendship. Like most Victorian women, she had been imbued with the moral ideal of the sacrifice of self, and there was no greater cause than the militant campaign to evoke this sense of purpose.

Constance Lytton had long been an advocate for prison reform. In describing her conversion to the militant campaign, she makes reference to a speech by Emmeline Pankhurst:

I felt taken hold of by the movement. Every sentence of it appeared to be true, dignified, strong, entirely respectful. This passage I more especially remember: You know that women have tried to do something to come to the aid of their own sex . . . I was in the hospital at Holloway, and when I was there I heard from one of the beds near me the moans of a woman who was in the pangs of childbirth. I should like you to realise how women feel at helpless little infants breathing their first breath in the atmosphere of prison. We believe that if we get the vote we will find more humane ways of dealing with women than that.

In prison, the exposure of the middle-class militants to the pain and suffering of the poorest and most abject women, incarcerated for petty theft, concealment of birth, prostitution or vagrancy, served only to confirm the need for major social reform. Imprisonment was an education for the suffragettes, and this hard-won knowledge invigorated their motivation and commitment to continue militant action in the battle for women's rights.

The fulcrum of the campaign was the unleashed passion of the women. The campaign of imprisonment, violence and broken health waged against them did not break their spirits but reinforced their strength and belief that their battle was just. The evangelical fervour of the militants, most especially Christabel Pankhurst, ignited a prairie fire among their ranks. To Lady Constance, Christabel was

the sunrise of the women's movement . . . The glow of her great vitality and the joy of her being took hold of the movement and made it gladness. Yet, her nature being so essentially a woman's, there was a vein of tenderness throughout her speech, and her strength lay in her steadfast, resourceful and brilliant intellect.

Militancy under Christabel's leadership, dedicated to "Deeds not Words", escalated from public demonstrations, stone throwing and imprisonment to hunger striking, arson and ultimately death.

In July 1909, George Bernard Shaw, a supporter of the militant campaign, wrote a topical sketch compiled from the editorial columns of the daily papers. It was banned by the censor on the grounds that it burlesqued public men. Prime Minister Asquith was presented as Mr Balsquith who, disguised as a suffragette, chains himself to a foot-scraper in order to reach the War Office to meet with the so-called General Mitchener. The stage directions read:

The Sufraget* takes off her tailor-made skirt and reveals a pair of fashionable trousers.
MITCHENER (Horrified): Stop, madam. What are you doing? You must not undress in my presence. I protest. Not even your letter from the Prime Minister —
THE SUFRAGET: My dear Mitchener, I am the Prime Minister ... (he continues) ... It has come to this: that the only way the Prime Minister of England can get down Downing Street to the War Office is by assuming this disguise; shrieking "Votes for Women", and chaining himself to your door-scraper.

The sketch continues and General Mitchener suggests that the militants be shot. Balsquith demurs but Mitchener is adamant:

MITCHENER: ... Military methods are really the most merciful in the end. You keep sending these misguided women to Holloway and killing them slowly and inhumanely by ruining their health; and it does no good: they go on worse than ever. Shoot a few promptly and humanely; and there will be an end

---

* In 1906 the *Daily Mail* first coined the term "suffraget" for the militant women of the WSPU. Prior to this, all women who had been involved in the campaign for the vote were known as suffragists.

of it at once of all resistance and of all the suffering that
resistance entails.
BALSQUITH: But public opinion would never stand it.
MITCHENER (walking about and laying down the law): There's
no such thing as public opinion.

The sketch, performed privately at the Court Theatre in
July 1909, had been written in response to the first
hunger strike by Wallace Dunlop, an artist, who had
entered the House of Commons and stencilled in large
letters on the wall of St Stephens Hall this aide-memoire
to the Government and members of Parliament:

WOMEN'S DEPUTATION JUNE 29. BILL OF RIGHTS. IT IS THE
RIGHT OF THE SUBJECTS TO PETITION THE KING, AND ALL
COMMITMENTS AND PROSECUTIONS FOR SUCH PETITIONS
ARE ILLEGAL.

Charged at Bow Street with "wilful damage", she was sent
to prison for one month.
Wallace Dunlop sent to the Home Secretary, William
Gladstone, an application to be placed in the first division
at Holloway Prison as befitted one charged with a political
offence. She announced that she would eat no food until
this right was conceded. Mr Gladstone did not reply, but
after she had fasted ninety-one hours, Wallace Dunlop
was set free. During the months from July to September
other militants followed her example, remaining in
prison on hunger strike for several days before being
released. In late September Gladstone intervened and
forcible feeding of the militants was introduced.
The following month in Newcastle, Constance Lytton, in
retaliation for the forcible feeding, was arrested after
throwing a stone, wrapped in paper, which carried the
inscription: "To Lloyd George — Rebellion against tyranny
is obedience to God — Deeds, not words." Sentenced to a
month's imprisonment, she went on hunger strike. After
two days she was released, the official reason being her
heart condition. Constance Lytton, however, believed she

had received preferential treatment because of her family and political connections: her brother was the Earl of Lytton and a member of the House of Lords. Women who were older and in far worse health than her were still being held and forcibly fed.

Determined to expose this unfairness, and the brutality of forcible feeding, she disguised herself as a working woman under the alias of Jane Warton. Arrested in Liverpool while protesting about forcible feeding in Walton Gaol, she was sentenced to two weeks in prison. She went on a hunger strike and was forcibly fed eight times before her true identity was discovered and she was released.

The year 1910 marked a truce for the militants as an all-party group in the House of Commons and the House of Lords attempted to pass a Conciliation Bill granting limited voting rights to women. But finally the Government blocked the Bill and in November the militant campaign resumed. A deputation sent to deliver a petition to the House of Commons received brutal treatment at the hands of the crowd and police. On Black Friday, 18 November 1910, Emmeline Pankhurst's sister, Mary Clarke, died from the brute force meted out against them.

Despite poor health, and a minor heart seizure, Constance Lytton returned to the militant campaign in November 1911: "I determined that I would do my work alone. I was afraid that, if I combined with others, I might fail them, through illness, when they counted on me." Arrested for smashing the windows of a post office on Victoria Street facing Westminster and the House of Commons, she was sentenced to prison and returned to Holloway.

The Women's War continued to escalate, and in March 1912 it culminated in a massive window-smashing raid on the fashionable streets of London – Regent Street, Bond Street and Oxford Circus. Thousands of pounds worth of damage was done. Emmeline Pankhurst wrote of this raid:

The panic stricken Government did not rest content with the imprisonment of the window-breakers. They sought in a blind and blundering fashion to perform the impossible feat of wrecking at a blow the entire militant movement. Governments have always tried to crush reform movements, to destroy ideas, to kill the thing that cannot die. Without regard to history, which shows that no government has ever succeeded in doing this, they go on trying in the old senseless way. The [WSPU] offices in Clements Inn were thoroughly ransacked by the police, in a determined effort to secure evidence of conspiracy.

Emmeline Pankhurst and Emmeline and Frederick Pethick Lawrence, the leaders of the Women's Social and Political Union, were convicted on conspiracy charges and imprisoned. Christabel Pankhurst, to evade trial, fled to safety in Paris to continue her leadership of the militant campaign. The militants continued to escalate their actions — now with dangerous acts of arson and the widescale destruction of property.

It is against this background that Constance Lytton wrote her journal. Partially paralysed as a result of a major heart attack in 1912, she learned, in the most painstaking manner, to write with her left hand. The desire and motivation to preserve and tell this story was not self-serving autobiography but an on-going political concern to get a reluctant and hostile public to understand the true nature of the militant campaign. The immediacy of her first-person testimony evoked the story of a militant during three critical years of the suffrage campaign: 1909–1912. The popular myth is that women were "given" the vote on the basis of their proven equality and emancipation during the First World War; in fact it was only part of a much more complex struggle, to which the militants, though small in number, made an important contribution. The lives of these women are not recorded in official histories, and works such as Constance Lytton's have been an important influence on my own research into other primary sources — journals, diaries and letters — for my book, *Shoulder to Shoulder* (1975), and the BBC drama series of the same name.

To understand the tone and mood of the disclaimer by the original publisher William Heinemann that precedes this prison journal is to understand a little of the public outcry — and sense of social outrage — that the militant suffrage campaign evoked:

The Publisher hopes that fault will not be found if he disclaims agreement with some of Lady Constance Lytton's views expressed in this volume, notwithstanding the fact that he is glad to offer it to the public. He feels that personal disagreement over details should not hinder him from publishing this splendid story of heroism and unselfishness.

The *details* that Heinemann does not refer to were the public acts of daring by the suffragettes — acts of defiance designed to challenge a traditional male-dominated government that excluded women.

Equally, these actions challenged the idealised concept of Victorian womanhood. Women were seen as gentle, genteel, reserved, soft-spoken, self-effacing, the effective spiritual guardians of the moral values of England. Within this female landscape, the militants were certainly seen as hooligans. Indeed, the first response of Constance Lytton, on meeting the militant suffrage leaders, was to criticise these confrontational "tactics" as unjustified, unreasonable, without a sense of political responsibility and as setting a bad example — a response totally in keeping with her own background and upbringing as well as popular opinion of the day. Much of the power in her journal lies in the authenticity of her response to the militant campaign. From critic to activist, the day-by-day documentation of her political awakening makes women's history vivid.

DEDICATION
TO PRISONERS

WHEN, for a short while, I shared your lot, I asked myself through all my waking hours if there were any friendly thought which could act beneficently for all prisoners, no matter how various the training of their previous lives, no matter whether distress of circumstance, drunkenness, selfish action, cruelty, or madness had been the cause which brought them into prison.

And there seemed this one thing. It is a single idea, but needs many words to give it shape.

Lay hold of your inward self and keep tight hold. Reverence yourself. Be just, kind and forgiving to yourself. For the inner you of yourself is surely the only means of communication for you with any good influence you may once have enjoyed or hope some day to find, the only window through which you can look upon a happier and more lovable life, the only door through which some day you will be able to escape, unbarring it to your own release from all that is helpless, selfish, and unkind in your present self.

Public opinion, which sent you to prison, and your gaolers, who have to keep you there, are mostly concerned with your failings. Every hour of prison existence will remind you of these afresh. Unless you are able to keep alight within yourself the remembrance of acts and thoughts which were good,

a belief in your own power to exist freely when you
are once more out of prison, how can any other
human being help you ?   If not the inward power,
how can any external power avail ?

But if you have this comforter within you, hourly
keeping up communication with all that you have
known and loved of good in your life, with all the
possibilities for good that you know of—in your
hands, your mind, your heart—then when you are
released from prison, however lonely you may be,
or poor, or despised by your neighbours, you will
have a friend who can really help you.

There will be people who visit you in prison,
and who watch over you at first when you come
out.   They will try to help you, but unless they
truly understand your lot, understanding your goodness as well as your badness, and sympathising with
your badness as well as with your goodness, they
will seem far off from you.   Who knows, though,
but what you may help them ?   In my ignorance
and impudence I went into prison hoping to help
prisoners.   So far as I know, I was unable to do
anything for them.   But the prisoners helped me.
They seemed at times the direct channels between
me and God Himself, imbued with the most friendly
and powerful goodness that I have ever met.

Prisoners, I wish I could give to you, for your
joy, something of the help you gave to me, and that
in many ways I could follow your example.

CHAPTER I

INTRODUCTION

SOME of the experiences which I have to record are of so unusual a character that I think it will help to a better understanding on the part of my readers if I briefly outline the drift of my existence before I became aware of the women's movement, and in touch with that section of it known as the " Militant Suffragettes."

My father had been dead fifteen years and I was thirty-nine years old in 1906, when my narrative begins. I lived with my mother in the country. Two sisters and two brothers had left the home when they were young—the sisters to marry, the brothers to train for and enter their professions. I assumed, as did all my friends and relations, that, being past the age when marriage was likely, I should always remain at home. In my early girlhood I had a yearning to take up music professionally ; again, after father's death, when unexpected financial misfortunes caused my mother great anxiety, I had longed to try my hand at journalism ; and once more, a few years later, I had the same ambition. But these wishes, finding no favour, had in each case eventually to be repressed, and in 1906 I had neither equipment, training nor inclination for an independent life.

I had been more or less of a chronic invalid through

the greater part of my youth.   An overmastering
laziness and a fatalistic submission to events as they
befell were guiding factors in my existence.   I was
passionately fond of animals and of children, music
was a great delight to me ; otherwise I was not given
to intellectual pursuits.   So far as I know, I was an
average ordinary human being, except perhaps for
an exaggerated dislike of society and of publicity in
any form.   I had many intimate friends, both men
and women, and also children.   Such mental training as I have known was chiefly due to intercourse
with them.   I owed to them, as well as to my
mother and many members of my family, a happy
life, in spite of considerable physical suffering.

In 1896 and successive years I had given secre-
tarial help to my aunt, Mrs. C. W. Earle, in the
writing of her wonderfully delightful books, beginning with " Pot Pourri from a Surrey Garden." She
insisted that, in return for my small and mostly
mechanical services, we should share the profits of
the sale.   The book ran into many editions, and she
held to her bargain, but I never felt as if I had a
right to the money.   Her widely sympathetic and
stimulating companionship had a great influence on
my mind.   Thanks to her investigations in theories
of diet, I became a strict vegetarian.   My health
gained in all directions and I gradually freed myself
from the so-called " constitutional " rheumatism
from which I had suffered since my infancy.   I
realised, too, that all these years I had caused untold
suffering that I might be fed, and determined that
in future the unnatural death of an animal should
not be necessary to make up my bill of fare.   My

vitality increased, but the notion of a vocation apart from my family and home remained as foreign to my ideas as it was then to the average British spinster of my class.

In the year 1906 my godmother, Lady Bloomfield, died. She had shown me much kindness and I had never found an opportunity to serve her in any way, the generosity had been all on her side ; yet, at her death, she left me some money, without any conditions as to how I should spend it. It gave me a strange new feeling of power and exhilaration. I look back upon this event as being spiritually the starting point in my new life, of which this book will tell, although, from the practical point of view, it seems only by a series of coincidences that my after experiences were evolved from it.

I looked about me with a view to spending the money. I had a fancy to put it to some public use. The commonly accepted channels of philanthropy did not appeal to me. I shifted my inquiries in other directions. I remember that at this time I was chiefly occupied with the idea that reformers were for the most part town dwellers, their philosophy and schemes attuned to those surroundings. There seemed to me need for a counteracting influence to attempt reform and regeneration on behalf of country dwellers. The noiseless revolution which had been worked in a few decades by the system of compulsory education seemed to me tainted throughout by the ideals of townsfolk. The influence of teachers and clergy, of public authorities in general, sets before the nation's children and their parents ideals which mould them into townsfolk.

Country craft and country lore grow less, and are less
honoured in every decade. There is no room for
them in the national curriculum. This tendency,
nevertheless, seems unnatural, imposed by a species
of force on a reluctant though inarticulate people.
Some temperaments cannot acclimatise themselves
to town dwelling. The life of cities will always
appear to them artificial, repellent from the physical
conditions it imposes and the mental outlook resulting from these. Rain, earth and air are better
scavengers than any municipal corporation. The
ceaseless cleansing, yet never making clean, of town
existence has from my childhood fretted my imagination and produced a sense of incarceration. In
towns, the earth is laid over with tombstones,
metalled roads or floors of wood. Avenues of bricks
and mortar shut out a great part of the sky, limiting
into a mere ceiling the heavens which should be our
surrounding. A town had always seemed to me a
" deterrent " workhouse at best, and often a punitive
prison besides.

The monster of industrialism, which followed in
the wake of the discovery of steam and the dethron-
ing of handicraft by artificially-propelled machinery,
may one day be bridled and controlled so as to be a
servant of humanity, a fellow worker in the day-to-
day glory of creation ; but for the present it is still
a wild beast, a dragon at large, dealing pestilence
and death with its fiery breath, combated in panic,
its evils evaded rather than faced, its power a nightmare breeding fear and subjection. Instead of
harnessing this new force to every branch of our
existence, ordering it to serve us at our command,

we have cringed before it, left our normal lives and
drained our energies to congregate in its grimy
temples and worship at its shrine. Poor, blind
force that it is, we are determined to make it an
idol, and for sake of the return in money which its
mechanical rotations produce, we have been willing
to sacrifice the interests both of the human beings
which should control it and of the soil, the land,
which alone can produce the raw material for its
task.

How to transform this Moloch from a tyrannous
master to a helpful, submissive friend, that was the
problem which seemed to cry out for solution above
all others. I looked around to see how the needs
of country folk were able to express themselves,
and everywhere there was presented to my inquiries
a complicated machinery of administration both
national and local—voting rights for election of
parliamentary, municipal, county, district and
parish councils. But this machinery was apparently
born and bred of urban conditions, super-imposed
upon the rural districts, in no way native to them,
not of spontaneous growth. This succession of
councils, instituted with the apparent purpose of
watching one another, and, if necessary, bringing
pressure to bear upon one another, were for the
most part lifeless formalities, having no organic life,
no breath of reality to set them in motion. The only
function which gives them any tangible vitality is
their power of imposing taxation and levying rates.
You find in the country districts that members of
these different bodies are the same individuals.
The parish councillor who is expected to bring

pressure to bear on the district councillor, who
again must appeal, if need be, to the county councillor, is one and the same person who, as likely as
not, is also the representative of the district on the
board of guardians, and he is sure to be selected
again to work the administrative machinery of
every new device that comes along for the ameliora-
tion of social evils. In other words, the elective
principle is a farce in rural districts. The electorate
are dead both to their powers and their duties.
They live, in fact, under a system which is anything
but representative. They live rather, under the
devitalised husk of the feudal system, the poorer
members of the community dependent, in the
worst sense, upon those who are their social
superiors, but no longer receiving from them any
security of well-being, and neither class extending
to the other, with rare exceptions, either the loyalty
or devotion which seem to have been bound up with
the feudal traditions of our forefathers. Was it
possible to wake up this inert mass, so that they
should co-operate with one another, and thus be
strong enough to grasp the present machinery of
national Government, and either utilise it or alter it
to one better suited to their needs ?

Each of my inquiries in turn led me back to the
individuals concerned, to the human beings themselves. What were their homes, their ambitions,
thoughts, beliefs ? What guidance do they give to
those who wish to serve them ? I groped my way
blindly and acquired knowledge only in a negative
sense by a series of failures. I gleaned two general
precepts from my investigations. They were these :

It is useless to try and help the lives of a community without consulting the individuals whom you hope to benefit, and that to benefit the life conditions of men does not necessarily benefit the life conditions of women, although their interests may be apparently identical as to social grade, locality, religious and other beliefs.

After a series of barren experiments, I stumbled by chance on a piece of social radium, a regenerative agency that bore good fruit and that contained an element of spontaneous joy most refreshing compared to the oppressive straight-jackets of national or private philanthropists. I heard of the revival of folk songs and dances. I went to see and hear them. The first performance opened the door for me into a new paradise. The Esperance Club of working girls had been the means of bringing to life researches of antiquarian musical students. This club had evidently been for many years an unusually successful social enterprise, but the discovery of a lost treasure in the shape of traditional songs and dances gave it a new inspiration. Both words and tunes of the songs have come, generation after generation, from the heart of the English folk. Each generation, each individual who has sung them, has added or omitted some little touch, so that in these songs, which have been mostly collected from old men and women over eighty years of age, is expressed the very soul of English national sentiment. The same with the dances. They were traditional in families or localities, they had been handed down from father to son, and were as truly folk dances as the songs were folk songs. Songs and dances alike are full of life on the

land and love of the land, of flowers, animals and
crops, of the daily lives of men, women and children.
Dramatic, tragic and comic incidents find spontaneous expression, and every one of them tells of
a vigorous and mainly joyous existence. The girls
of this club learnt the Morris dance first from two
Oxfordshire countrymen. Both the dances and
songs were acquired easily " by a sort of spiritual
sixth sense," as if the rhythm and meaning of them
were latent in their being and were easily re-
awakened. The girls not only learnt quickly, but
were inspired to teach others, young girls of seventeen
and eighteen showing an amazing facility and power
of organisation in this matter. One of these came,
at my eager request, to teach in our village, and,
after one week, men, women and children were alive
with these friendly, joy-giving, native arts. The
following year a girl teacher came to us again with
renewed success.

In the autumn, 1908, I was invited by the secretary of the club, Miss Mary Neal, herself a wonderful
organiser, to share a seaside holiday with her girls.
In those days I never left home save for family
reasons, or for some very exceptional matter. I,
therefore, refused the invitation. I happened to
mention the proposal the next day to my mother.
She said : " Why don't you go ? " I immediately
went, little realising that this visit would lead to a
most unexpected series of experiences.

CHAPTER II

MY CONVERSION

IT was in August—September, 1908, at "The Green Lady Hostel," Littlehampton, the holiday house of the Esperance Girls' Club, that I met Mrs. Pethick Lawrence and Miss Annie Kenney. I was two or three days in the house with them without discovering that they were Suffragettes or that there was anything unusual about their lives. But I realised at once that I was face to face with women of strong personality, and I felt, though at first vaguely, that they represented something more than themselves, a force greater than their own seemed behind them. Their remarkable individual powers seemed illumined and enhanced by a light that was apart from them as are the colours and patterns of a stained-glass window by the sun shining through it. I had never before come across this kind of spirituality. I have since found it a characteristic of all the leaders in the militant section of the woman's movement, and of many of the rank and file. I was much attracted by Mrs. Lawrence, and became intimate with her at once on the strength of our mutual friendship for Olive Schreiner. We had, besides, many other interests and sympathies in common. The first Sunday that we were together, the girls of the club were asked to come in early that evening, so

that Jessie Kenney, Annie Kenney's sister, who had
only recently been released from Holloway, might
tell them of her prison experiences. I then realised
that I was amongst Suffragettes. I immediately
confessed to them that although I shared their wish
for the enfranchisement of women, I did not at all
sympathise with the measures they adopted for
bringing about that reform. I had, however,
always been interested in prisons and recognised
from the first that, incidentally, the fact of many
educated women being sent to gaol for a question of
conscience must do a great deal for prison reform,
and I was delighted at this opportunity of hearing
first-hand something about the inner life of a prison.
I listened eagerly and was horrified at some of the
facts recorded. Amongst these I remember specially
that the tins in which the drinking water stood were
cleaned with soap and brick dust and not washed out,
the tins being filled only once or at most twice in
twenty-four hours ; the want of air in the cells ; the
conduct of prison officials towards the prisoners.

Having betrayed my disapproval of the Suffragette "tactics," which seemed to me unjustified,
unreasonable, without a sense of political responsibility, and as setting a bad example in connection
with a reform movement of such prominence, there
was naturally something of coolness and reserve in
my further intercourse with Mrs. Pethick Lawrence
and the Kenneys. But before their brief stay at the
club came to an end, I achieved a talk with each of
the leaders.

One evening, after incessant rain, Annie Kenney
and I marched arm-in-arm round the garden,

under dripping trees. I explained that though I had always been for the extension of the suffrage to women, it did not seem to me a question of prime urgency, that many other matters of social reform seemed more important, and I thought class prejudice and barriers more injurious to national welfare than sex barriers. I was deeply impressed with her reply. She said, in a tone of utmost conviction : " Well, I can only tell you that I, who am a working-class woman, have never known class distinction and class prejudice stand in the way of my advancement, whereas the sex barrier meets me at every turn." Of course, she is a woman of great character, courage and ability, which gives her exceptional facilities for overcoming these drawbacks, but her contention that such powers availed her nothing in the face of sex prejudices and disabilities, and the examples she gave me to bear out her argument, began to lift the scales of ignorance from my eyes. She was careful to point out that the members of her own family had been remarkably free from sex prejudice, and her illustrations had no taint of personal resentment. She explained how the lot of women being not understood of men, and they being the only legislators, the woman's part had always got laid on one side, made of less importance, sometimes forgotten altogether. She told how amongst these offices of women was the glorious act of motherhood and the tending of little children. Was there anything in a man's career that could be so honourable as this ? Yet how often is the woman who bears humanity neglected at such times, so that life goes from her, or she is

given no money to support her child. I felt that
through Annie Kenney's whole being throbbed the
passion of her soul for other women, to lift from
them the heavy burden, to give them life, strength,
freedom, joy, and the dignity of human beings,
that in all things they might be treated fairly with
men. I was struck by her expression and argument, it was straightforward in its simplicity, yet
there was inspiration about her. All that she
said was obvious, but in it there was a call from
far off, something inevitable as the voice of fate.
She never sounded a note of sex-antipathy; it was
an unalloyed claim for justice and equity of development, for women as for men.

Then Mrs. Pethick Lawrence and I, during a
day's motoring expedition, achieved a rare talk out.
She met all my arguments, all my prejudices and
false deductions with counter-arguments, and above
all with facts of which I had till then no conception.
I trusted her because of what I had learnt of her
personality, her character, mind, wide education
and experience, and was to a certain extent at once
impressed ; still I only half believed many of the
things she reported, the real purport of her statements did not yet sink into my soul as they were
soon to do, fact upon fact, result upon result, as I
found out their truth for myself.

During my stay at Littlehampton I witnessed a
scene which produced a great impression upon my
conscience. One morning, while wandering through
the little town, I came on a crowd. All kinds of
people were forming a ring round a sheep which had
escaped as it was being taken to the slaughter-

house. It looked old and misshapen. A vision
suddenly rose in my mind of what it should have
been on its native mountain-side with all its forces
rightly developed, vigorous and independent. There
was a hideous contrast between that vision and the
thing in the crowd. With growing fear and distress
the sheep ran about more clumsily and became a
source of amusement to the onlookers, who laughed
and jeered at it. At last it was caught by its two
gaolers, and as they carried it away one of them,
resenting its struggles, gave it a great cuff in the
face. At that I felt exasperated. I went up to
the men and said, "Don't you know your own
business? You have this creature absolutely in
your power. If you were holding it properly it
would be still. You are taking it to be killed, you
are doing your job badly to hurt and insult it
besides." The men seemed ashamed, they adjusted
their hold more efficiently and the crowd slunk
away. From my babyhood I have felt a burning
indignation against unkindness to animals, and in
their defence I have sometimes acted with a courage
not natural to me. But on seeing this sheep it
seemed to reveal to me for the first time the position
of women throughout the world. I realised how
often women are held in contempt as beings outside
the pale of human dignity, excluded or confined,
laughed at and insulted because of conditions in
themselves for which they are not responsible, but
which are due to fundamental injustices with
regard to them, and to the mistakes of a civilisation
in the shaping of which they have had no free share.
I was ashamed to remember that although my

sympathy had been spontaneous with regard to
the wrongs of animals, of children, of men and
women who belonged to down-trodden races or
classes of society, yet that hitherto I had been
blind to the sufferings peculiar to women as such,
which are endured by women of every class, every
race, every nationality, and that although nearly all
the great thinkers and teachers of humanity have
preached sex-equality, women have no champions
among the various accepted political or moral laws
which serve to mould public opinion of the present
day.

Nothing could have exceeded the patience, the
considerate sympathy even, with which both Annie
Kenney and Mrs. Lawrence endured my arguments,
arguments, as I now realise them to have been,
without any genuine element, stereotyped and
shallow. Before we parted, Mrs. Lawrence said to
me, and it was the only one of her remarks which
savoured in the least of the contempt which my
attitude at that time so richly deserved, " You are
sufficiently interested in our policy to criticise it,
will you be sufficiently interested to study its cause
and read up our case ? "

For two months I " read up " the subject as I had
never read in my life before ; I took in the weekly
paper *Votes for Women*, the only publication which
gave events as they happened, not as they were
supposed to happen. I attended as many meetings
as I could, and the breakfasts of released suffrage
prisoners, whereat the spirit behind this movement,
its driving force, seemed best exemplified. Above
all, I watched current politics from a different point

of view. I still held back from being converted, I criticised and argued at every turn, over every fresh demonstration of the W.S.P.U., but I began to realise of what stuff the workers in the movement were made ; what price they paid for their services so gladly given ; how far removed they were from any taint of self-glorification, and how amazingly they played the game of incessantly advertising the Cause without ever developing the curse of self-advertisement. I have never been amongst people of any sort who were so entirely free from self-consciousness, self-seeking and self-vaunting.

At this juncture of my conversion I was much concerned with the arguments of Anti-Suffragists. I wrote a pamphlet to refute their points of view, as generally presented in newspapers and magazines. I was always, as it were, stopping on my road to combat their attitude. It was only after considerably longer experience that I realised the waste of energy entailed by this process, since the practical opposition which blocks the way to the legal removal of sex disability is not due to those men or women who have courage to publicly record their opposition, but to those who take shelter in verbally advocating the cause, while at the same time opposing any effective move for its achievement. Anti-suffrage arguments or agitations should, of course, be met whenever they present themselves, but it soon became clear to me that in private intercourse many people put them forward without any conviction, merely as a way of opening the conversation, and while at heart much more interested in the positive than the negative side of the question.

The same is true of public audiences. The assertive
claim to the value of voting rights for men, wherever
these are denied, is perennially educating the public
to our contention ; one has but to catch them
" at it " to illustrate the claim of women. The
drawbacks resulting from laws and customs based
on sex bias are also constantly put forward by
Anti-Suffragist men themselves, when they are not
considering the possible infringement of their own
monopolies. Lord Cromer has headed the agitation
against freedom for women in Great Britain. When
he was responsible for the welfare of Egypt, he wrote,
concerning the Prophet Mahomet : " Unfortunately
the great Arabian reformer of the seventh century
was driven by the necessities of his position to do
more than found a religion. He endeavoured to
found a social system. The reasons why Islam as a
social system has been a complete failure are mani-
fold. First and foremost Islam keeps women in a
position of marked inferiority." He quotes Stanley
Lane Poole in corroboration : " The degradation of
women in the East is a canker that begins its
destructive work early in childhood, and has eaten
into the whole system of Islam." Lord Cromer
then draws conclusions worthy of the most ardent
Suffragette : " Look now to the consequences
which result from the degradation of women in
Mahomedan countries. It cannot be doubted
that the seclusion of women exercises a baneful
effect on Eastern society. The arguments on this
subject are indeed so commonplace that it is unnecessary to dwell on them. It will be sufficient to
say that seclusion, by confining the sphere of

women's interest to a very limited horizon, cramps
the intellect and withers the mental development
of one-half of the population in Moslem countries.
. . . Moreover, inasmuch as women, in their
capacities of wives and mothers, exercise a great
influence over the characters of their husbands and
sons, it is obvious that the seclusion of women must
produce a deteriorating effect on the male population, in whose presumed interests the custom was
originally established, and is still maintained "
(" Modern Egypt," Vol. II., chapter entitled
" Dwellers in Egypt," pp. 134, 155, 156, First
Edition). The contention of woman Suffragists
could not be more reasonably presented. Add to
this the belief of Englishmen in the power of the
vote to lift from degradation and to widen the outlook of citizens ; their attitude towards rebellions
on behalf of constitutional rights by Russians,
Turks, Persians, and Uitlanders of South Africa ;
the principles of every constitution in which
Britishers have had a hand, notably in Australasia
and South Africa, and the case is complete. To
meet the Anti-Woman Suffragist arguments, it is
only necessary to quote their own utterances.

My own researches had shown me not only the
grievous harm to women from the inequalities of law
and custom with regard to them, but that in many
matters concerning men, and in practically all questions relating to children, the help of women was
needed with an urgency that would no longer justify
delay. I learnt that before resorting to militancy
the women's organisations had for many years past
succeeded in obtaining a majority of supporters in

the House of Commons, and the backing of leading
men of both parties.   It was startling to realise that
the professed advocacy of such men as Lord Beacons-
field, the late Lord Salisbury and Mr. Arthur
Balfour had not moved the Conservative party in
any way to assist their cause.   When the Liberal
Government was returned to power in 1906, under
the leadership of Sir Henry Campbell Bannerman, he
himself was a declared Suffragist, as were all but a
few of the men of most influence in his Cabinet,
including Mr. Birrell, Mr. Buxton, Mr. John Morley
and Mr. John Burns.   Sir Edward Grey and Mr.
Haldane had themselves introduced a Woman
Suffrage Bill in 1889.   Mr. Lloyd George, Mr.
Runciman and Mr. Winston Churchill, who joined
the Cabinet in 1908, were strong verbal advocates of
votes for women.   The women had tried repeatedly,
and always in vain, every peaceable means open to
them of influencing successive Governments.   Processions and petitions were absolutely useless.   I
saw the extreme need of their position, the in-
effectiveness of every method hitherto adopted to
persuade these professed Suffragists to put their
theories into practice.   But I still held aloof from
completely backing their militant action owing to
mistrustfulness bred of ignorance as to its true
nature.

After six weeks I reached the stage when I had
little left to say against the movement and my
enthusiasm for the workers in it was considerable,
but on the whole my attitude was of a negative
order.   I was still not prepared to back my theoretic
approval by action when, on October 13, Mrs.

Pankhurst, Mrs. Drummond and Christabel Pankhurst were arrested for issuing the famous handbill calling upon the people of London to witness the women's deputation to the Prime Minister and to help them " rush " the House of Commons.

At a crowded meeting at the Queen's Hall the previous day, Monday, October 12, the leaders announced that a warrant had been served upon them and that at any moment the police might come in and arrest them on the platform. The meeting was enthusiastically in their favour and the announcement caused an outburst of indignation. This, however, was instantly suppressed by the leaders, who explained that they were under a compact with the managers of the hall never to use these weekly meetings for any insubordinate demonstrations ; that if the police arrived and proceeded to arrest them they would only be carrying out their orders ; that if this happened, no interference, not a murmur of resentment must come from the audience. After a few moments they settled down under this decree with reluctant but strikingly obedient resignation. Before long the police were announced to be at the door. After some moments of interchanging messages with the leaders on the platform, during which the suspense in the hall was tremendously taut, the police left saying that the women arrested would have to report themselves at Bow Street the following morning. The next day, Tuesday, October 13, I called at the W.S.P.U. offices in Clement's Inn to offer my sympathy. I regretted that I was still not sufficiently in agreement with their militant policy to join the deputation, but

inquired whether there were any lesser services which
I could render them. I was asked to try and approach the Home Secretary with a view to securing
1st Division treatment for the prisoners as political
offenders instead of ranking them, as hitherto, with
criminals in the 2nd and 3rd Divisions. From the
first I had been in sympathy with this demand. To
publicly maintain that the Suffragists, even if their
breaking of the law were proved, had anything in
common with the ordinary transgressor for selfish
ends, appeared to me ludicrous as well as tyrannous
on the part of the Government. I therefore
willingly undertook the task, although I was convinced that my efforts would meet with no immediate success. I had already grasped this much
of the spirit of the militants that rightness of aim is
the factor controlling their actions ; likeliness of
achievement, in so far as this depends not on themselves but on their opponents, is not a matter to be
considered. Looking back at the advance of their
cause since militant action began in October, 1905,
it seems to me that its amazing rapidity has been
chiefly due to the unswerving carrying out of this
principle. At every stage the militants selected a
line of conduct, not in itself rebellious, but on the
contrary, morally and constitutionally in accordance
with accepted opinion and law. It has been the
ignoring or deliberate repression of their lawful
claims which produced disturbances. The un-
reasoned punishments which followed in no way
altered the women's need nor their determined
claim for legal redress. The sufferings of their
comrades merely heaped fuel on the fires of their

enthusiasm and inevitably exposed the reactionary nature of the Government's attitude towards them. I did not obtain 1st Division treatment for the prisoners, but my observations during that memorable day made me a complete convert to the policy of militancy.

From about 4 in the afternoon to 11.30 at night I was incessantly on the move between Clement's Inn, the House of Commons, Bow Street Police Station and the private residence of the magistrate. I had ample opportunity of noticing the nature of the crowd summoned by the famous handbill and of studying the attitude of mind of the authorities, of the Home Office, the magistrate, and of the police towards our movement. The facts which I noted that day as a spectator were typical, and corroborated afterwards in every respect when it came to my own experience. The decisions of the Government as expressed through the Home Office were pre-determined and detached from any consideration of the political demand which was the root cause of the women's rebellion. The magistrate's attitude was obviously affected, whether directly or indirectly, by the Government's lead. The political nature of the offences of which our prisoners were accused was not admitted ; their purely nominal crimes were nevertheless punished with a severity that was unheard of had they been judged as ordinary disturbers of the peace. It was clear that the political motive of their actions was recognised sufficiently to justify the authorities in assuming that these actions would be continuous, an example to others, and a dangerous appeal from

an organised body, but the reason was ignored
when there was question of an inquiry into the
political motive itself. The police showed a much
more straightforward and impartial attitude whenever the conduct of our case was left entirely in
their hands. They never for a moment looked upon
the suffrage prisoners as ordinary rowdies, they
realised that our motives were political and our
actions peaceable, but that our appeals were met
in a quite different spirit from those of other political
agitators. The police, of course, in turn came
under the influence of those in authority over them,
and when under orders would knock us about in the
streets, and accuse us in the courts, according to
the requirements imposed upon them. Under this
pressure, individual policemen would occasionally
act with brutality and unfairness, but in the main
their treatment of Suffragists was in striking contrast to that of the magistrates, the Home Office
and the Government. A great number of police
constables are better versed in the suffrage question
and the woman question generally than most
politicians. They have been obliged to attend our
meetings. They know both the political and moral
ethics of our policy. I have heard more intelligent
reasoning about votes for women from policemen
(both when my identity was known to them and
when it was not) than has issued, with but rare
exceptions, from the House of Commons.

During the afternoon and evening of this day I
had my first experience of a suffrage crowd, immense
in numbers, embracing every shade of opinion
on the question, from enthusiasm in favour to

contemptuous or angry hostility, largely interspersed
with curiosity-mongers who were fascinated by the
fight although without interest for its cause. There
were men and women of all classes, but rowdyism
was plainly not there, and from that day forward I
was convinced of the fact, self-evident enough in all
conscience, that the women never appealed to
hooliganism and that they had nothing to gain
from and nothing to offer to that element in the
mob. The women, and the men too, who fight in
this cause, or assist it ever so remotely, have never
been and never will be of a self-seeking type, nor are
they lovers of disturbance for its own sake.

I first of all tried to interview the Home Secretary,
Mr. Herbert Gladstone,* at the House of Commons.
I did not see him, but a friendly member of Parliament acted as messenger boy between us. I
asked : (1) Would he use his powers to ensure that
the three prisoners should be sentenced to the
1st Division, and not to the 2nd Division as though
they were common criminals, which obviously they
were not ? *Reply :* As the prisoners were not yet
arrested he could not possibly adjudicate on the
question of their sentences. (2) If I returned at
six o'clock, the hour when they were to surrender to
the summons, would he then give me an answer ?
Reply : He had not the power, the question rested
with the police-court authorities ; he had determined never to interfere with sentences. (3) Would
he give me a permit or some sort of facilities to
approach the magistrate ? My messenger told me
that it would be useless to put this question, that

* Afterwards Lord Gladstone.

Mr. Gladstone was in a state of great anger over the whole proceedings, and that, even if he had the power, nothing would induce him to help the Suffragettes to 1st Division treatment. I then went to Bow Street Police Court. The crowds were dense in Parliament Square, Parliament Street, and Trafalgar Square, but extremely orderly. When I reached Bow Street it was past six o'clock and the magistrate had left. On inquiring where I could find him, I was ushered into an inner room before a superintendent who wore a flat cap, not the usual policeman's helmet. He was very civil, but told me it was against the rules to give the private addresses of magistrates and that Mr. Curtis Bennett would not be back until ten o'clock the following morning for the Court. I put various other questions. Though offering no practical assistance the answers led me to realise a strangely unexpected atmosphere of sympathy, and after a few moments hesitation I found myself telling this superintendent the full purport of my mission. To my intense surprise he not only expressed much approval, but burst out with a torrent of abuse against the Government—" Why to goodness couldn't the Prime Minister receive the women's deputation same as any other ? The brunt of the whole business falls on us, and it's the beastliest job we've ever had." Then he added, " The prisoners are here now, in the cells, would you like to see them ? " I felt almost overwhelmed that so unworthy and half-hearted a follower as myself should be the one to have this grand opportunity, but, of course, I availed myself of it without a moment's hesitation.

I was shown through a series of passages and up a flight of stairs, where a wardress was in charge. This October day was damp and foggy with the first sense of autumn chill, but as I was led on towards the cells the atmosphere became perceptibly damper and colder at every step, as in a vault. I realised for the first time the actual meaning of the word " puanteur," which haunts the pages of Dostoievsky's account of his imprisonments, the smell, as it were, of deadness pervading, I should imagine, every building, however cleanly washed, which is built and used to incarcerate human beings solely for punitive purposes. I had never seen Mrs. Pankhurst except on a public platform at moments when she was surrounded by public enthusiasm and personal devotion, such as are rarely accorded even to great leaders. My critical faculty is easily aroused by success, and although I recognised the single-mindedness of her aims, the uprightness of her character, the vigour of her intellect and convincing oratorical gifts, the charm of her personality and, above all, the magnificent power of her leadership, yet I had hitherto not felt drawn to this remarkable woman. It was with no sense of hero-worship that in reply to the wardress' friendly question, " Which of the ladies do you wish to see ? " I answered, " Mrs. Pankhurst." She went to a cell door, many of which lined one side of a passage as the horse-boxes of a stable, and drew aside the shutter of a small grating. I looked through into a kind of animal's den, dimly lit and furnished only with a bare wooden bench running along the side of the wall, and terminating in

a sanitary convenience. Standing erect as she moved
towards the grating, was a woman whose appearance struck awe into every fibre of my being. A
splendour of defiance and indignation pervaded her
face, yet she was controlled and her attitude conveyed no suggestion of personal grievance. From
that moment I recognised in her, and I have held
the vision undimmed ever since, the guardian pro-
tector of this amazing woman's movement, conscious not only of the thousands who follow her lead
to-day, but of the martyred generations of the past
and of the women of the future whose welfare
depends upon the path hewn out for them to-day.
I seemed to grasp prophetically and all at once the
characteristic qualities which I learnt later on by
closer observation and experience. I saw that the
quality of sternness, which presented so unyielding
a front to every opponent and every obstacle,
drew its force from deep fountains of understanding, of sympathy and of love. While she
most perfectly fulfilled her mission of pioneer, and
shirked none of the responsibilities accruing to the
lead, yet the efficiency and glamour attending the
fulfilment of that mission were due to her recognition
of the elements behind her, as an arrow-head
derives its force from the construction of the whole
weapon. The seemingly miraculous power of leadership with which the controllers of this militant
movement are gifted is due to the fact that they too
are fellow servants of a cause which they recognise
is of infinitely greater importance than themselves
or any other individual, they share with the humblest
member of the rank and file the sense of loyalty

and bond-allegiance to a common ideal—the welfare
of women throughout the world.

I was advised by Mrs. Pankhurst how to turn my
services to the best account and not to mind
about the 1st Division, as they themselves could
plead it in court, but to get them released for that
night or they would not be able to plead properly,
from fatigue. After a fruitless search of some
hours for the magistrate in the wilds of West
Kensington and a return to the office at Clement's
Inn for further instructions, I at last ran my quarry
to ground somewhere near Olympia. The magistrate, Mr. Curtis Bennett,* received me courteously,
but his face promptly assumed an official-defensive
expression on learning my quest. If I had come
to ask him about the trial next day he must request
me not to proceed, since he must keep his mind unbiassed. I explained that I was altogether new to
the rules of the game which he had at his fingers'
ends. That, as I was ignorant which questions I
might or might not put to him, it would be best for
me to unburden myself and for him to select which
of my demands he could answer. He saw the reason
of this and kindly consented to the arrangement.
In reply, he could make no statement as to which
Division he would sentence the prisoners, nor could
they be let out on bail that night, because of the
late hour at which they had responded to the sum-
monses. As to taking them food and bedding, that
was a matter for the police to decide, it was beyond
his jurisdiction. I was thankful to hear this,
knowing that the police were not likely to offer

* Afterwards Sir Curtis Bennett, who since died in 1913.

objections when matters were left solely to their
care. I went back to Mrs. Pethick Lawrence, and
in a few minutes we had taken bedding and rugs
and were off to the police station at Bow Street.
We found that a Member of Parliament, Mr.
James Murray, had visited our friends and ordered
everything they wanted from an hotel, making
them as comfortable as possible for the night.

The next day their trial took place. After the
evidence of the police had been taken, Christabel
Pankhurst asked for an adjournment, in order to
take legal advice and to prepare a defence. This
was granted for one week. During the interval,
Christabel secured the attendance of Mr. Lloyd
George, Chancellor of the Exchequer, and of Mr.
Herbert Gladstone, Home Secretary, as witnesses
for the defence. The adjourned hearing of the case
on October 21 lasted from 10.30 to 7.30 at night,
with only two short intervals. The trial was
immensely impressive, the three figures stood up at
different times, and it was obvious to all who listened
to the case that they were fighting against evil and
were in all things most essentially good, so that one
was awed by them. When the two members of the
Cabinet gave evidence, the futility of the part they
played was most obvious and they presented an
appearance that was petty and contemptible to the
last degree. There were a great many other witnesses, of whom I was one, in support of the contention that the crowd on the evening of October 13
was an orderly one, and that no violence was done.
At 7.30 Christabel Pankhurst said she had still fifty
witnesses to call, and the case was adjourned to

Saturday, October 24. It was owing to Mrs. Pankhurst's speech on this occasion that I felt taken hold of by the movement. Every sentence of it seemed to be true, dignified, strong, entirely respectful. This passage I more especially remember : " You know that women have tried to do something to come to the aid of their own sex. . . . I was in the hospital at Holloway, and when I was there I heard from one of the beds near me the moans of a woman who was in the pangs of childbirth. I should like you to realise how women feel at helpless little infants breathing their first breath in the atmosphere of a prison. We believe that if we get the vote we will find some more humane way of dealing with women than that."

Mrs. Drummond made me feel faith in the woman's movement, her type was most lovable, full of daring for the enemies of woman, full of patience in working for them, full of the most noble kind of humility in her reverence for them.

Christabel Pankhurst was the sunrise of the woman's movement, I cannot describe her in any other way. The glow of her great vitality and the joy of her being took hold of the movement and made it gladness. Yet, her nature being so essentially a woman's, there was a vein of tenderness throughout her speech, and her strength lay in her steadfast, resourceful and brilliant intellect.

With the exception of declining to give a pledge to keep the peace for twelve months, a pledge which these women were quite unable to accept, they had been guilty of no offence. Mrs. Pankhurst and Mrs. Drummond were each sentenced to three

months' imprisonment, and Christabel Pankhurst
to ten weeks' (two and a half months) imprisonment.
It was like darkness when these three were in prison.
Mrs. Pethick Lawrence and Sylvia Pankhurst,
Christabel's sister, kept the weekly meetings going
at the Queen's Hall in a splendid way. Sylvia is an
artist by profession and an artist at heart, but whenever the women's movement wants her she is there
for its bidding. She looked all that is most modest
and humble, but speaking seemed to come as a
second nature to her as to everyone of the Pank-
hursts, and at times I could not have believed, but
for having heard and seen, the splendid political
speech which came from that young girl. During
this time I lived in the country and seldom came to
London. I needed no converting now and my only
wish was to convince my mother.

CHAPTER III

A DEPUTATION TO THE PRIME MINISTER

THROUGHOUT this month of January, 1909, I became convinced that I should be justified in offering myself as a member of the next deputation to the Prime Minister to demand the removal of women's disabilities to the Parliamentary franchise. I became a member of the Women's Social and Political Union, and on January 28 I wrote to Mrs. Pethick Lawrence offering myself for the deputation. I did not tell anybody but her of my decision. On the 30th I received her answer, accepting my offer.

On February 24 I went up to London from Homewood, without telling mother of the plan and actually without saying good-bye to her, as she went out to the village before I started. I wrote her the following letter at King's Cross Station, but did not post it till later in the day :—

"Wednesday, February 24, 1909.

"MY ANGEL MOTHER,—I don't know whether I shall post this to you or see you first. I want to have a letter ready.

"Don't be startled or afraid. I have something to tell you which—with the help of recent presentiments—you, I know, are half expecting to hear.

" If you ever see this letter it will mean that after joining the deputation I have been arrested and shall not see you again until I have been to Holloway. For months I have been planning this letter to you, but now that the time has come, it is not any easier to write for that.   Of course, my hope has been all along that I should be able to take you into my confidence, that I should have the perhaps all-undeserved yet heaven-like joy of knowing that though you could not share all my views, yet that you would understand why I held them, and, granted these, you would further understand my action and the great sacrifice which I know it means to you. My darling Muddy, you will never know, I trust, the pain it is to have to do this thing without your sympathy and help—with, on the contrary, the certainty that it shocks you and hurts you and makes you suffer in numberless ways.   Hardly a day has passed but what I have tried to feel my way with you, tried to convert you—not to my theoretic views, difference there does not matter, but to my intended conduct in connection with them.   Every day I have failed.   If I decided to do this thing, absolute secrecy was necessary, for, the whole of these police regulations being arbitrarily ordered and special to the case, they would never arrest me, not, I mean, unless I really broke the law, if they knew who I was. Unless I had your sympathy and understanding, it was, of course, hopeless to count on your secrecy.   I had two alternatives, to give up the plan, or to keep it and deceive you about it.   I chose this last.   For your sake I have tried never to tell you an actual lie in words.   I have not done this, and that is, perhaps, why you have your suspicions. But to my conscience that is no easier. It was my intention to deceive you, and I have deceived you, and, for all practical purposes, successfully. Once the intention is to deceive, it seems to me not to make any difference how it is done.

" You will be angry. If it could be only that. But you will be hurt through and through. As I write the words their meaning is acute in my mind and heart. You will hardly care to know, but I must tell you what has decided me to take this torturing step.

" Prisons, as you know, have been my hobby. What maternity there lurks in me has for years past been gradually awakening over the fate of prisoners, the deliberate, cruel harm that is done to them, their souls and bodies, the ignorant, exasperating waste of good opportunities in connection with them, till now the thought of them, the yearning after them, turns in me and tugs at me as vitally and irrepressibly as ever a physical child can call upon its mother.

" The moment I got near the Suffragettes the way to this child of mine seemed easy and straight. But I knew the temptation to think this must make me doubly sure of my ground. I have felt from the first that I could not take this woman's movement merely as an excuse for Holloway. I have waited till my conviction was genuine and deep at every point, and till the opportunity occurred for facing the police regulations in a way possible to my whole nature, temperament, conscience. There are several other things which the Suffragettes do, which I would not and could not do.

" I finally made up my mind in about the middle
of January, and soon after wrote to Mrs. Pethick
Lawrence. Enclosed is her answer. I had not
recently been seeing them, or going to meetings, or
in any way specially communicating with them. I
took the decision entirely on myself, in no way con-
sulted her nor asked her advice; even had they not
accepted me in the deputation I should have joined
outside.

" About the physical discomforts part of Holloway,
don't be distressed for that. These are already
nothing to what they were. And I am such a muff,
what remains of hardship will be wholesome for me
—really ' reformatory ' for me as imprisonment
seldom is to others. If I could only know that you
will help me face it, it would be nothing to me. It's
my journeying after the hobby that sucks up my
soul like a tide, my Nile sources, my Thibet, my
Ruvenzori. If you, my splendid Mother, will only
help me in spirit that the little spark of Sven Hedin
shall not fail in me. I am no hero, but the thought
of other travellers' much worse privations on that
road will, I believe, fizzle up my flimsy body enough
for what is necessary, and if only I knew you were
helping me in your heart I should not, could not,
fail, Muddy darling.

" You can't forgive me now, but perhaps you will
some day. Whatever you feel towards me, whatever I do, I shall still be always

" Your most loving and devoted

" Con.

"The account papers, tradesmen addresses, wages
paper, are in the lift-up place of desk on dining-room

writing table. I expect I shall be away from you a month. The others will cling round you. If I were going a trip abroad you would not resent the separation. In my little warm cupboard nest in Holloway my only thought of the outer world will be of you. I shall try anyhow to get back to you to-night.

" Con."

I went to 4, Clement's Inn, lunched there with Mrs. Pethick Lawrence, Christabel, Mrs. Pankhurst and Mrs. Tuke; Miss Neal came too. She kindly undertook to post my letter to mother and buy me a brush and comb and toothbrush in case we should be sent to the 1st Division.

I had a cracking headache and felt quite dazed. They kindly put me to lie down in the upstairs rest room boudoir, where Mrs. Pankhurst and Christabel had remained hidden from the police on October 14, 1908.

At about six o'clock we had supper. I ate next to nothing. Miss Elsa Gye, who had been summoned by telegraph to come and assist me through the Deputation, was at supper. She was a delightful girl, young and fresh-looking. I had been told that she was just engaged to be married, and I felt it was horrible that she should risk weeks of imprisonment solely because of me.

I had disguised myself by doing my hair in an early-Victorian way, so that the police, if on the look out for me, should not recognise me and so be tempted not to arrest me; for people whose relatives might make a fuss effectively are considered awkward customers.

At about seven Miss Gye and I set out and hailed
a taxi.   I found I had left my ticket behind for the
Caxton Hall Meeting.   So I flew back to Clement's
Inn to get it.   It was a raw, cold night, but I had
been advised to dispense with my muff and boa, as
these, I was told, would almost certainly be torn
to shreds " in the hustling " ; this gave one a
rather gruesome warning of what was to be expected
from the handling of the police.   We were each
given a copy of the resolution which was to be put
to the meeting.   As we drove to Caxton Hall, it
suddenly struck me that I had not sufficiently
learnt up my part.   "What does one have to do ? "
I asked.   " I suppose I must do something to show
that I mean business."   " Oh, no," my companion
answered, " you needn't bother about what you'll
do.   It will all be done *to* you.   There is only one
thing you must remember.   It is our business to
go forward, and whatever is said to you and whatever is done to you, you must on no account be
turned back."   That seemed to me at the time, and
has seemed to me ever since, to be the essence of our
militant tactics.   I afterwards heard it yet better
summarised by Mrs. Pankhurst : " Our demand is
just and moderate.   We press our cause reasonably
and in a law-abiding spirit, but in such a way that
we give the Government but two alternatives—
either to do us justice or to do us violence."   My
companion also told me that if the police became
too violent, I could cut matters short and ensure
instant arrest by the semblance of making a speech
or collecting a crowd round me for that purpose,
since these offences constituted a breach of the

peace. Miss Gye and I sat in the body of the hall, we had on the "Votes for Women" sashes and were to join the Deputation unostentatiously as it left the building.

The appearance of the Deputation on the platform was remarkable for the look of dignity and pathetic earnestness of the members, many of them white-haired, and one or two young and pretty girls.* The speeches seemed to be very much to the point. I could hardly listen to them for the distracting thought of when my mother would hear about me and what she would think and feel; but I had no wish to shirk, and never for a moment did I doubt that I had done right.

Many friends had seen and not recognised me, at which I was delighted. Others did recognise me, and seeing I had the sash on, which meant the Deputation, they looked immensely surprised.

Presently the Deputation came down from the platform, formed up in couples, headed by Mrs. Pethick Lawrence, and marched out of the hall. Miss Gye and I joined in behind the sixth or seventh couple. We were thirty women in all. By this

* The Deputation was composed of our leader Mrs. Pethick Lawrence, Miss Daisy Solomon, Mrs. Vans Agnew Corbett, Miss Una Dugdale, Miss Madeline Petre, Miss E. H. Chesshire, Mrs. Caprina Fahey, Miss M. Barnet, Miss Margaret Davies Colley, Miss Margaret E. Rodgers, Miss Mary Allen, Miss Ellen Pitman, Miss Maud Freeman, Mrs. Katherine Richmond, Miss Mary Lethune, Miss M. Adair Roberts, Miss Leslie Lawless, Miss Caroline Townsend, Mrs. Tyson, Miss M. Tyson, Miss Ainsworth, Mrs. Lamartine Yates, Miss M. E. Thompson, Miss Helen Kirkpatrick Watts, Miss Kate Walsh, Miss Sara Carwin, Mrs. Saul Solomon, who was not eventually arrested, and Miss Elsa Gye and myself brought the number to twenty-nine.

time I had a feeling of exhilaration that the moment
for my own independent action had come at last.
I had a vague notion that I should have to encounter
physical difficulties, but since I had merely to meet
them and endure them, knowing that I could lay no
claim to overcoming these by physical powers of
which I was deficient, the way from that moment
seemed plain and easy. I felt proud to be one of
the active ones at last, to be the companion of these
women in particular, whom I had watched on the
platform, and to know that the Deputation was
headed by one of our leaders who had first revealed
the woman's movement to me.

The following resolution was put to the meeting
and carried with acclamation : " That this Parliament of women expresses its indignation that while
every measure in the King's Speech vitally affects
the interests of their sex, and while heavier financial
burdens are to be laid upon woman tax-payers, the
Government have not included in the programme for
the session a measure to confer the Parliamentary
vote upon duly qualified women. The women here
assembled call upon the Government to introduce
and carry into law this session a measure giving votes
to women on the same terms as to men.

"A Deputation is hereby appointed, to whom is
entrusted the duty of forthwith conveying this
resolution to the Prime Minister at the House of
Commons and eliciting his reply."

A copy was then handed to each member of the
Deputation.

Of all the undesirable possibilities before me, I
dreaded most lest by some horrible twist of fate the

leaders of the Deputation should be refused admittance, and I, if recognised, should have the lonely privilege thrust upon me of being received. I had never made a regular speech, and two attempts I had made at narrating my experiences of the previous October to a village audience had not been reassuring. My own point of view was definite enough, but I did not feel equipped to speak for others. When deciding to go on the Deputation I had, however, taken stock of my representative character and asked myself for which group of women I should stand, what was my atom's share in this movement if I did not strain after any vicarious office but merely added my own personal weight to the scale ? Without doubt I myself was one of that numerous gang of upper class leisured class spinsters, unemployed, unpropertied, unendowed, uneducated, without equipment or training for public service, economically dependent entirely upon others, not masters of their own leisure, however oppressively abundant that might seem to the onlooker. In a class where property runs with primogeniture, the first-born, if a female, is overlooked. In a class the whole status of which is based on property, on wealth to live at ease and in luxury, property is only dealt out to women, if at all, after male relatives have been served first, and then, as a rule, in much less proportion. Posts of honour and remuneration are barred to them in nearly all professions, in even those few they are allowed to enter. They remain almost invariably without honour of titles or lands or wealth, even where their services have been sought. Posts of Government are exclusively for men, with the sole

exception of the Sovereign.   Trained to luxury and
untrained to remunerative work, they are for the
most part dependents from childhood to the grave.
A maiming subserviency is so conditional to their
very existence that it becomes an aim in itself, an
ideal.   Driven through life with blinkers on, they
are unresentful of the bridle, the rein and the whip,
uncritical of the direction in which they are driven,
unmindful of the result to others as well as to themselves of their maintainer's beliefs and policy, whatever they may be.   The bride at the sacred ritual of
her marriage festival hears from her husband the
words, "With this ring I thee wed, with my body I
thee worship, with all my worldly goods I thee
endow." She knows at the time and she learns yet
more intimately as life goes on that those words have
no practical bearing, and that at her husband's
death the greater part of even that property which
had been seemingly made over to her during his life-
time will pass from her hands at the wane of her
lonely existence, when she needs it most, into those
of her son or some more distant relative.   The
literal, practical, interpretation of that husband's
vow—yes, of the vow even of good and well-
intentioned husbands — most usually is : "With
this ring I thee bind, with my body I thee control,
with none of my worldly goods I thee endow."   As
a widow more often than not she sinks, because of
her financial position, to a social state out of touch
with all her past life.   But at least the wives, the
widows, generally have children through whom their
powers of service to their families and to the community in general are to a certain extent developed

and recognised, and which give them a certain insight into the realities of existence. They also have known well-being and vicarious honour through their husbands. But to the single woman, the old maid of later years, the paralysing worship of incapacity dominates life, the chain of limitations and restrictions is but seldom broken, and never overcome save by exceptional force of character or ability. Even then how often it is only the beating of wings against unyielding and maiming bars ; freedom, if attained, rendered useless by lack of preparation in the competition against trained and privileged beings of the male sex, and the vain ambition ends in a seeming mutiny, nothing more—a distortion, an abnormality, an untidiness of creation.

I could stand indeed for the superfluous spinster, but who would listen to a messenger from this mute array, who cares for the blind, the lamed, the maimed and the dumb ? The fearful unnecessity of their disablement awakes no pity, no heart softens at thought of them, no politician would feel his conscience pricked by the narration of their grievances. A yoke so submitted to, so uselessly endured, can claim no reverence of martyrdom. But before condemning those who submit to it, I wish that our critics could realise what it means to be born under this yoke and then try to shake it off.

It is easy to see that if women are to appeal effectively to a modern parliament for the rights of liberty and representation which so long have been recognised among men, it must be through the working women, the bread-winning woman. Her situation is easily comparable to that of the working-

class man who quite recently has had himself to
fight in order to win his denied claim to freedom, a
fact which he, and others for him, still remember.
The aristocracy, the landed proprietor, the middle-
class trader, each in turn was driven to claim and
fight for these same rights.   But their struggle was
of long ago, their security in this right has remained
unshaken for so many generations that they have
clean forgotten what it would mean to be without it.
It is by the side of the most recent victors that
women must put in their claim.   With this class,
the working-class women, though at all times at one
with them in point of sympathy from theoretic
understanding of their troubles and needs, I
was not in direct touch and had no first-hand
experiences that I could share with them.   I read
the petitions of factory workers, of the sweated
home workers, of the professions—teachers, nurses,
medical women—with respect and whole-hearted
sympathy, but how could I stand for them when I
was not equipped to represent them ?

This was my state of mind until, walking from
Holloway to the City in one of our Suffragette
processions, I heard for the first time with my
own ears the well worn taunt " Go home and do
your washing." This awoke in me a magic response.
Since the days of my earliest childhood washing
had held great charm for me, and as a result I
had revered the washers exceptionally.   In my
youth, the pursuit was associated exclusively with
laundry-workers, but in later years I realised that,
except in that small proportion of houses where
servants are kept, every woman is a laundrymaid,

and that in every house throughout the land, or
indeed throughout the world, the cleaning and the
washing are done mainly by women, by wives and
mothers, their girl children or women servants.
Washing, the making clean that which had been
dirty, and making the crumpled and uncomfortable
things smooth, was my hobby. I was an amateur
scrubber and laundry-woman in the same spirit as
other unemployed females dabble in water-colour
drawings or hand embroidery. But much as I
personally enjoyed occasional experimenting in the
craft, it was easy to imagine how irksome the
occupation might become if one were driven to it
week by week with no release, under unsuitable
conditions, without the necessary equipment, in a
small house or single room, surrounded by children,
with a stinted water supply, inadequate firing
utensils, a weary body and a mind distraught as to
how to exist from day to day. From the moment
I heard that " washing " taunt in the street, I have
had eyes for the work of the washers. If there is
one single industry highly deserving of recognition
throughout the world of human existence and of
representation under parliamentary systems, it
surely is that of the washers, the renewers week by
week, the makers clean.

I determined, if I should find myself the solitary
representative of the Deputation and its untrained
spokeswoman, I should point to the collars and
shirt fronts of the gentlemen who received me and
claim the freedom of citizenship for the washers.
As I stepped out from Caxton Hall, through the
grime of a foggy February evening, I caught sight

of white collars here and there in the crowd, like
little flashing code-signals beckoning to us across
the darkness. The gnarled hands, the bent backs,
the tear-dimmed eyes of those that had washed
them white seemed to cry out, " Remember us.
Don't be afraid to speak for us if you get through
to the presence of those who know nothing, heed
nothing of our toil." I said in my heart, " I shall
remember, and I shall not be afraid in their presence."

We had scarcely stepped into the street before we
found ourselves hedged in by a ∧ shaped avenue
of police, narrowing as we advanced. They asked
no questions, said nothing, but proceeded to close
upon us from either side. My companion and I kept
together. Very soon all breath seemed to have been
pressed out of my body, but remembering the order
of the day, " Don't be turned back," I tried to hold
my ground even when advance was out of the question. Miss Gye, however, soon realised the situation
and pulled me back, saying, " We are not yet in
Parliament Square; we must manage to get there
somehow; let's try another way." The police had
forced themselves between the ranks of the Deputation, keeping them apart and trying also to sever the
couples, but Miss Gye and I managed to regain hold
of each other. I had not been able to reconnoitre in
the morning as I had intended. The whereabouts
of Caxton Hall was unknown to me, and in the
darkness I felt quite at sea as regards direction.
We soon got clear of the police and found ourselves
in a friendly crowd who half hindered, half pushed,
us along. But I was already so incapacitated by
breathlessness I could not lift my chest and head.

I had repeatedly to stop, and, but for the kindly assistance of my companion and an unknown man and woman of the crowd, I should have been unable to get any further. The main body of the Deputation had made for the strangers' entrance of the House of Commons, near the House of Lords. I saw none of them again until we met in the police station. In Parliament Square we soon became entangled in a thick crowd, some of them friendly, as many not, the great bulk curiosity-mongers. Miss Gye and I were, of course, recognisable as members of the Deputation by our sashes, and though at first whenever the police or the crowd pushed us apart she managed to return to me, we eventually got completely separated and lost sight of each other. My two stranger friends in the crowd, however, not being marked by badges were always returning to my help. The occasion most literally turned out to be one for " deeds, not words." Being doubled up for want of breath, I could scarcely see where I was going, but my instinct led me to avoid the police in every way that I could. They were placed about in twos and threes in no apparent special formation, but now and then one came to a whole line of them, standing shoulder to shoulder. I was during most of the time physically incapable of speech. I only twice was able to express myself in words, on both occasions when I was lifted off my feet and relieved of the toil of dragging my own body. First when the crowd wedged me up against a policeman, I said to him : " I know you are only doing your duty and I am doing mine." His only answer was to seize me with both his hands round the ribs, squeeze the remaining

breath out of my body and, lifting me completely
into the air, throw me with all his strength. Thanks
to the crowd I did not reach the ground ; several
of my companions in more isolated parts of the
square were thrown repeatedly on to the pavement.
Another time a policeman turned me round and,
holding my arms behind me, drove me ahead of him
for several yards at a great pace. So that his
violence would not land me on to my face I exerted
what pressure I could to steady my feet. No doubt
this looked very " violent " on my part to some of
the crowd who jeered and booed. I said to them, in
gasps : " You ask women to behave in a womanly
way ; do you think this is treating them in a manly
way ? " Twice again I was thrown as before
described. I offered no resistance to this whatever,
and being of light weight for my size, I feared that
I was becoming a specially desirable victim for the
experts in this line. Each time I was thrown to a
greater distance and the concussion on reaching the
ground was painful and straining, though in each
case the crowd acted for me as sort of buffers.
When seized for the throw there is also a feeling of
wrenching throughout the body. But I gained in
the direction of the House nevertheless, always
assisted by the crowd. The stranger woman in
particular, a German lady who was tall, well-built,
and of considerable strength, had managed to keep
near me. Three times, after each of the " throws,"
she came to my help and warded off the crowd while
I leant up against some railings, or against her
shoulder to recover my breath. Several times I said
to her, "I can't go on ; I simply can't go on." She

answered, " Wait for a little, you will be all right presently." At the time and ever since I have felt most inexpressibly grateful to this stranger friend.

I was goaded on most of all, perhaps, by the fear that I should be taken off by an ambulance—I heard that some were about—and, if so, that all I had achieved so far would have to be faced again, probably with renewed difficulty. Flashes of vivid light and the sound of a slight muffled explosion came about from time to time. I did not know what these were, they added to the sense of incomprehensibleness and general confusion. It was only towards the end of the day I realised that they were the newspaper photographers' flashlights. The irony of their attentions seemed great.

It was cheering to find that in spite of everything I had gained ground and was quite near to the House. The police were now far less numerous, standing only in small groups of twos and threes. Several of these to my surprise let me pass quite close by them unmolested. The prospect of actually entering the House seemed now not unattainable. My utterly dishevelled condition, my inability for want of breath to stand upright or to string more than two words together at a time, should have enhanced the nightmare of possibly being admitted to the presence of the Prime Minister. But strange to say that fear had left me. The instinct for achievement engendered by the rebuffs of the police, the indignation aroused by the fact that such treatment of a deputation of voteless citizens had been deliberately ordered and sanctioned by the Government, had for the moment cured all fears as to my personal

inadequacy as a spokesman. I found myself at the
gates of the members' entrance. No crowd was near
and only two policemen stood, ordinary wise, at
either side of the gate. They did not seem to be
noticing me. I straightened my back to assume as
much of a normal appearance as possible. I passed
through the gate. At this the policeman nearest to
me turned and seized my arm. Expecting to be
thrown as before, I tried to hold my ground and said,
" Please let me pass," or words to that effect.
Another policeman promptly took me by the other
arm and I was led off at a great pace. The effort to
try and realise what was happening seemed to use up
the last remnant of physical power at my disposal.
I supposed I was being led away, as I had been
warned was sometimes done as a means of dis-
heartening the women, to some distant and lonely
street. But there was nothing of roughness or
insult in the attitude of the police who held me. I
thought perhaps I had fainted or fallen without
knowing it and that they were ambulance men. I
felt unable to cope with the problem, my eyes shut
and my head fell forward. We seemed to be going
a long way. " How shall I ever get back from
here," I wondered. Presently there was an alteration in the sounds of our footsteps and in the
gestures of the men. I opened my eyes and looked
up. Close in front of me, over a doorway, was a blue
lamp with the words " Police Station " printed upon
it. I knew then that I had been arrested. The
discovery was positively life-giving. To think that
it was over, that the struggle would not have to
begin all over again ! I was able to lift my head

a nd walk fairly easily ; the crushing sense of failure
w as gone.   When anticipating events, and trying to
pr epare myself for the various stages of the ordeal
before me, I had supposed that one of the worst
moments would be this of being actually " had up,"
when I should find myself in the police station and
know the first step towards prison had been taken ;
that there could be no going back.   When it came
to actual experience, Cannon Row police station had
all the attractions of a harbour after a storm.   From
the moment I set foot inside this domain of the
police nothing could exceed their courtesy and even
sympathy.   In a large, nondescript kind of waiting
room I was taken up to a table at which a policeman
sat making entries in a ledger.   I was asked my
name, address, age, vocation, etc.   I wondered
whether I was the only one that had been arrested,
but presently two more of the Deputation came in.
The delight at seeing again some of my companions
was very great ; it was only then I fully realised how
the isolation from the others had added to the toil
and gruesomeness of the struggle in Parliament
Square.   We were taken up to a large sort of club
room, in which there were billiard tables.   Several
of the Deputation were already there.   We were
eager, of course, to hear each other's experiences.   I
quickly realised that I had had an unusually good
time of it.   Several of them had been thrown on to
the ground, some kicked, one had had her thumb
dislocated, another had a sprained ankle.   One had
her face streaming with blood from a blow on the
nose.   Before long Mrs. Pethick Lawrence joined us.
It was a curious sensation on seeing her, of mingled

delight that she was with us again, and indignation
that a woman such as she is should have been
arrested. The word quickly went round that we
were to conceal as best we might our various
injuries. It was no part of our policy to get the
police into trouble. Except where they were given
definite orders to the contrary, they did their best
for us, and whenever they themselves controlled the
situation their good will towards us was most marked.
I remember that the most difficult thing to disguise
was the wounded nose of Miss Dugdale, when a
policeman came up to inquire whether any were
hurt or if a doctor were wanted for us.

It was here, at Cannon Row, that I first tasted the
delights of that full, unfetterd companionship which
is among the greatest immediate rewards of those
who work actively in this cause. No drudgery of
preliminary acquaintanceship has to be got through,
no misdoubting inquiries as to kindred temperaments or interests. The sense of unity and mutual
confidence is complete and begins from the first
unhesitatingly. It was most noticeable, as it had
been to me before when a mere looker-on, that this
unity, so far from tending to produce uniformity of
type, had the very opposite effect, it enhanced
individuality. One felt like so many different bolts
and cranks and wheels of a machine, each bringing a
different quality to serve a different purpose for the
smooth working of the whole. For the first time in
my life I felt of some use ; since we all were so
different from each other, it seemed we could each
contribute something to the general solidarity of
experience, of opinion, of conduct.

The throwing about had brought on an aggressive cough which at first checked my ardour to brisk up with my companions. I found refuge in a distant bow window where there was a seat, and where I managed to allay the worst of my cough. Presently a wardress appeared. I asked her if we might have a glass of water for myself and one other woman who had a badly hurt ankle. She was most kind and quickly brought several glasses. I wrote a letter to my mother, reassuring her as to our having got through all right, assuming that some account of the way the women had been treated would appear in the press the next morning, and knowing how great would be her anxiety in consequence. As I recovered from the excessive spasms of the cough, I was able to talk to some of my companions. I felt, for about the fiftieth time since I had come in touch with the W.S.P.U., ashamed of myself in their presence. They were drawn from many different grades of society. Several were women of considerable intellectual gifts, a good many were from the leisured class, some belonged to the working class. Most of them could look back on lives of much more useful service to the community than I could boast, many had made sacrifices greater than my own to join the Deputation, several were running much graver risk, physically, in facing the hardship of prison than I incurred. Some had to face a situation in their homes more distressing even than my own. My little share of difficulty and sacrifice, of risk and dread, which had completely filled my horizon for so many weeks, seemed insignificant enough now. Time passed very slowly, but rather from intensity of interest, acuteness of minute observation, than from boredom. We were to be detained until the House of Commons rose. At last at about eleven the light in the Clock Tower went out and our good friend, Mr. Pethick Lawrence, appeared and bailed us out for the night. One by one we again passed before a seated head constable and his book, and were handed an official paper requiring us to appear at Bow Street the next morning.

I had made no arrangements as to where I should spend the night, my chief concern having been to keep secret my share in the day's proceedings till they were over. I felt stunned and cold as ice. I was in a sense, of course, satisfied and glad that, at least, I had shared what the other women had endured, but for the first time during that day it had come before me forcibly that, not only the Government, but the general public too were to a great extent responsible for the official treatment of the Deputation. I shuddered when I remembered the crowd of curiosity mongers, most of them " respectable " looking people who had treated the whole thing as a kind of cock-fight, and who took sides with the baiters or the baited, according to their apparent likeliness of victory. It was revolting, the kind of thing I could not have believed of a London crowd unless I had myself witnessed it. It made me feel ashamed to the marrow of my bones.*

* I met a lady, Winifred, Lady Arran, in July, 1911, who told me that she had been in Parliament Square and had seen our Deputation. She saw and recognised me. "But," she said, "you seemed not to realise that all the men in the crowd were for you."

I took a four-wheeler and made for my youngest sister's house in Bloomsbury Square. On the way, by as it seemed a strange coincidence, I passed my eldest sister, who was just emerging from a theatre with a friend. I stopped and spoke to her. She apparently did not notice my dishevelled condition or suspect that I had been with the Deputation. She told me that she too was staying in Bloomsbury Square. Arrived there, I found my hostess in bed. I asked her if she could put me up. "You've been with the Deputation?" she asked. "Yes." "You've not been arrested yourself?" "Yes." Her look of mingled sympathy and satisfaction was life-giving, I shall never forget it. Both my sisters were immensely kind and helpful. The house was full, and I shared a bed with my eldest sister. All night she kept her strong arm round my heart and steadied my throbbing body which, owing to the attentions of the police, continued to shake all night. Several times in the night my sister said with great distress, "Oh! Con, you are not fit to go to prison;" but she, of course, was thinking only of the physical side of things. We were able to discuss what best could be done to comfort Mother. Neither of my sisters ever tried to persuade me to take advantage of any possible way out from imprisonment if it should be offered at the trial. They knew my decision could only have been taken after deep and prolonged consideration and for reasons good enough in my estimation to outweigh all those against.

CHAPTER IV

POLICE COURT TRIAL

In the morning we telephoned to mother, supposing she would have received my letter, telling her of the trial at Bow Street that morning, but begging her not to come up for it unless she specially wished to do so. This telephone message was, unfortunately, the first news that reached her of my arrest, and was a great shock to her. She could not have caught a train that would have brought her in time to Bow Street; my eldest sister, Betty Balfour, and my eldest brother, Vic, went down to her later in the day. I felt happier than I had done for a long time. I knew that the first news would be the worst to her, that had now reached her, all else would seem unimportant in comparison; the most difficult, most dreaded part of my job was over. I felt less ill in health than the day before, only played out. My one anxiety was lest I should break down physically and be dismissed from the prison at once "on medical grounds." The wish to avoid this contingency was about as stimulating a tonic as could be desired. It had exactly the same happy effect upon me as some people seem to derive from a glass of brandy.

My sister, Betty Balfour, drove with me in a hansom to Bow Street. A considerable crowd was waiting outside the police station; we elbowed our

way through them with great difficulty and only by
the help of the police, to whom we appealed to ease
matters " for one of the accused." I felt dazed with
the press of people. Before long I found myself in a
sort of loose-box guard-room, or wide passage, where
all my fellow criminals and many of their friends
were assembled. Many of my personal friends were
there and most heart-gladdeningly kind to me. I
had concocted a short speech, explaining the reasons
of my action. I was told it was not very likely that
the magistrate would allow me to deliver it ; my
friends kindly helped me to condense it as much as
possible. It consisted of about four short para-
graphs, sentences bearing on the reasonableness,
justice and urgency of our demand. I remember
nothing of it but these words : " I have been more
proud to stand by my friends in their trouble than I
have ever been of anything in my life before."

Presently there was a roll call and we were all told
off to the various policemen who had taken us
prisoners. I had been so exhausted at the moment
of my capture the night before that I had not realised
what sort of a human being underlay the helmet and
uniform responsible for my arrest. In the morning
I saw that he was a particularly pleasant-spoken and
obliging man, who seemed to understand all about
it from our point of view. He explained what I had
to do. We were first congregated in a sort of waiting-
room with a wooden bench round the wall, and then,
as our time drew near, we were called out into a
narrow passage where the particular policemen who
were charging us stood facing us against the opposite
wall. It looked as if we were *vis à vis* partners waiting

for a country dance to strike up.   We went into
the court as our names were called.   I was thankful
that I knew a little of the hang of the business from
having been present at the trial of Mrs. Pankhurst,
Christabel Pankhurst and Mrs. Drummond.   It is
the absolutely unknown element in these kinds of
ceremonies that adds considerably to their fearful-
ness.   My name came rather early on the list.   I
was thankful that at least this time I had not to go
into the awe-inspiring witness-box.   Sir Albert de
Rützen was the magistrate; he seemed old for
the work.   His manner throughout was querulous
rather than dignified.   The feeling of publicity and
exposure struck me as completely odious; I was
extremely nervous and rather dazed.   I remember
thinking, "If I feel like this, what must it be for the
ordinary prisoners, whether guilty or not, who, day
after day, file into this court ? "   I had a vague
sense that friends were present amongst the crowd
at the back of the court, but the mechanism of the
official proceedings and the individuals who worked
it seemed all at enmity with us—all, that is, except
my partner the policeman.   His look, manner and
voice were so friendly that the set phrases in which
he told of my conduct in Parliament Square and
consequent arrest had a strangely incongruous and
unreal ring about them.   Not that he accused me of
anything very terrible.   He reported that I had
pushed past him exclaiming, "I must see Mr.
Asquith, I must get to Mr. Asquith."   I had never
said anything of the kind, but no doubt, in the
policeman's estimation, this was a remark in keeping
with my actions, and he thought it most probable

that I had said words to that effect. I did not comment on the charge. It seemed all to be known and settled beforehand, and the processes which had to be got through seemed more or less farcical and unreal. When allowed to speak, I managed hastily to blurt out some of my speech, but I felt that nobody listened.

The sentence was one month, with the alternative of being bound over to "keep the peace." I was immensely relieved that there was no fine. At the same time the length of the sentence was a surprise and somewhat of a shock, although I had prepared myself for it. It seemed hardly believable that what I had done was really considered worthy of four weeks in prison. I must, nevertheless, have heard, though the fact did not penetrate into my mind, that Miss Joachim and several others had, less than a year ago, been given three months for this crime of going on a deputation—they, like myself, were first offenders.

On leaving the court we were taken downstairs to the cells. Four or five of us were put together. I was in one with Miss Daisy Solomon, Miss Elsa Gye, my guide and friend of the day before, Miss Dugdale and a sympathetic young girl unknown to me. These cells are narrow compartments, unfurnished, except for a wide wooden bench running the entire length of one wall and terminating in a lavatory seat. This was unconcealed and without any means of drawing water from within the cell. It was periodically flushed with water by a pulley communicating with all the cells from outside. The door had a small grating of iron bars, through

which one could look and speak to people outside.
Many of our friends came by in the passage and
spoke to us through this grille.   They also brought
us some sandwiches and fruit—very acceptable.
This was the worst moment for the friends, and
several mothers who came to say goodbye to their
daughters must have left feeling very miserable.
I felt thankful that my mother was not there.   For
me, it seemed the best moment for many a long day.
My part was over, so far as initiative and activities
were concerned, the rest required only enduring,
always a much easier job to my lazy temperament.
My sisters and youngest brother came to bid me
goodbye.   Some   other   friends   came   and   said
" Well done," or words of that kind.   Christabel
Pankhurst came.   She said " Thank you," and
seemed grateful for my share in the day's work.
This was a most unlooked-for honour and joy,
from that moment I felt a very privileged and
happy person.   The sound of her voice and the
look in her eyes remained stamped upon my mind,
and played the part of a sort of talisman of consolation whenever the trials of my imprisonment
weighed upon my spirits.

As for the physical hardships of prison, these had
been the first items to be measured and prepared
for when deciding to go on the Deputation ; of all
the anticipatory difficulties they had been the least,
and it was a comfort to think that now, before long,
one would know the worst in this respect.   I felt
considerably exhausted still from the battering
about the day before, and I had a craving to be
alone.   Unlimited hours of " solitary confinement "

were the most desirable paradise I could vision to myself.

It was a time of longer waiting than I had ever thought a single day could contain. Already one began to taste that peculiar feature, most markedly characteristic of the whole of prison life, that of being in ignorance of what is going on outside your cell, of why you are being kept there, and of what will happen to you when the keys jangle, bolts rattle, the door is thrown open and you are ordered out. We passed the time recommending to each other various dodges of how to keep in touch while in prison. Knocks on the cell walls with a brush or boot, and at the hour when the wardresses went to meals it was said to be possible to communicate by speaking on the hot water pipe, which runs through all the cells, at the point where it touches the wall. We were to maintain the right to talk to each other at associated labour. Mrs. Pankhurst had obtained the right to speak to her daughter when they were in prison together. Otherwise the silence rule, at all other times we were told, was very rigidly enforced. I showed my companions some leg and arm exercises which I urged them to do, so as to counteract the want of exercise and general stagnation of life which makes so many people ill in prison. We had great fun over this. We were all able to send messages and little scraps of letters to our relations. I was distressed that the stranger girl seemed to have no friends, and no one came to the grille to ask for her. It spoilt the pleasure of our visitors. She seemed of a very retiring and unassertive nature, and I did not like to make inquiries

as to how we could help her communicate with her
friends for fear that she had none. Happily, just
before the passage was cleared of all visitors, three
kind-looking women came to the window and she
sprang up. They were her friends.

The courtesy of the police continued, and
Christabel Pankhurst and a few others were allowed
to remain talking to us for some time after the
general public had been sent out of the passage
communicating with the cells.

Knowing that we had yet a long day before us, we
in turns took advantage of the lavatory end of the
cell, the others mounting guard in a group round
the grating to ensure privacy. This was my first
experience of the publicity attending this process
throughout prison life. It is, without doubt, one of
the greatest trials to the better-educated prisoner;
my sympathy went out especially to the younger
members of our Deputation and to all young
prisoners.

At about 2.30 there came a jangling of keys,
rattling of bolts, and the cell doors were thrown
open. We came out and lined up in the passage
outside, and our names were called out in the order
of our arrest. There were again some delays and
waiting in different passages. One seemed to be
dealt with much like goods at a custom house,
certain facts about one being recurringly inquired
after, investigated, noted in a book, and the goods
then passed on for the same process to take place
elsewhere. Eventually we filed out into a courtyard
where the prison van, " Black Maria," as the hull of
a great dead ship, awaited her cargo. The grim

appearance of that celebrated vehicle had always
been a signal to me, when passing it in the street, for
having to repress an instinct to follow it, an awed
reverence for the distressful plight of those inside it,
an almost maddening craving to know what had been
the cause of their law-breaking, the nature of their
crimes, how far their present degradation could
morally uplift them, what was happening to their
human belongings, what would happen to themselves when they were once more free, whether
indignation, revolt, dull indifference, remorse, or the
harrowingly abject penitence so frequent in suffering
beings was uppermost in their minds. Now I
myself was one of the criminals. I should know the
sensations from actual experience, literally from
within. Of course I in no sense regarded myself as
a criminal, and was aware of a detached spectator's
commentary running through my mind all the while.
It suddenly struck me, perhaps, after all, this is a
sensation common to many criminals. A good
number of them no doubt either know they have not,
or think they have not, committed the offence for
which they are condemned. Many, while admitting
their acts, probably have a moral standard with regard to them quite different from that which controls
the law. Others, perhaps, like myself, think their
acts were entirely justified and right; some, again,
would feel consciously and aggressively at war with
all recognised standards.

I had several times seen men arrested and male
prisoners in the streets, travelling, outside prisons
and police courts, but I had never seen any women
prisoners. Suddenly the picture of them and of

women's crimes came into my mind with a rush.
Who were the women who, day by day, trod the very
stones on which my feet now stood, whose eyes
would look up, a few minutes after mine, to the
terrifying form of Black Maria ? How and why had
they broken the law, in what way were they enemies
of Society ? The impress of their feet seemed to be
one with mine, and up from that criminals' pavement
their mind seemed to get into my own. Child-
burdened women who were left without money,
without the means or opportunity or physical power
to earn it, who had stolen in order to save their lives
and that of their children,—thieves ! Women who
from their childhood had been trained to physical
shame, women who at their first adolescence had
borne children by their own fathers under circumstances when resistance was inconceivable. Women
who had been seduced by their employers. Women
deceived and deserted by their friends and lovers.
Women employed by their own parents for wage-
earning prostitution. Women reduced to cruelty
after being for years the unconsulted churning mills
for producing in degradation and want and physical
suffering the incessant annual babies of an undesired
family. Women who had been stolen in their bloom
and imprisoned for purposes of immoral gain. If
amongst such women, such criminals, there are
many who are professionally thieves, prostitutes
" by choice," immoral " past redemption " as it is
called, sodden with drink, undermined by drug
taking, their maternity transformed into cruelty,
their brains worn to madness, what cause is there
for surprise or reproach, and what hope is there of

cure by imprisonment ? Before they took to these muddy lanes have they not been driven out from the fair road ? What was their training, what their choice from the start ? Are not the doors of the professions and many trades still barred to them ? Their right to work, a fair value for their work is it not denied to them ? When they undertake the burdensome but joyous labour of maternity, is there any security to them of physical respect and choice, of economic security, of rewardful honour and social influence ? Where is the recognition of the woman's great service, how is she helped to render it suitably and efficiently; does the State, the race, the family, the individual, see to it that she has her reward ?

I moved forward after the others. Black Maria looked like a sort of hearse with elephantiasis— warranted to carry many coffins concealed in her body and to bear them to as many graves. She fairly set one shuddering. To get inside her seemed a sort of living death, certainly, most literally, entry into another world. For a moment I hesitated and thought, " Suppose I refuse to get in ? " The mere notion called up the forces arrayed against one and made me realise my utter helplessness. The gates, the bolts, locks and chains, the cells we had just left, the court and magistrate, the high walls all around, the enormous policemen on every hand. The one who stood at the open door of the van said, " Come along, please." His words were civil enough and linked one back to the normal outer world, but his voice and beckoning gesture were authoritative and the sense of physical power seemed to wedge one in.

It was clear that henceforth all one's actions would
be initiated and carried out without choice, solely
by necessity of obedience.

The policeman who had special charge of us for
the journey was a man of jovial disposition, and he
cracked witticisms as he played his 'bus-conductor's
part. We readily responded to his mood. An
antidote was needed to the grimness of the proceedings, but the merriment was by no means all
forced. As soon as I laid aside the remembrance of
the real prisoners and limited the outlook to that of
our own immediate experience, the comic element
was rampant and seemed to dig one in the ribs,
making me laugh with heartiness. We were all, it
seemed, playing some ludicrous, babyish game,
unsuited to our years, but all the more absurd for
that. The 'bus-conductor-policeman got inside ;
we followed him one by one into the narrow central
gangway that forms the spinal marrow of Black
Maria. On either side are tiny separate cells, like
the compartments of a cupboard, the doors of which
when opened completely obstruct the passage so
that only one prisoner at a time can be admitted or
released. On first getting in it seems quite dark,
and the sensation of being rapidly pushed into a
very small hole, squeezed back, the door shut and
locked to the accompanying sound of banging and
much jangling and turning of keys, is extremely
disagreeable. The cell contains a seat and is
ventilated by a grating in the door, by groups of
small holes on either side, in the floor at one's feet,
and by a wire-netted ventilator running under the
roof of the van, as in a 'bus. The cell was so small

that my legs, which are long, had to be tucked up
almost under my chin ; I could imagine that in hot
weather the want of air would be oppressive, but
though the sense of being so closely confined was
disagreeable, the draughts from the ventilators
seemed to play upon one almost excessively and I
felt very cold. When the cells were all filled the
passage was duly packed with prisoners, standing
one against the other like tinned sardines. As the
van was not high enough to admit of standing
upright, this must have been a most tiring position.
Presently there was a final shutting and locking of
the outer door, in which was a small grating window,
as we know it from the outside. Then followed a
rumbling jerk and Black Maria's great overcharged
body began her long, jolting drive to Holloway.
The sensation reminded me of a bathing machine
when it sets out for the sea, but the noise and
jolting and darkness were all greater in degree.
We tried to communicate with each other, to find
out who was in which cell and who was standing in
the passage. We started singing the Women's
Marseillaise and other of our songs. Those in the
passage managed to put a scarf with our colours
through the ventilator under the coachman's seat,
others passed a scarf through the grating window
of the door at the opposite end. These feats
were, of course, communicated to the whole Maria-
full of us, and the news that the police were
allowing the scarves to remain was greeted with
much cheering. Possibly, the driver was unconscious of his magnanimous action, since the scarf
end, I expect, flowed out somewhere near his feet.

The colours every now and then were seen and
loudly cheered by friends in the street. This woke
in me an appreciation of the colours and understanding of their meaning in a way I had not
grasped before. There is so little need for symbolism in these days of print, newspapers, advertise-
ments, etc., but our movement has had to combat
all the conditions of an era of darkness, ignorance,
and barbaric repression. When newspapers will not
accept, publishers will not print, and booksellers
will not sell the true facts concerning us, then a
rapid means of irrepressible communication had to
be sought through the symbolism of colours, purple,
white and green—justice, purity, hope. Wherever
you see them you know we are there, and you know
our meaning.

I joined in the songs for as long as I could and
in the counter-cheering whenever we had a cheer
from the streets, but I soon withdrew into the
luxury of my solitude. I was exhilarated and
happy in mind, but my physical exhaustion was
considerable. The physical tax of the Deputation
and the nervous tax of the trial proceedings had
strained my powers to their uttermost. At last I
was alone with myself. The sense of release from
the necessity of keeping up appearances, of having
to put on a good front, was great. I wondered how
often the occupants of my cell in that black hive
must have felt the same after the anguish, suspense,
complication of fears, connected with their trial. I
noticed that if for a moment I entertained the idea
of initiative, action, the wish to touch normal
existence, to be and behave like an ordinary being,

then the sense of subjection, of being buried alive was all but insufferable and might quickly drive one to the verge of insanity. But the physical exhaustion which leads to the craving for inanition, for solitude and privacy, turned that locked-up slice of the van into a welcome sanctuary.

After a long drive, for seemingly the better part of an hour, the sounds changed and Black Maria quivered over a courtyard pavement, filling us with expectations of arrival. The jolting and noise ceased, the doors were unlocked, one by one as we had been packed in we emerged again and were quickly ushered into Holloway Prison, through what seemed a back door in a yard surrounded by high walls. It made no particular impression upon me. It might have been another police court, less dingy and more clean.

CHAPTER V

HOLLOWAY PRISON

WHEN we arrived at the prison we formed up along a passage in the order of our arrest. We were taken in charge by two or three wardresses who, without a word or sign of greeting, went through the routine of taking our names, ages, sentences, etc. Then we were removed into waiting cells, three or four of us to each one. I found myself, to my joy, in a cell with our leader, Mrs. Pethick Lawrence, Miss Leslie Lawless and Mrs. Fahey, daughter of the great sculptor Gilbert. Strength came back into my bones with delight at being with Mrs. Lawrence. She having been in the prison before gave us various directions and advice. The cell was small and old, the walls and ceiling were dirty, the window of grained glass looked extremely dingy; but Mrs. Lawrence said that in all probability we should eventually be put into new and very clean cells. There was only one stool. Mrs. Lawrence had to sacrifice herself and sit on it, as we none of us would do so in her presence. We ranged ourselves at her feet on the floor, some of us leaning back against the wall. I was very happy to meet Mrs. Fahey, her father and mine had known one another; everything about her had the indication that she was a good woman and probably would become a great one.

I remember vaguely that conversation turned

on to personal yarns as to how we had severally
fared during the Deputation, what had first brought
us into the movement, the experiences of ex-
prisoners. We were to try and claim associated
labour and the right to speak to each other at that
time. All other rules so far as we could grasp them
were to be rigidly observed. If anything in the
prison routine seemed to us unjust we were to petition
the Home Secretary about it, or ask for an interview
with the Governor. If we were ill or felt that any
part of the prison life was being seriously injurious
to our health, we were to ask to see the doctor. But
my recollection of the two or three hours spent in
this cell are vague and shadowy. I was at the end
of my tether, and the craving to be alone overtopped
everything else. Soon after we were inside a light
was lit from without, and I noticed for the first time
a curious aperture in the thick wall to the left of the
door. A piece of grained glass near to the passage
side of this hole, shielded the light which was lit
from outside. The cell was thus lit up with rays as
from a bull's eye lantern. These details interested
me very much. I was fascinated in a grim sort of
way by the " eye " in the door of which I had heard
so much. An oval wedge-shaped indentation in the
thick nail-studded door, at about the height of one's
head, was finished off in the centre by a small
circular bit of glass about the size of a large eye-
glass. On the passage side of the door this was
overlaid with a bit of wood which could be turned
aside like the flap over a key-hole, for the warders
and others to take a look at the prisoner, unobserved,
whenever they chose.

Presently there was a rattling of keys, the lock
turned with what seemed a thundering sound and
the door burst open. I thought it must be some
remarkable and unexpected event that had caused
so much hurry and noise, a fire perhaps had broken
out, but this was my first introduction to the prison
door drill ; the thunder and rattle and haste I was
soon to learn were the invariable accompaniments of
being visited for no matter what cause. The door
was opened only a very little way. No face was to
be seen, but a hand thrust in four tins of food and
loaves of bread on to a little shelf in the corner of the
cell nearest to the door. This was our supper—the
last meal before the night. The little brown loaves
looked appetising, and we were hungry. The kind
of breakfast one eats before one's first " trial " is
nothing sumptuous, and the sandwiches brought in
by our friends made an excellent but not too substantial lunch. The slice of cold pressed meat lying
at the bottom of a dirty-looking tin was not attractive, and the cocoa in a can of the same metal was
positively repellent. We most of us ate some bread,
one was bold enough to try the cocoa, no one sampled
the meat. I thought I would keep my loaf as a
sleeping draught for whenever bedtime came to
this seemingly endless day.

Some time after supper had been let in upon us,
the door was again opened and " Lytton " was
summoned to an unknown presence. I was conducted to a room where a lady in a bonnet stood
waiting to receive me. She was the Matron. She
told me in a civil and considerate manner that she
had a letter for me from my mother which she had

been allowed to give to me. I wondered if my mother
were ill or inordinately distressed at my sentence.
I had a great longing to take the letter, but I had
prepared myself for special privileges being extended
to me and I was determined not to profit by anything of the sort unless I could also secure it for my
companions. I asked : " Is it not against prison
rules that I should have the letter ? " She looked
surprised, but promptly answered, " We make the
rules as the occasion calls for, and you have been
allowed to receive this letter." " Will the other
Suffrage prisoners also be allowed to receive letters ?"
She hesitated, but eventually said decisively, " No."
" Then I am afraid I can't have this letter either."
In spite of my effort to conceal it, I think she saw or
guessed my great desire to have the letter, for the
look in her eyes became very kind and she pleaded
with me to take the letter. I shook my head. Then
she told me it was within the ordinary rules that she
should read the letter to me. I hesitated for a
moment ; there might be something sacredly private
in the letter and it seemed such desecration that
strangers should know what my mother felt. Then I
glanced at the envelope and realised that it had been
officially opened and probably read already. So I
agreed. The letter had been written under the
agitation of the news about me and was not easily
legible in places, so that the matron, although she did
her best, could not decipher some passages, and the
tension of deferred anxiety as to its contents made
my mind and hearing dull from overstrain. As a
result, I received the impression that my mother was
more angry with me than was actually the case.

She did not speak of being ill or broken down herself, and I felt I could bear everything but that ; but the imagined degree of her disapproval shadowed the whole of my imprisonment without cause. However, when I was handed the letter on my release and read it for myself, I found in it so much more sympathy than I expected that the rebound of joy made up for everything. My mother had sent it by her maid to London, telling her to deliver it into the hands of the Governor with a covering letter to him asking him kindly to give it to me. She had thought out all this most considerately so that at least I might be reassured about herself, and be spared any unnecessary anxiety. The maid, on arriving at Holloway Prison, had sent my mother's card up to the Governor as a passport to his presence and asking if she, the maid, might see him. He understood it to mean that mother herself was there, and he came rushing down the stairs in hot haste to greet her ! Poor man, how relieved he must have been to find it was only her maid !

After the Matron had finished reading the letter I, for the moment, forgot all wish to restrict my privileges into line with those of other Suffragettes. I asked, " Can I write an answer to this letter ? " " No." " Nor send a message ? " The Matron shook her head. On returning to my companions in the waiting cell I told them what had taken place. My mind was filled with thoughts of my mother and I remember no details until the door was again thrown open and a wardress told us to line up in the passage, preparatory to inspection by the medical officer. It was good to see the rest of the Deputation

once more. We were told to open our dresses and
underclothes at the neck so that our chests might be
examined. There was some further waiting, during
which time I was able to take note of the wardresses,
several of whom were waiting about and superintending us while others came and went. They were
fine-looking women, young and vigorous, most of
them had good figures and all of them had beauti-
fully-kept hair which gave me a deal of pleasure to
look at. They wore uniforms more or less in the
style of hospital nurses. Most of them wore dresses
of dark blue cloth with nurse-like, small black
bonnets and strings. Some had holland dresses
with aprons, and black velvet bows on their heads.
They held themselves very upright, and their general
bearing brought to my mind certain types of the
chaperon's bench at Court balls.

I had made up my mind to ask the doctor for a
few medical privileges. I dreaded lest he was
coming round to inspect and question us as we
stood in the passage, or that we should have to go
before some " board " or " committee " of men.
To my relief I found that we were being shown into
a room singly, and when it came to my turn I found
there only one individual, a young man sitting at a
table with a big book in front of him. I stood
beside him and answered his questions with regard
to my age, whether I was married or single, what
illnesses I had had, etc. He then tapped my lungs
and examined my heart with a stethoscope. An
infancy and youth of chronic rheumatism had
affected my heart, and the treatment I had received
as member of the Deputation had taxed it severely.

Moreover, the news of my mother's distress, the prison
sounds of keys and bolts, the look of the cells, and
my fears lest the doctor should take alarm at my
flimsy physique and order my dismissal from the
prison, each added considerably to my agitation of
that moment. The doctor's impassive face and
manner changed to one of concerned inquiry after
testing my heart. He asked many questions, and
seemed with difficulty to believe when I told him
that strict vegetarianism had cured my chronic
rheumatism and that it was six years since I had
anything of an attack. I asked to be allowed
flannel underclothing and vegetarian food. It was
a new and strange experience to be so closely
examined by a doctor and not to learn anything of his
verdict. I longed to ask him "What are you going
to report about me?" but I knew that I could do
nothing if he should answer "Dismiss you," and I
was anxious to end the interview as soon as possible.

After the medical examination we were soon
taken off, separately, to the changing room. Here
my trinkets, money, watch, the combs in my hair,
and everything in my pocket were taken from me
and a list made, which I had to sign. I had a
great longing to keep my handkerchiefs. A wardress
sitting at a desk with a large book on it asked a
further string of questions as to age, name, address,
place of birth, previous convictions. As I gave
"Vienna, Austria," for the place of my birth, my
father having been in the diplomatic service, I
thought how impossible it would have seemed had
some seer foretold, at the time of my birth in
an official residence, that I was destined to be

imprisoned in Holloway as a common criminal. A
description of the prisoner's personal appearance
was also entered in the book. It was a comic
moment when the wardress looked up with her
head on one side, as any portrait painter might do,
to investigate the colour of one's hair and eyes.
During all these processes I had a first opportunity
of noticing the manner of the wardresses which so
many Suffragette friends had described to me, but
which had conveyed no clear impression to my
mind. I noticed that there was no inflection in the
voice when speaking to prisoners, nor did the
wardresses look at them when addressing them.
As a prisoner, it was almost impossible to look in the
eyes of my keepers, they seemed to fear that direct
means of communication ; it was as if the wardresses wore a mask, and withdrew as much as possible
all expression of their own personality or recognition
of it in the prisoner. At first, the impression
received was as of something farcical. I remember
that it amused me immensely and absorbed my
attention with a sort of fascinated curiosity. But
this soon went off, and made way for a chilling,
deadening impression. When later on I saw it
applied to the ordinary prisoner, to my companions,
to our leader, Mrs. Pethick Lawrence, it aroused
in me a feeling of indignation and strong resentment.

One corner of this room was divided off by a
curtain. I was told to go behind it and take off my
clothes. As I removed them one by one I wondered
what would have been my experiences by the time
I should see them again. I was handed a cotton
chemise, woollen stockings and a petticoat. In this

queer get-up I was taken to be weighed and then
shown to a bath. The bath compartments were
close together in a passage, like stalls in a stable,
each one only just large enough to contain the bath
and a few inches of standing room at one end.
The door was of the cow-shed order, about three
feet deep, space above and below, and without a
fastening. As I was ushered into one of these, an
ordinary 3rd Division prisoner handed me a bundle
of clothes and a pair of laced shoes. She had a
charming, sympathetic face, and I never shall
forget the look of deep kindness in her eyes and in
her voice as she whispered to me, " If the shoes are
too small, ask the officer and she'll let you have a
larger pair." My tired body, my very soul, seemed
to bask in comfort at her words. I looked and
nodded my thanks to her, afraid to speak, for I had
been warned how we might get the prisoners into
trouble by breaking the silence rule with them.

" So this is the bath of evil fame," I thought,
as I put down the bundle of clothes on the floor and
pulled the cowshed door after me. For the most
part, whatever bit of prison life I had heard about as
specially objectionable seemed to me less bad than
I had expected, and being prepared I was forearmed
to put up with it without grumbling. But the much-
abused, dirty bath which had been so often described
by our prisoners, surpassed all expectations. The
paint was blistered and broken to a surface of mottled
unevenness in a way to gather the scum from the
water into a thousand crevices every time the bath
was used. Whatever the original colour of the paint
might have been, it was now of a dull mud colour,

sufficiently dirty-looking to arouse every sort of suspicion, but not dark enough to conceal the marks of the scum most recently added to the crevices. A large but well-worn scrubbing brush was the only washing appliance, whether for the purpose of scrubbing the bath or the bather was not stated, probably it was used indiscriminately for both. I had been given a small towel of oatmeal-coloured coarse linen striped with red, and a piece of soap wrapped up in a rag of white flannelette. The water was clean and delightfully hot. I tried to concentrate my mind on these two great merits and to raise a sense of present luxury by remembering that this was the last bath I should be able to indulge in for a week. The soap had a smell of disinfectant like dog soap, clean and hygienic enough, no doubt, but under the circumstances a disagreeable reminder of its anti-verminous properties. The towel, which at first sight seemed ludicrously small and inadequate for the purpose of drying a body so large as mine, disclosed with use an almost miraculous faculty for not absorbing moisture. It left one to dry by dint of friction ; my admiration for this towel grew even greater on closer acquaintance with it. Then came the moment for the clothes. They certainly looked a most repellent heap, and it was some time before I recognised their respective uses, and could decide in what order to put them on. I was pleased to see that the flannel garments promised by the doctor were there. Some of my companions, although they asked for and received permission for the same privilege, did not get any flannel clothes until the second week, and some not through the whole term

of their imprisonment. Warmth being my first
consideration I started off with a low-necked flannel
shirt without sleeves. It was patched in many
places, the patches being so coarsely joined that one
could easily trace their pattern from sensation while
wearing it. The flannel was of numerous shades of
yellow and grey, stained in many places, and freely
marked with the broad arrow stamped on in black
ink. The original cut of the shirt had evidently
been nondescript. It was very short, reaching
barely below the hips and low at the neck, and the
patches set in at random had added variety and
counter design in many directions. It looked like
the production of a maniac. For propaganda purposes it was an absolutely priceless garment and I
determined that, if possible, it should accompany
me out of prison, for the enlightenment of those
critics who are appalled at the leniency of the prison
treatment of Suffragettes. Next I put on a chemise
of unbleached, coarse cotton, striped with red, fairly
high at the neck, but without sleeves. This however, was long to the knees and from its ample
voluminous width was one of the most warmth-
producing of the garments. A pair of stays made
without bones but exceedingly stiff and straight in
shape. They had no fastenings and had to be laced
up each time ; the lace had no metal tag so that it was
a slow process. These stays were so unyielding that
I found it impossible to tie my petticoats around the
sheer precipice of their make, and the very next day
I had the courage to dispense with them. Flannel
drawers, short like footballing " shorts," ditto of
unbleached cotton. A very short flannel petticoat.

An old-fashioned under-petticoat of coarse, linseed-coloured material, thickly pleated into a cotton band at the waist—it stuck out almost like a crinoline. Then came the dress, skirt of dark green serge, pleated in same way as the petticoat and tied with black tape strings, the shirt of same material fastened by a single button at the neck ; this was the only garment with long sleeves. A blue check apron which tied in the shirt and gave a very neat appearance. Finally, a small Dutch cap of starched white calico, tied under the chin with tapes. These caps are full of stains, from hairpin rust, etc., when seen from within, but outwardly they have an extremely clean and attractive appearance, redeeming the degraded look of the dress and decidedly becoming to many of the women. They pleased me immensely from the first and were a constant joy to my eyes in all my imprisonments. Two check dusters were supplied, one as a handkerchief to hang from the apron string, one to be folded diagonally and worn round the neck, under the serge shirt. I always have thought this the most comfortable neck covering imaginable and the short time it takes to put on was a daily renewed pleasure compared to the complicated neck apparatus of more civilised modern garments with their innumerable hooks and eyes, pins, brooches, etc. The drawback to this duster-necktie was that it was identical with the handkerchief-duster, and, as they were changed from week to week, there was no means of knowing whether one's neckerchief of one week had not been the nose kerchief of another prisoner on previous occasions. As the clothes came from the laundry

with many stains, unironed, unmangled, and looking
in many respects as if they had not been washed,
this detail of the handkerchiefs remained throughout
my time in prison one of the most trying of the
physical and minor disagreeables. All the clothes
were marked with the broad arrow, if light in colour
they were marked with black ink or some kind of
tar-like sticky substance; if the clothes were dark,
as the petticoat and dress, then with whiting. The
stockings were of thick, rough wool, most irritating
to the skin but warm. I never had a pair that were
long enough to cover my knees, and as the drawers
stopped short of the knees in the opposite direction
I had the chance of sampling the knee part of
a Highlander's dress. I thought it very uncomfortable. Woollen strips were given for garters ; I
thought these practical and hygienic. Last of all I
turned to the shoes. They were immensely heavy
and looked large enough for a giant, they were new
and exceedingly stiff. After a great struggle I
managed to get them on, but they were so uncomfortable that I remembered the advice of the kind
woman and took them off again. I supposed that
now would be my only chance of asking for another
pair, and, although I never have been able to muster
much courage in facing rebuffs, I had an impression
that I should not grow any bolder as prison life went
on. It is comparatively easy to plead or protest on
behalf of some general principle, but to do so for
personal advantage was a more effortful business,
and yet it seemed foolish to go in for needless discomforts when a remedy had been almost officially
suggested. I gathered up my soap and towel and

put my head over the cowshed door to inquire if I
might come out. My eyes fell on a prisoner waiting
in the passage. She was of the 2nd Division, for she
wore a green dress; those of the 3rd Division wear
brown. Her face had a genial expression and broke
into a radiant smile as our eyes met. I thought I
had never seen a more attractive-looking being. In
spite of the subservient humility which the prison
uniform conveys, the look of self-mastery and consequent dignity was prominently expressed in every
line of her face and of her whole form. I felt drawn
to her by a feeling of mixed curiosity and sympathy
and determined to communicate with her if possible.
It never occurred to me that she was a Suffragette.
She was Mrs. Pethick Lawrence, as the smile in her
eyes betrayed before many moments had passed.
My delight at recognising her was quickly succeeded
by an almost irrepressible wave of indignant feeling
that she should be subjected to these outward
symbols of criminality and shame. However little
they were able to degrade her, the authorities had
sentenced her to wear them with that intent. The
futility and injustice of their action seemed to me at
that moment about on a par with each other.

A wardress told me I might come out. I picked
up my shoes and went with them in my hand to an
" officer " who seemed to be the most authoritative
person present. I said to her, " I find these shoes
are rather small for me. Could you kindly let me
have a bigger pair ? " She seemed not to have
heard what I said, did not look my way, but shouted
past me into the air, speaking in a loud voice, very
rapidly, and without any variety of intonation in a

way that sounded strange and unnatural, as if she
were proclaiming an edict written by another person:
" It's — no — good — complaining — about —
those; they're — the — largest — size — in — stock;
you — can't — have — any — others — so — you'd
— better — make — the — best — of — them." As
soon as I realised that she was answering me I felt
very curious and interested. " So that is what it
means," I thought, " being in prison." It required
no flight of the imagination, no tags of theory, to
understand what the effect of this manner would be
on an ordinary prisoner.

Mrs. Lawrence and I waited together in the
passage. Presently a wardress came up to us with
a paper in her hand and began reading out the
prison rules, which we were told had to be strictly
observed under pain of punishment. There were a
great many dealing with a variety of subjects. She
read very fast like a wooden automaton, as if she
herself were weary of this too frequent job.
Although I had heard of many of the rules before
from previous prisoners, I could with difficulty catch
the drift, and it struck me how little the ordinary
prisoner would be able to glean from this hurried
reading of rules absolutely new to her, framed in
official language often far beyond her compre-
hension.

We were then led off through various corridors,
taken out of doors and into another building, weighed
a second time, and taken up a staircase. At the top
we were told to remove our shoes and carry them in
our hands. In the passage there were cells with
locked gates that looked very grim, and locked doors

behind them. One door opposite the stairs was open
and the gate only closed. This was unlocked for us
and we were ushered into a large high room. A fire
burned brightly at one end and beds were ranged on
either side of the walls. It was evidently a hospital
ward. We were shown to the beds nearest the fire-
place, on either side of it, and told they would be ours.
Mrs. Lawrence came over to me and whispered,
" They have put us in hospital." The one thing on
which my hopes had centred throughout that seemingly eternal day was the prospect of being completely alone at the end of it. Now that was not to
be. For the first time I was taken unawares, had
made no preparation for the contingency; I felt quite
unnerved and could have sobbed like a child. The
fact that I was to remain with Mrs. Lawrence was my
only consolation.

The ward was large and high, with big windows
of grained glass at either end, opened at the top by
pulleys so that one could not see out, but the
ventilation was perfect. There were grating ventilators as well as the windows. It was well warmed
by hot pipes running the length of one wall and by a
large coal fire. The furnishings of the fire-place
were both comic and grimly suggestive. A cage of
thick iron bars covered it, from the mantelpiece to
the floor, the cage had a central gate fastened by
a padlock and inside this prison was a poker chained
to the side of the grate, as if it could not be trusted
not to run away and escape through the iron bars
of the cage. I looked round to see how much
of lunacy, or violent criminality, such as were
suggested by these precautions, was represented

amongst the present inmates.   There were ten beds
in all, but only four or five occupants; most of
them were already in bed—one looked extremely
ill.   A wardress, like a nurse, in a holland gown,
came in accompanied by a 3rd Division prisoner
carrying a wicker tray fitted with bottles con-
taining drugs—the " poison-basket " I called it;
it returned regularly twice a day.   A dark-looking
mixture was poured into a little cup and handed to
me.   I explained that I never took drugs and begged
to be excused.   " You've got to swallow that to-night
—those are my orders, there's no choice about it. You
can ask the medical officer about it to-morrow."   I
supposed that responsibility for my refusal would
fall upon the wardress, so I drank it down.

We were given slippers to replace the coarse
nailed shoes which were not allowed to be worn in
hospital on account of the polished wooden floor.
The slippers were of yellow leather, blackened by
much use.   They were extremely dirty, both outside
and in, and I made up my mind never to wear them
without the protection of a stocking.   Mine were
not a pair, each one had an independence of size
and shape which seemed to endow them with almost
human   personality;   but they were comfortable,
and I grew strangely fond of them before the end
of my time.   Our beds were already made; we
were each brought a night-gown of coarse, unbleached calico striped with an occasional red line
and marked at intervals with the broad arrow in
tar-like ink; it had long sleeves.   We were also
provided with a short, grey flannel dressing-gown
and a small tooth-brush.   We were told to undress

and to tie up our day clothes in our aprons, all but
the caps ; these being both white and starched
were treated with the utmost reverence. I discovered that this arrangement was most detri-
mental to the appearance of the apron the next day.
Some prison rules, however trivial and apparently
unimportant, are rigidly enforced, others after the
first instructions are never referred to again. This
was one of those, luckily, for an appearance of
neatness in the prisoners depends entirely upon the
cap and apron. I soon ventured upon a different
plan of damping the apron over night, folding it
evenly as for ironing and binding it tightly round
the heating pipe whenever I could secure a share of
that much sought-after luxury, for the pipe was not
on my side of the ward. This device was successful
to the point of giving me a ludicrous amount of
pleasure. When the clothes were dealt out from
the laundry once a week they looked as if they had
been washed in cold water by a child, but the hot-
pipe dodge soon gave them quite a presentable look.
In the free world I am accustomed to sleep in
flannel sheets, woollen under-clothes, and a hot
bottle, also with two flannel pillows. The prison
equipment was, of course, not of that order. I
took off the dress, stiff petticoat, stays and neckerchief, but kept on all the rest of the day clothing
and wore it under my night-gown. I also kept on
the night-gown in the day time, as it was the only
under-garment with long sleeves. This flagrant
break of the regulations on my part was either not
observed or was winked at by the authorities while
I remained in hospital.

The bedsteads were of iron, the bedding much more luxurious than I had expected—two mattresses, a pillow, three blankets and calico sheets, unbleached, with red stripes, and marked frequently with the broad arrow, as was the rest of the bedding. My sheet, where turned over at the head, had a large stain, as if oil had been dropped upon it. The stain was dry, but, nevertheless, extremely objectionable to look at. I remade the bed, putting the other end of the sheet at the top, only to find that the stains were everywhere. I seem to have been specially unfortunate in my outfit on arrival, for both this sheet and my flannel shirt were more revolting in appearance than anything I saw again in the whole course of my imprisonments. In one respect I was lucky. My dress skirt, though painted here and there with the broad arrow and not new, was yet quite clean and of a convenient length ; some of us had to submit to a skirt that touched the ground, an undesirable length in a place where dust abounds abnormally and no clothes brush is available, or else so short that the legs were disagreeably exposed and gave the appearance of a child's dress. My dress shirt was quite new, had evidently not been worn before, a luxury which I much appreciated, since the sleeves were worn next to the skin and it was made of non-washing material.

At each end of the bed was a small iron shelf. At the head were kept a pint mug for water, toothbrush, soap, towel, brush and comb. On the shelf at the foot were a Bible, prayer book, hymn book, small devotional book, called " The Narrow Way,"

and an instructive book on domestic hygiene,
" A Perfect Home and How To Keep It." This contained two chapters on the necessity of perfect
ventilation in sleeping rooms, the want of which gave
rise to ceaseless complaints from the Suffragettes
in the cells, and the attempt to instruct prisoners
by means of a book, while denying them the primal
need therein declared to be essential, seemed a
cruel as well as a rather ludicrous form of sarcasm.

We proceeded to undress. I took down my hair,
which in those days I wore puffed out round the
head by means of fluffing the inner hair. The hair
brush was of the size and shape of a small shoe
brush, black and with black bristles which, in this
particular brush of mine, were almost worn away.
The comb was like a doll's comb, exactly the size
of my first finger. Though my hair was not particularly abundant, I struggled in vain for the first
two days to get it completely disentangled with
these utterly inadequate tools. There were no
looking glasses anywhere in the prison except, so I
heard it rumoured, in the doctor's room, but I never
saw it when there. I did not attempt to dress my
hair, but did it up in a tight " bun " at the back of
my head. This not only seemed to me most suitable
for the prison cap and dress, but also I had an eye
to seizing the advantages of the prison life. If one
was not to have the comforts and luxuries of free,
civilised existence, I thought one had better shed as
many as possible of its burdens ; I have always
ranked hair dressing as one of these. Some ex-
prisoners had told me that the hair pins we took
into prison in our hair would have to suffice us till

our release. Others said that more could be
obtained for the asking. I very soon found out
that asking for extras of this kind generally produced a refusal and often something of a scolding
as well, so that I limited my requests to those which
would, I thought, be of general advantage to others
as well as to myself. I never saw any hair pins
being given out, and by the day of my release my
own supply had fallen to three. Despite this lazy
decision on my part I had the greatest admiration
for those prisoners who took a contrary view and
who in the teeth of difficulties, such as no looking
glass, an ever-diminishing supply of hair pins, and
the brush and comb as described, yet managed to
produce elaborately dressed heads of hair. Amongst
the Suffragettes, a large proportion of them had
remarkably beautiful and abundant hair, which
when, towards the end of my sentence, I saw them
in the exercise yard gave me an immense amount of
pleasure. Some of these managed to dress their
hair in puffed out and fashionable ways. Amongst
the ordinary prisoners I remember one in particular
who, in the way of hair dressing, excited my admiration almost to the point of awe. She could boast of
no good looks, her face and her hair were of almost
the same shade of pale sand-colour. Through all
the week-days, whenever I saw her, a generous
portion of her front hair was rolled up with bits of
the thin, brown toilet paper, of which a practically
unlimited supply is served out to each prisoner, and
which is put to a great variety of uses. On Sunday
morning the curl papers were there as usual, but on
Sunday afternoon the bond-hair was made free and

a glory of frizzled hair encircled and brightened her poor, tired face. This adherence to outer-world Sabbatarian tradition and conformity to the requirements of orthodox public opinion had a meaning, an artistic and moral expression almost, in prison, such as they lack when occurring in ordinary life. The good-will and neighbourliness of which, no doubt, they were the outward symbol, had met with their reward, for this woman was allowed a share in some of the more privileged duties of the prison service.

I felt very tired as I laid down in the bed, but my brain was screwed to a pitch of nervous excitement that drove away all possibility of sleep. The bed and pillow were stonily hard. My pulses beat against the pillow; the stuffing of it gave back a sort of rattling echo to every beat. A naked gas jet immediately in front of my eyes was alight all night. At a long table underneath it sat a wardress reading or sewing at her own clothes. One of the patients in a bed next but one to mine seemed to be very ill. She tossed and turned continually, as if in a high fever, and her voice sounded parched as she coughed or called out in a half delirious sleep. My distress for her grew as I watched her. The wardress took not the smallest notice of her. I kept on scheming as to how I could help her, but my courage repeatedly failed me. At last I could bear it no longer. I went up to her bed and whispered, " Is there anything I can do for you ? " She answered, " I should like a little water." I took the pint mug of white earthenware from the shelf behind her. It was empty; I took it to the wardress. "May I get that patient some water?" I asked. She nodded assent. I went to a washing-stand with two jugs and basins on it that stood against the wall opposite the entrance door. The wardress beckoned to me and pointed towards another door which led to a small vestibule giving on to a sink and lavatory. This door was kept locked in the day time, but now it was open, another door leading from the vestibule to the landing being locked at night. I drew some fresh water from the tap. The water in Holloway seemed to be like mountain water, better than any I have ever tasted in a town—I suppose because the dry air in prison combined with much dust makes one very thirsty. The prisoner thanked me most gratifyingly and told me she was very ill with influenza. I ventured to whisper before leaving her, "Are you a Suffragette?" "Rather," came the prompt reply, and her face brightened at the word. She was a nurse, Miss Povey, of the Freedom League. The wardress herself had a hard, hacking, bronchial cough, which must have hurt her a good deal. I longed to suggest various things to her to ease it, but I had not the courage. Though I was immensely tired, all possibility of sleep seemed to go further and further from me, and I was too much on view for my thoughts to rest on my home and our people. Finally, I settled down to watching the wardress and the other prisoners, and wondering who they were and what their crimes. I had never seen many people in bed at night before. It was amusing to watch their various ways of lying and gestures, but none of them seemed to be really asleep, or only for very short spells at a time. The wardress had meals brought to her, and there would be short snatches of whispered conversation with the wardress who brought them in. It seemed to me that it must be an appalling way of passing one's time. There was not the interest of a night nurse nor the excitement of a policeman on the beat. There was a large clock at one end of the ward above a swing door leading to a lavatory. It was an unexpected luxury to be able to watch the time.

CHAPTER VI

THE HOSPITAL

At about 5.15 a.m. the stillness of the prison was broken by many sounds. One of the unexpected things in prison life are the number of sounds one hears which one cannot interpret at the time, and which are never accounted for afterwards. One early morning sound, or rather wrenching noise, seemed to come from the ward or passages below our own, as if a giant iron fender, with the fireirons loose and rattling within it, were being dragged from one end of the building to the other.

At home I am no early riser, and I had looked forward with most cowardly dread to the prison routine in this respect. The puritanical elements in my character, which hitherto had failed to drill the rest of me on this point, took on a triumphant air of sanctimonious glee with the expectation that a fundamental reform would be wrought in me by at least this portion of my punishment. But neither the fears of my vices nor the hopes of my virtues were realised. To rise at 5.30 requires no heroism, under any conditions, when you have been allowed to retire to rest at 6.30 or even earlier ; but when in addition your bed is extremely uncomfortable, your pillow seems stuffed with thunder, you have with difficulty been able to keep warm, and when you have scarcely been able to sleep a wink all night, then the virtue necessary to make you rise early is *nil*.

At 5.30 punctually, a little 3rd Division prisoner, who slept in one of the infirmary cells along our passage, came in to clean the grate and light the fire. She moved very quickly and did her work with precision and dexterity. She had a most attractive and lovable face, refined features and a beautiful expression. I wondered for what crime she had been sent to prison. She wore several stripes on her arm denoting good conduct during a protracted sentence.

Soon after this the wardress came near my bed and said it was time to get up. She told me to make my bed and gave me what she called a duster for the purpose of cleaning the iron bedstead. The duster was a strip of thick sail-cloth, which moved the dust but refused to absorb it. I dusted every part of the iron, turned the mattresses and re-made the bed. A thin counterpane of blue check gave a rather pleasing finish. This had to be folded in a particular way at the foot of the bed so as to fall over the side in rectangular fashion. The wardress came up to show me how to do it. It required a certain dodge which pleased me very much, as did all the other old-maidish fads of the kind in the prison routine. But I found that no two experts achieved this bed-cover fold in quite the same way. On that first morning several of the prisoners, two wardresses, and one of the overseeing wardresses ("officers" is the correct term) came up to my bed and refolded the corners of the bed cover, saying, "You haven't got that quite right," or "That's wrong; this is the way you should do it."

We took it in turns to wash. Hot water was brought by the 3rd Division servant of the ward in jugs. There were two crockery basins on the wash-ing-stand, which stood against the wall in the centre of the ward. Such appointments seemed positively luxurious, but one detail was sorely lacking, and its absence marred all the rest—privacy.

When dressed a superintendent " officer " came into the ward. She looked extremely severe. She asked, " Had I dusted my bed thoroughly before I made it ? " " Yes." " Had I turned up the movable half of the iron frame, and dusted it under-neath ? " " No, I did not know there was a part that turned up." She said that was wrong, that another morning I must be sure and do it, but she did not tell me to make the bed again. I was fortunate, for I heard afterwards that this same officer took hold of the bedclothes and threw them all off without explaining to their owner anything of what it was about.

Breakfast was brought in at about 6.30. The patients who were well enough to be out of bed laid the cloth and put out plates from a small cupboard hung on the wall near the door. Then a wardress and two 3rd Division prisoners carried in the hot milk and tea in large cans, loaves of bread, a small supply of butter and boiled eggs. The tea was ladled out from the cans with a long tin spoon and poured into the earthenware mugs. It looked as if it must make a great mess, but was always very skilfully done. The mugs and plates, I was pleased to notice, were made of leadless glaze. In ordinary life I have always considered hot boiled milk a very disagreeable drink, but that morning, after the long wide-awake night, it seemed to me positive nectar. In hospital we were allowed white bread ; it was of excellent quality, made of seconds flour. Tea and eggs are no part of my diet, so I was limited to the milk and bread and butter, but they were dealt out abundantly, all except the butter, which was fresh and of fairly good quality. Those of us who were well sat at the table all together and waited on the patients in bed. We were not supposed to talk to each other, but we were allowed to communicate to a certain extent in whispers. We were very much amused at each other's appearance in the strange clothes and cap.

After breakfast we cleared the table, the gate of the ward was unlocked and we carried the crockery to baskets on the floor in the passage. From there the 3rd Division prisoners took them and washed them out in the bath room cell next door. The hospital wardress had to stand at the gate all the time that we were doing this. Some wardresses allowed us sometimes to come and go freely ; others, or the same wardresses on different days, would allow only one of us out of the ward at a time. This and all other rules of the kind would hardly ever be told to us in so many words, but suddenly the wardress would step out and block the way, laying her hand upon us without a word as if we were animals. This being handled when there is no occasion for it seems very insulting. Like all these prison methods, it seemed curious and interesting when first done to oneself, but aroused a feeling of indignation when one saw it being done to others.

It gave one the feeling of belonging to a race apart,
something degraded and imbecile, despised not only
for the particular crime one had committed but as an
all-round inferior being. The moral influence of
this kind of treatment is rubbed in afresh through
every hour of prison life and has a bad moral influence
on both prisoners and wardresses. It seemed,
moreover, quite unnecessary.

After breakfast the chief wardress who had
reproved us for not lifting up the movable section of
the beds, beckoned me to her—" Take off your
slippers. Bring your shoes ; you have to go before
the Senior Medical Officer." This made me anxious.
I knew quite well that I was not in a state of ill-
health to cause the release of an ordinary prisoner ;
I knew, too, that many suffrage prisoners had been
kept in prison when much more seriously ill than I
was. But I remembered the specially constructed
rule which had sanctioned a letter being delivered
to me, and I was on the look-out for more privileges
of the kind. The wish was strong in me to have
personal experience of the inflictions which a Liberal
Government thought suitable to woman Suffragists,
to share every incident of the treatment which my
leaders and friends had suffered in our cause and to
gain some experience of prison life from within for
the sake of one day being equipped to work for
prison reforms.

Outside the ward I was told to put on my shoes.
I hated those shoes with the vigorous hatred of a
child. The laces had no tags, my fingers were very
cold, and being hurried up by the wardress made
them the more awkward. I was given a cloak of

green cloth and taken downstairs. The staircase
was of stone and, with my feet encased in these thick
unyielding shoes, I was afraid of slipping. I laid
my hand on the banister to steady myself. " If you
must have hold of that rail, can't you use the
uprights ? Don't you see the top's polished, you'll
soil it." This remark was made by the wardress
who shouted past me with a sort of bark. At the
foot of the stairs she pulled at my cloak, " Got it on
inside out, is that how you mean to wear it ? " This
was said in the same voice, but I thought I caught
something of a twinkle in her eye as if she were not
without a sense of humour and would welcome an
appeal to the same. I noted this for future experimenting, but was at the moment unable to take
advantage of it. I felt mentally stunned, physically
cowed, morally indignant, a blend of sensations
which I think must be common to many prisoners.

The doctor's room was a sort of office well lit by
several large windows. The Senior Medical Officer
was a different man from the doctor who had
inspected us the previous night. I had expected a
struggle on the question of tonics, but to my delight
he quickly agreed that I should survive without
drugs. He spoke in an ordinary voice, his expression
of face and the things he said were quite natural, he
treated me as though I were an ordinary mortal.
After even twelve hours of prison customs this seemed
a remarkable and gladdening thing. Up till that
moment I had incessantly wished that I should some
day be able to tell the officials the entirely harmful
impression conveyed by their manner to the
prisoners. It was obvious that this official manner

was quite detached from the individual personality
of those who assumed it.   They looked and spoke in
this way, not to serve their private ends, but in com-
pliance with some strangely mistaken tradition, as a
matter of conformity.   When under the heel of it,
one felt a conviction that no reform of prison regulations would alter the maiming influence of prison life
until this tradition were altered.   Now, on the
contrary, I felt equally desirous of proclaiming that
here was an individual with an innate gift to usefully
fill the part of prison official ; he had mastered the
fundamental matter of treating prisoners as he would
treat other human beings.   I think this doctor tried
some slight persuasion to obtain my release by consenting to be bound over.   He quickly saw, however,
that my imprisonment was not due to any hasty or
unconsidered act, and he did not press the matter
for long.

It was agreed that I should go back to bed for the
benefit of my heart condition.   After the prolonged
strain I was only too glad to do this.   The morning,
however, was taken up with many visits of inspection.   The Governor made his rounds in a formal
way and never relaxed his official muscles, but he
seemed kindly, nevertheless, and I felt sorry for
him having to play what I supposed was a disagreeable game for him.   The matron wore a quite
different expression from when I had seen her the
evening before.   She looked very tired, and I
wondered whether any part of her work gave her
satisfaction.   The Chaplain, too, looked ill and I
thought what a harrowing life his must be, always
pouring out sympathy for sorrows and sufferings

that he had no power to relieve. He came up to my
bed with a smile and said, in a voice well-flavoured
with contempt : " Well, you must have done something very wicked to find yourself in here ? " I was
surprised, supposed he meant it for a joke; supposed,
too, that possibly from his point of view it was an
entirely comic thing that we should be in prison.
But it seemed odd that his imagination and
sympathy should not at least have led him to inquire
first what was our point of view in the matter, and
he seemed not to consider it possible that our actions
should have entailed self-sacrifice and the pain of
bringing anxiety to those we loved. I answered :
" If I had thought what I did very wicked, I should
not have done it."

At ten o'clock hot milk was again brought into the
ward for those who wished for it, also fruit, but, to
my great relief, this was optional. The morning was
taken up with cleaning the ward. The 3rd Division
prisoner by a series of processes and with the aid of a
long-handled polisher, first swept, then beeswaxed,
then polished the wooden floor. She did it with the
skill of an expert and her graceful gestures were a
pleasure to watch. She never paused for a moment
in her work except when the entry of some official
necessitated a temporary suspension.

Then followed a polishing of metal fixtures and
dusting of the walls, shelves, books, etc. To my
great joy, the patients not in bed were ordered to
take part in the dusting. It was a means of prac-
tising my favourite hobby of cleaning, also of keeping
warm, of helping the little 3rd Division prisoner, and
occasionally exchanging a whispered word with her,

though this was rarely achieved. The dust was
continuously stirred throughout the morning, moved
from the floor, then from the wall. The grey fluff
that came from the bedding and floated about the
floor gathered a certain amount of dust as it was
swept up and eventually burnt in the fire, but no
damping or reasonable process to get rid of the dust
was used, so that shelves, books, beds, were no
sooner dusted than they were again covered as before.
On one or two occasions I ventured to damp my
duster, but this, of course, made it very dirty, which
result met with disfavour. It was no doubt felt
that as the more vigorous patients had nothing
much better to do, they might as well go on dusting
throughout the morning. In an ordinary home the
daily processes of sweeping and dusting always seem
to me absurdly laborious, elaborate and inadequate ;
the workers at these household crafts having had
so little share in the application of modern invention
to their toil, and little appeal on behalf of public
service and utility has been made to women of higher
education and greater leisure than the workers themselves. The housecraft of prison, as one watched it
day by day, pressed one's thoughts on to the subject.
The collecting of dust by means of damp cloths
immediately followed by a dry rubber would
certainly be more effective.

At about twelve the midday food was served, it
was the most solid meal in the twenty-four hours.
It consisted every day of fried fish, potatoes, cabbage,
bread, butter and a custard pudding or boiled rice
pudding made with eggs. I, being a vegetarian, did
not eat fish. After some days I had the courage to

ask for a rice pudding made without eggs and was allowed this. The food was good and well cooked, but the absolute monotony of the bill of fare was a great trial to some of the prisoners, more especially the bed patients.

In the afternoon, those who were allowed out exercised for an hour walking round and round a yard with high walls to it. We were exercised at a different time from ordinary prisoners. We were not allowed to talk to each other and had to walk single file one behind the other at a given distance apart. As there were never more than four or five of us from the hospital a certain amount of laxness was allowed. We could go our own pace, the faster walkers from time to time overtaking the slower and now and then one was allowed to stop and lean up against the wall. The weather was cold, we had frost and snow, during most of my time in Holloway, and being used to furs, gloves and muffs, I felt the cold very much especially in my hands. The only extra garment for out of doors was an unlined cloth cape with hood attached. This was warmer than it looked. I used to do arm exercises as I walked to stir my blood. The discomfort of the shoes prevented any joy in walking, there was no yield in the soles and the hard leather pressed the feet in a way to make every footstep a consideration. I have sensitive feet and may have suffered more in this respect than others, but to judge from appearance the tread and gait of all prisoners is laborious and artificial, affecting the hang of the whole body, on account of the shoes.

I did not go out for the first two or three days.

In the afternoon the sense of fatigue overcame one. Unless the patients were ill enough to undress and get into bed, they were not allowed to lie on it, we, however, sometimes sat on a chair close to the bed, leaned our heads upon the pillow and slept.

Some read books, others did needlework, others tended the bed patients.

I am a little deaf, and found it a tiring business after no sleep at night to hold intercourse by means of whispers, the only form of conversation allowed, but nevertheless this was far the most interesting occupation available. People are inclined to be communicative, although total strangers to each other, when cut off from their homes and friends and all sharing the same fate. I heard life stories in Holloway hospital that would fill many novels. I wondered, as I have always done, how it is that people can trouble to read books when romance, adventure, comedy, tragedy and pathos are to hand at all times in more living form and with far greater variety of event and character.

At about five the supper was brought in, the food being the same as at breakfast. I sometimes kept back a potato from the midday meal to eat cold with the bread and butter. As soon as this was cleared away we were let out in turns to the bath-room, where a hot foot bath was provided, and privacy. This was a most welcome luxury. Two mornings after we had been in, a screen was put round the washing table so that the morning ablutions became more effective. From this time forward I experienced nothing to complain of in the washing line.

These first days of prison, although immensely

interesting, were, nevertheless, longer in point of time than anything I remember in life, not excluding early childhood. The novelty of every detail and the fact that observation was sharpened to a pitch only known at moments of great emotion, no doubt partly accounted for this.

I knew that my eldest sister had intended to come and visit me as soon as she could get a permit ; I supposed she would have no difficulty. The first and second day went by and she did not come. I became a prey to a morbid depression of spirits. Being completely cut off from previous existence, one rapidly fell into the belief that all friends and belongings had discarded and forgotten one. This state of mind was one of the most melancholy experiences of prison. It seems childish and absurdly unreasonable when remembered after release. It nevertheless was bitterly real at the time, and a few hours within prison walls were sufficient to develop the illusion. As with so many other prisoner sensations, it is akin to child life, engendered from complete helplessness, subjection to others, ignorance and uninformedness as to what is happening outside the cramped horizon of the life to which one is subject. The sense of continuous expectancy and comfort for present distressful monotony in the belief that undreamed of good might happen at any moment is also very similar to the mental outlook of children.

The next day, February 26, Mrs. Pethick Lawrence was summoned out of the ward. She came back radiant, having had a visit from her husband. Her happiness and the news she brought back of the outer

world shed joy upon us all, but, nevertheless, I had
the feeling all the more strongly that my own people
had forgotten me, since they, I argued, could have
obtained the same privileges as Mr. Lawrence.   The
ordinary prisoner is usually allowed a visitor only
after the first month of the sentence has expired.

The members of the Freedom League were in great
excitement, expecting that their leader would be
coming to prison that day and very likely be sent to
hospital. She had been arrested at the head of a
deputation when the other members of the Freedom
League had been imprisoned, but her case had been
remanded.   In the afternoon the prayer card at the
head of one of the spare beds was altered to one of
Roman Catholic prayers. This was taken to indi-
cate beyond doubt the coming of Mrs. Despard. I
read the Roman Catholic card and thought it compared favourably, in point of suitability to prisoners,
with the selection made by the Church of England.
The hymns, biblical passages and prayers were more
tender and personal and less concerned with mis-
doing. They were rather childish, but, as I have
pointed out, prisoners resemble children.

In the evening, when the curfew hour of our
bedtime was already past, a stranger prisoner, a very
remarkable looking woman with white hair, a fine
face, and stately carriage came into the ward, and
was immediately recognised by her followers as their
deservedly beloved leader. She came up to greet
Mrs. Lawrence, and they were about to shake hands
with cordiality when the wardress interfered, angrily
forbidding them to touch one another.

When the poison basket came round that night, I

noticed with admiration and envy Mrs. Despard's dignified but effectively determined refusal of the proffered tonic. She discarded the hospital whisper and said out loud to the drug dispenser : " I have never taken medicine in my life and I am not going to begin now ; I will explain to the doctor to-morrow." She was a most vigorous lady. I have never heard of a prisoner before or since who slept soundly through the first night of sentence. She walked round the exercise yard, too, at a pace beyond my powers. I was fortunate in achieving one very interesting conversation with her, when she told me of how the women's workrooms instituted under the recent Local Government Board's Central Unemployment Fund had been closed down, on the ground that they were not self-supporting, although they were worked at less loss and at far less cost per head than some of the workshops for unemployed male workers. £28,000 was said to have been spent on one farm colony for men which had produced only £1,000 return. Yet there was no complaint, no talk of closing down because of its unremunerative character. £750 had been allotted for widows' and single women's workrooms. These, too, were worked at a loss as there was not sufficient sale for the clothes they made, and because of this loss, small in total and far smaller in proportion than in the men's work, the room was closed. To our great surprise Mrs. Despard was released " on medical grounds," after serving only a week of her sentence, although she was in robust health. The weekly paper *The Christian Commonwealth* had taken up her case and the House of Commons was circularised by

the editor, Mr. Dawson. This is supposed to have
moved the Home Office to clemency.

One of the patients who slept in a separate cell,
but came to the ward for meals, had a particularly
attractive face and personality. She was exceptionally gentle and courteous in her manner, but her
outward calm nevertheless suggested a reserve of
inward force ; her eyes had a way of lighting up
suddenly with sympathy, pathos, or fun. I longed
to have a free talk with her. Her name was Mrs.
Clarke ; she was one of three Suffragettes, the others
being Miss Irene Dallas and Miss Douglas Smith, who
had been arrested on a deputation to Downing Street
on January 24. I had sent in my name for the larger
deputation to the House of Commons. I had
been invited to go instead on this smaller one to
Downing Street, but I had refused. When I saw the
women afterwards who had undertaken this much
more disagreeable job than mine, I felt again
thoroughly ashamed of myself. I should say they
were all three unusually sensitive to the odiousness
of the errand which had appalled me to the point of
shirking it. I did not realise until after she had left
the prison that Mrs. Clarke was a sister of Mrs.
Pankhurst.* These three were released on the
morning of February 27. We could just hear the
sounds of their welcome and the band playing
the *Marseillaise* outside the prison, but, of course,
could see nothing through the high, grained-glass
windows. One was filled with a great longing to

* Mrs. Clarke was released from Holloway the second
time on December 23, 1910. She died on December 25,
1910.

join them. This was after only thirty-six hours
of prison, I imagined what it must be to those
under long sentences when a fellow prisoner is
released.

On that day, Saturday, at about the time for our
exercise, one of the superior officers came into the
ward and, singling me out from the others, ordered
me to leave my slippers, bring my shoes to put on
outside and follow her. I had already learnt the
order of the daily routine, and every event that was
slightly exceptional filled me with hope that my turn
had come for a " visitor," but I had had several
disappointments in this line and so steeled myself
not to expect too readily. I was taken across the
yard of the main entrance and ushered through a
part of the prison where I had not been before to a
row of rooms looking like small offices with glass
doors, giving on to a passage. On the door to which
I was led was written the word " Solicitor," and
almost before I had time for joyous conjectures as
to who my " visitor " could be, the door was opened
and my sister, Betty Balfour, was facing me. It was
like seeing the sun after a long time of darkness. I
only then realised to what an extent the gloom of
prison surroundings and anxiety about my home
people had taken hold of my mind. The sight of my
sister did not dispel them, but seemed to take me
from within their grip to an independent position
outside of them, the physical trials of my fellow
Suffragettes in our ward, the anti-happiness get up
of the prison building, clothing, food, equipment, and
the general vitality-destroying framework of the
prison system and its officials, seemed suddenly to be

a thing apart from me instead of one with my very self.

We were told to seat ourselves on opposite sides of a small table and not to touch each other nor pass anything from one to the other. The door was left open and the wardress sat just outside so as to hear, and if necessary control our communications. She was a benignant, kindly woman whom I had not seen before ; she reminded me of Madeleine de Rohan, of the Theatre Français, in *Le Monde où l'on s'ennui*. She was dignified, gentle, sympathetic. I was nevertheless afraid of her, or rather of the office which she filled, and wished her miles away. I never saw her again, either during my month in Holloway or on the many occasions when I have since revisited it on behalf of other prisoners. I have tried several times to write down my impressions of this " visit " from my sister. I have to own myself beaten. The joy of it seems so exaggerated, I cannot trust myself to convey it for publication. All prison sensations are exaggerated from the point of view of those out of prison, that is their essential characteristic. Still more exaggerated must a genuine description of them seem to a prison official who is used to witness without sharing them. For men and women who have experienced them, it is never again possible to discredit their intensity or to be contemptuous towards those who try to give expression to them. My own recollections of prison are isolated from other parts of my life by a kind of halo of reverence. Awe comes over me whenever they are in my mind ; this awe and reverence are twice as powerful in connection with those moments

when joy had her turn, and these rare occasions of
gladness outweigh from their importance the much
more numerous experiences of gloom, anxiety, anger
and physical suffering.

After twenty minutes of eager and joyful ecstasy
of communication, during which I drank in the sight
and sound of my sister's loved personality, the
wardress told us that our time was up and I was
taken away. My sister and I were allowed to kiss
each other before parting. When I got back to
hospital I had three very distinct sensations. That
of having experienced a good thing which was over ;
distress at not being able to impart my joy to my
companions nor discuss it with them, since none of
them knew my sister ; indignation when I realised
that no ordinary prisoner, who needed the help of
joy so much more than I did, and no Suffragette
prisoner without influential friends, would be able
to have a similar experience until after the first
month of imprisonment. In the practical sense
more especially, for the settlement of business and
family affairs, it is on first being imprisoned that
letters and interviews are needed by prisoners.

The glow of my own happiness, however, triumphed
over all else until bed time, when with a perversity
born, I suppose, of the accumulated fatigue of recent
days and nights, the one flaw in my sister's visit came
uppermost in my thoughts and possessed my brain
with an unconquerable tyranny. Some days before
the deputation, she had been in correspondence with
a leading Conservative M.P., one whose lifelong
belief in Woman Suffrage had become a little rusty.
The questions he put to my sister proved that he had

not kept pace with recent events in the movement
and was unaware of the tremendous demand made
by women themselves for the vote as evidenced by
the resolutions, petitions, and unreceived deputations of organised societies of working and professional women, quite apart from the unions that had
sprung up everywhere expressly in support of the
Suffrage. I had sent her a collection of printed
evidence to this effect for the benefit of her correspondent and I inquired of her eagerly that afternoon
as to the result. She told me that she had unfortunately lost the papers. I was annoyed and
wasted several minutes of our precious time together
in reproof. The memory of my anger came back to
me now in exaggerated dimensions. Why had I
allowed myself to be reproachful to her ? She had
been so dear to me, so prompt and efficient in her
efforts to come and see me, so comforting in her
wealth of sympathy, and I had rewarded her with
reproaches ! As I went back over the scene, my
heart was wrung with longing to send her some little
message of good-will and my inability to do so
appeared to me then as nothing short of a tragedy.
For the fiftieth time in those first hours of imprisonment I seemed to be and to feel like a child, at the
mercy of fluctuating emotions extreme in their
intensity. I longed to be alone, but that night the
ward patients kept unusually wide awake and I
had to restrain myself over and over again. As
the night wore on, the avenue of beds became less
troubled, a sense of privacy grew in proportion and
at last I gave way to my grief and sobbed. I
covered my face in the bedclothes, but in spite of

this precaution the wardress heard me and before long she came and stood by my side. I expected a scolding. She very seldom took any notice of the patients till morning, I knew it was her business to reprove me, but on looking up at her face I saw that the customary mask-like expression had vanished. She was kind, she inquired tenderly why I was crying, sat down on my bed and held my hands, told me that my sister would not remember my reproaches but would be unhappy if she knew of my present distress. She did not laugh at me, she showed as much sympathy as a friend. It was a great surprise. She stayed talking to me in whispers for a considerable time, though looking continually towards the door as if in fear of being detected in a kindness, for through the night as through the day, she was liable to unseen inspection through the locked gate and open door, or through the spy-hole of the door when closed. I was most deeply grateful to her, it was a delightful discovery that underneath her rigid exterior she was an unspoiled human being. I longed to return her kindness and ventured to propose that I should rub her chest to ease her hacking cough. At first she would not hear of it, but at last, after I had fetched some ointment from the bed-head of one of the patients who had a cough, she consented and allowed me to open her dress. She seemed much afraid and told me she would probably be dismissed if we were seen. My attempts to allay her distress eased my own mind of its childish trouble, for which reason she had probably allowed me to help her. I would gladly have talked to her all night about prisoners, the working conditions of wardresses, her

own life, but this, of course, was forbidden. She
soon went back to her table, her face resumed its
former expression and I never again held any intercourse with her.   If the horrors of prison existence
are enshrined in an atmosphere of nightmare, the
rare happy moments have the glamour of a good
dream.   This kind act of the night-wardress remains
as one of the sunlit flower patches of my time in
Holloway.

The next morning after the superior officer had
been her rounds taking temperatures, she beckoned
me to her.   "What have you been complaining
about ? " she asked sharply.   " I haven't been complaining," I answered.   "Yes, you have—you complained of something to a visitor."   I then remembered that, when reassuring my sister as to my health
and to prove to her the genuineness of my statements as to prison conditions being in no way
harmful to me, I had mentioned two things which
proved rather trying, viz., that my underclothes and
stockings were too short to cover my knees, and the
fact that one small towel had to do service for all
purposes during a week.   I reported this to the
wardress, but explained that I had mentioned these
not in complaint but to prove to my sister that my
discomforts were insignificant.   "Well," she retorted, " next time you have anything to complain of
come to me with it—if not I shall get into trouble."
This seemed the very reverse of prison regulations,
for usually the trouble was caused by anything out
of the ordinary being granted to a prisoner.   From
that time forward I was supplied with two towels,
one of them renewed every week, and two rolls of

flannel bandages were brought to me to cover my knees. I supposed that the ordinary cells, to which I expected soon to be transferred, would be much colder than the hospital, so I held the flannel bandages in reserve. After I came out of prison I heard that my family were troubled, knowing how dependent I was upon warm underclothes, especially at night. My eldest brother had interviewed the head of the Prison Commissioners Department, Sir Evelyn Ruggles-Brise, who had said that I should at once be supplied with bed-socks. Bed-socks, of course, do not grow in prisons. They were represented, I suppose, by my flannel bandages, but the official statement had the desired result of quieting my family's anxiety.

CHAPTER VII

SOME TYPES OF PRISONERS

THERE was no chapel for us on Sunday and it seemed an unusually long day. My thoughts yearned towards my home people, and I rehearsed the joy of my sister's visit over and over again. The excitement of seeing her had now given way to a wholesome and relaxed fatigue and I looked forward to another night with a sure expectation of sleep. In the evening at about six o'clock, our bed time, a new patient was brought into the ward. She was carried in by 3rd Division prisoners, helped by a head officer, sitting upright in an ordinary armchair with carrying poles attached to the arms. She looked extremely ill and ashy pale. She was evidently in great pain, though she did not groan or call out. There was nothing in the way she was treated to suggest a surgical case, and I concluded that she had been brought in for some fever or acute internal complaint ; from the look on her face I thought it not unlikely that she might die in the night. She was a stranger to me and after the first few minutes my instinct was to turn away and not look at her, remembering the distressing sense of publicity which I myself had felt so acutely on first coming to hospital. The news quickly spread in the ward that she was a member of the Freedom League, by name

Mrs. Meredith Macdonald. She had several friends
in the ward, but they scarcely recognised her when
she was first brought in.   They told me that she had
fallen down that morning in the exercise yard, which
was slippery from frost, and had injured her leg at
the hip joint. I soon got to know her myself and
talked much with her. No nurse was in attendance
on her during the night, only the ordinary night
officer (wardress). The anguish of acute suffering
in this newcomer and her harrowingly unassisted
condition, drove all thoughts of my own people from
my mind and all question of sleep from my eyes.
The accident had taken place at about 9.30 a.m.
She had slipped over a small gutter and fallen with
great suddenness to the ground. She lay for several
minutes stunned in the snow. The wardress in
charge ordered her to " go into the middle," where
those who cannot walk fast drag round in a smaller
circle, but she did not attempt to move. Some of her
fellow prisoners came to her assistance, they were
immediately ordered away by the officers. She
looked across the yard to the wardress of her own
corridor who then came to help her. " I have hurt
my thigh," she said ; " I think I had better go
in." The wardress answered, " Very well." As
soon as she began to walk she felt pain in the hip
bone and put her hand on the wardress's shoulder for
support. It was a very short distance to her
block (D X) of the building and on reaching it she
was handed over to another wardress who suggested
she should sit down and rest before going up to her
cell. She was about to do this when her right leg
collapsed completely under her and she would have

fallen, but that a wardress held her up and put her
into a chair. She was then told to go upstairs
"before you get any stiffer." The leg was useless,
but by help of the double banisters she hopped up
two flights to her cell, an older wardress from the
upper corridor lending her assistance. She had no
control over her foot and said to the elder wardress
that there must be something wrong. The wardress
answered, "I am afraid you have injured the muscles
and that is a very painful thing," and offered to put
her to bed. She could not face the additional pain
of being undressed. About half an hour later a
doctor and the hospital superintendent visited her,
and she was subjected to extreme pain by a reckless
testing. She herself suspected a fracture and suggested having recourse to X-rays as the only means
of satisfactorily testing this. She pleaded the special
need in her case of, if possible, retaining her walking
power on account of her young children. The doctor
sent her a draught to ease the pain, but this was
quite ineffective. She lay in her cell all day unable
to keep still for long on account of the pressure of
the injured part on the mattress, and yet every move
was exquisitely painful. In the evening the doctor
came again and renewed his agonising overhauling.
She was then removed to hospital, the chair in which
they carried her, having no foot rest, the injured
leg came in frequent contact with the porters, causing
her the intensest pain. It is not surprising that she
looked more dead than alive on reaching the ward.

The injury and the rough methods of investigation
combined produced a feverish and most painful
condition in the patient. The case was taken over

by another doctor (Dr. Sullivan) who at least handled
the injury much less brutally, but no attempt was
made to treat it surgically.   A slight wound in the
lower part of the leg was occasionally dressed and
bandaged by the hospital wardress, who visited us
twice a day when temperatures were taken and drugs
distributed.   There was no other nursing whatever.
The doctor's examinations consisted only of measure-
ments to compare the length of the injured leg with
the healthy one.   Nothing was done, in recognition
of fracture, to reset the bones or keep the limb in one
position, no weight was applied to stretch the shorter
injured leg ; there seemed to be no aim in the doctor's recommendations beyond that of helping to
restore a bruised bone by as nearly a natural use of
it as the patient could be urged to make.   A circular
air-cushion was supplied and extra pillows ; also a
night table by the side of the patient's bed, and a
bed pan was kept in the ward which could be used
for bed-patients with the voluntary assistance either
of the wardress in charge or of the fellow-prisoners.
Mrs. Macdonald was kept in bed for the first few
days, but the extremely painful pressure from lying
on the injured bone with the legs in flat position
caused her incessant restlessness, and before long she
begged leave to get up and sit in an armchair.   This
was allowed and soon she was urged to move about,
walk and use the leg as much as possible.   In spite
of the most heroic efforts, the last recommendation
was impossible.   She moved about leaning on a
chair by way of crutch and getting up or sitting
down with the help of her fellow-prisoners.   The
complete loss of control over the injured leg pointed,

in my estimation, to much more serious harm than
mere bruising.   I felt the greatest indignation from
that first evening of her entrance among us at the
way this prisoner was treated.   Her suggestion about
the X-rays was ignored, her request to the Governor,
and eventually her petition to the Home Secretary,
that she might be visited by her own doctor was
refused.   When the doctors talked with her about
her case they seemed to pay no attention to her own
views, but rather accentuated the official prison
manner of ignoring individuals as though she had
been a child or an irresponsible person.   Yet there
was no trace of exaggeration or a tendency to work
up grievances over her own case.   Through all her
acute and continuous physical suffering she showed
keen powers of observation and a sense of humour
that constantly relieved the nightmare of horror
with which I watched her pain.   Her heroism under
physical suffering surpassed anything I have ever
come across or imagined possible.   During the
nights I was with her in the ward, about four or five,
I slept very little myself and whenever I looked at
her she was awake.   I did not once see her asleep
by day or night while I was with her in prison.   It is
only since seeing her in free life that I have been
able to compare her face under normal conditions
and realised the intensity of distress which must
have caused the continually strained expression she
had in Holloway, varied at times by contortions due
to acute pain.   Yet she spoke little of her sufferings,
seldom complained of anything, never once was
irritable under her trials or indignant at the treatment of them, never once groaned or cried.   She was

uniformly patient, gentle, self-contained, considerate
of others.

I still was unable to get any sleep at night, but
when a few days had gone by I ventured to make up
my bed so that I faced the wall instead of the ward.
This gave a greater sense of privacy and sheltered my
eyes from the blinding light of the naked gas jet.
I very much missed a habit I have of doing various
physical exercises before going to bed.   About half-
way through the night I made amends for this by going
to the little ante-room near the sink and lavatory,
the door of which communicating with the ward was
left unlocked at night.   Here, taking it corner ways,
there was just room for me to stretch my arms full
length.   I consider it was thanks to this midnight
practice that I was able to keep my digestion in
better order than is usual among prisoners.

Hospital patients are not allowed to go to the
daily service in chapel, but occasionally we were
taken down to a morning service, in the nature of
family prayers, which was held in the ward below
ours.   This was given over mostly to feeble-minded
patients, several of whom were in bed.   My place
was always the same, close to the bed of a woman
whose face will haunt me, I think, as long as I live.
I never saw her move, she lay quite flat, her head
alone appearing above the bed clothes.   She took no
part in the service and seemed to be unconscious of
it.   She was young, her skin was remarkably smooth
and devoid of expressive lines, but yellow as if she
had jaundice.   Her appearance illustrated to me the
meaning of despair more clearly than I have seen it
hitherto in any living being.   She was entirely

passive and unresentful, but if hope had tried to
enter into her mind it would find no lodging there.
It seemed to me that neither life nor death had anything to offer her, nor was there anything she
possessed of which they could rob her. While I
stood or sat through the service my back was turned
on her, but when I knelt down I was facing her.
One could not feel pity for her—there was a rigid
dignity and detachedness about her as of someone
living in an atmosphere different from our own. All
my thoughts and prayers were bent towards her, but
I never had the sensation of in any way communicating with her.

I noticed regretfully that there were no hymns,
hardly any passages from the Bible were read, the
prayers selected were of a dolorous order, and the
greater part of the time was taken up by an address
from the chaplain. He spoke to us of the temptation in the wilderness, how that Christ was tempted
in the same way that we are, but that He was good
and we were bad. He instanced how wrong it
would be if, when we were hungry, we yielded to the
temptation of stealing bread. At this remark an
old woman stood up. She was tall and gaunt, her
face seamed with life, her hands gnarled and worn
with work. One saw that whatever her crimes
might have been she had evidently toiled incessantly.
At this moment her face wore an expression of
strained intensity as though some irresistible tide of
inward emotion had forced her to act. The tears
streamed down her furrowed cheeks as she said in a
pleading, reverent voice, " Oh, sir, don't be so hard
on us." The wardresses immediately came up to her,

took her by the shoulders and hustled her out of the ward ; we never saw her again. The Chaplain did not answer nor even look at her, and continued his address as if nothing had happened. A feeling of passionate indignation took hold of me, succeeded by the feeling of helplessness and irresponsibility which stifles vitality and above all every good impulse in prison. Sympathy for the ejected prisoner, dis-agreement with the man who officially represented the teaching of Christianity, neither of these thoughts could find vent in words or actions ; they become stored up in a brooding, malignant attitude of resentment towards the whole prison system, its infamous aim, its profound unreason, and the cruelly devitalising distortion of its results.

When we were back in our ward the Chaplain came to visit us. This time, he knew who I was. I asked him about the prison library which was under his charge. I wished to send some books when I was free, amongst others George Moore's story of " Esther Waters." I thought that novel ought to be in every woman's prison because of the heroic and triumphant struggle depicted in it of the mother of an illegitimate child. I asked the Chaplain if he knew it and would allow me to send it. He answered that he did not know the book, and added, " But your ladyship is such a good judge of literature, I should leave the choice of books entirely to you." Whenever officials visited the ward we were supposed each to stand at the foot of the bed allotted to us. Complete silence was the rule. This remark of the Chaplain's was, therefore, overheard by many of my fellow-prisoners. From that moment I was nick-named

" your ladyship."   As soon as the official round was
over several of us came together and, as was inevitable, compared the attitude of the Chaplain towards
the prisoner who had appealed to him during his
address and towards myself.   It was on this occasion
I first noticed that the dress-jacket I wore was
different from those of my companions ; mine was
evidently quite new and without the broad arrow
markings.   A fellow-prisoner, Miss Povey, member
of the Freedom League, to whom I had brought a
glass of water during the first night, came to my
rescue.   She was now sufficiently recovered to be
out of bed during part of the day.   She had a great
sense of humour and immediately responded to my
need.   We seized a brief moment when the wardress
was standing in the doorway, we took shelter behind
the open door and swopped each other's serge shirts.
She was small made and for once this portion of the
clothing had been more or less well adapted to our
respective sizes.   The sleeves of my shirt were half
a length longer than she required, and though she put
a large tuck in them they retained their superfluity
of size.   The sleeves of her shirt did not reach my
wrists and as the solitary button at the neck did not
secure the closing of the jacket down the front, I had
continually to be pulling it together again in the
course of the day.   It was marked in many places
with the broad arrow, but had been so well worn,
as the lining of the neck and cuffs attested, that the
white paint of the markings had almost chipped off
in several places.   From this time onward it became
a sort of game to watch for the privileges that were
accorded to me.   Prisoners who had been in before
explained that until I came there were never knives

and forks supplied as we now enjoyed, the fare, too, had been made more luxurious.

After three or four days I had practically recovered from the effects of the treatment meted out to the Deputation, and, but for the want of sleep and its results, had regained my normal health. I was very anxious to leave the hospital, partly because I wanted to share the lot of the bulk of my Suffragette companions and to ensure that they should benefit by whatever unusual privileges were accorded to me. Secondly, I wished to know from my own experience the routine life of ordinary prisoners and to see more of them, which I supposed would be possible away from the ward. Finally, my appetite for solitude grew from hour to hour. I feared that continued lack of sleep (I am a slave to sleep) might tell on me in a way to seriously handicap my health and cause my friends and belongings anxiety after my release, which could easily be avoided. Consequently, every morning when the Governor and doctor came on their round I asked leave to go to " the other side," as the ordinary cell buildings were called. My monotonous request was as monotonously refused from day to day. The Governor replied that I must first obtain consent from the doctors, the doctors insisted that my heart was in a condition to make the routine of floor-washing, plank bed, etc., injurious to me. One of the doctors did not trouble to continue feeling my pulse, he simply dismissed my request to be moved with the statement, " As for you, you are suffering from serious heart disease, you can't be let out of hospital."

To harden myself for the cell routine I shared
more and more in the cleaning processes of the ward.
Besides the emptying of basins and dusting the walls
as high as my arms could reach, the big table had to
be moved for floor polishing, and I helped the little
3rd Division ward-cleaner with this. She was very
small and worked unremittingly all day. She used
to flush very much over the floor-polishing, although
she was most dexterous with the heavy, long-
handled polisher, and did all her duties with admir-
able labour-saving skill and sequence. I wondered
how much her heart condition was considered. I
felt a great interest in her. Her face, expression, and
manners were those of an essentially good woman,
she was intelligent, had a sense of humour, was
loyal to both the officials and her fellow-prisoners ;
she seemed in every way above the average of
mortals. I wondered what offence against the law
could have brought her to prison, she had several
bars on her sleeve, implying a long sentence. I
found she had committed one of the most grievous
crimes which it is possible to commit, the most
unnatural, and opposed to all that lies at the root
well-being of a race or nation. She had killed her
own child. Yet when I came to know the facts, it
seemed to me that her actions were fully accounted
for, and even had her child-killing been more
deliberate than it actually was, it was impossible to
condemn this action in a human being who had been
squeezed by such opposing forces. Her story was
told me in snatches partly by the other prisoners,
partly by one of the wardresses, and partly by herself as I used to kneel by her side to put floor refuse

into the fire at the rare moments when the enormous
padlock of the fender door had been released. Her
story was this. She was a servant, and had been
seduced by her master. She, of course, was dismissed from his service. When the child was born,
he had at first contributed to its support, but after
a while had ceased to do so and disappeared, leaving
no address. She had taken the greatest pride in
bringing up her child, a boy, to whom she was
devoted. Her cell was one of those just outside
the general ward. It was sometimes used for the
reception of visitors to hospital patients who were
too ill to go across the way. When this happened
she always asked the prisoners eagerly on their
return, " Did you see the photo of my boy ? "
Having been in prison many months she was
allowed to receive and keep this photograph. To
return to her story, as time went on the struggle to
maintain herself and her child was considerable.
She made a friend, a man of her own class, who knew
her history, respected her for her good motherhood
and promised to marry her as soon as a sufficiently
good job came his way. Before long the job was
said to have been offered him, marriage was in
sight, and they plighted their troth with the seal
which knows no undoing. The work failed, marriage
prospects paled, her friend deserted her and she
found herself faced with the prospect which she now
understood only too well, of disabled health, unemployment, disgrace, and a second child to maintain
unaided. She kept on at her employment—in a
laundry—until the very hour of her premature
confinement. Then worn out in body and spirit,

and quite alone at the moment of her trouble, she had in her distraction and misery strangled her baby. She went on with her work at the laundry. It was the father of her child who gave her up to the police ; according to one rendering, he did so because she was so ill he thought it the only way to secure for her " a rest." She had an uncle, a citizen of London, a publican, who used his influence on her behalf at her trial so that she was condemned on the charge of " concealment of birth," not of child-murder. Prisoners are allowed visitors once a month, but no one had been to see her for several months. I determined I should be one of her visitors as soon as I was again free, so that we might hold a sustained conversation of a kind impossible to fellow-prisoners.

I often tell the story of this girl as an example of the neglect of women's interests and the consequent need for the recognition of their citizenship so that legislation and administrators of the law should be responsible to both sexes. My listeners have sometimes commented : " But what difference could the vote make ? and how could legislation alter these admittedly tragic situations ? " At this very time (March, 1909) the women of Norway who had recently been enfranchised, but had not yet exercised the vote, were drafting a bill for the protection of illegitimate children. I think there could not be a better example of how a fundamental change could be made in both the educative and protective side of legislation as between men and women, preeminently just and without any reactionary vindictiveness on the part of women. The essence of this

law is simply recognition of the fact that every child
has two parents and that the burden and responsibility of producing children should, therefore, be
shared by both in so far as law can secure equality.
According to this Norwegian law, *the mother is given
the right during pregnancy to inform the local authorities of the name of the father. The man whose name is
given may deny responsibility within fourteen days.
If he does not, he is registered as the father ; if he
denies it the burden of proof rests with the mother.
The father can be compelled to support the mother for
three months before* (in England the law gives her no
claim upon the father until after the birth of the
child), *and, in certain instances, for nine months after
confinement, and he is bound to support the child until
it is sixteen years old.* A man at the time of intimacy
is comparatively willing to undertake his share of
these situations ; after the lapse of many months he
is more inclined to try and shirk them. In the case
of denial on the part of the man, how much easier it
would be for the woman to prove her case when the
friendship had been recent and witnesses could be
brought forward in support of corroborating evidence. Ten or twelve months later such witnesses
have often dispersed or their memories grown hazy.
Owing to the undefended, economically unsupported
position of these mothers, certain results inevitably
follow—loss of respectable situations and consequent
necessity for the women to have recourse to more
precarious, more laborious, and worse paid employment, with their lowered social status pressing heavily
upon them in every direction. These conditions,
reacting on the exceptional physical state of the

mother, claim their inevitable toll from the life-
blood of the child. It is not surprising that the
deaths of illegitimate children are nearly double
those of children born in wedlock ; for 1911, the
statistics, the latest issued, show deaths of infants
under one year in England and Wales, in wedlock
249.37 per thousand births, illegitimate 489.99.
With the mother's maintenance secured, something
tangible is being done to save the health as well as
the life of future generations. *The woman can draw
the amount of her claim through the local authorities
who recover it from the father.* This is an immense
safeguard. Constantly under the legal conditions
here, when the mother's claim has been proved,
admitted by the father and paid by him for a few
weeks, he moves away before long, leaving no
address and the woman, even if she knows of his
whereabouts, cannot enforce her claim without
irksome and difficult legal procedure. It is far
easier for the public authority to pursue him, but
even if this proves in some cases impossible, it is
better for the State to lose its money than the life or
health of its citizens. The State always pays in the
end. *The child has the right to bear the father's name
and, in the event of his intestacy, has the same rights
of succession as his legitimate children.* Just imagine
how this clause would alter the outlook of parents
when educating their sons, more especially in
those spheres of society where such unions on the
part of men are almost invariably with women
of a lower class than their own, and it is these
unions which produce tragic and evil results far
more socially and racially injurious than illegiti-

mate unions among men and women of the same class.*

Another of the hospital patients, a member of our Deputation, Miss Leslie Lawless, was gravely ill with her lungs. She seemed in a high fever and we were very anxious about her. The prison clothes hang loosely upon one, and, though this is healthy in principle, they seem draughty and cold after modern garments, such as close-fitting undervests, etc. She had caught a severe chill waiting about for more than an hour in the draughty passages after the reception bath. She had been very ill and suffered much in her cell before being brought, only after the third day, to hospital. Mrs. Duval, a member of the Freedom League, was another really suffering patient. She had come up to London to see the results of the Freedom League Deputation. She was walking about the street when the Deputation had already been arrested. She was not taking part in any form of disturbance or demonstration. She was arrested on the ground that she was " known to be one of them." Two gentlemen, total strangers, who witnessed her arrest, volunteered to come into court and speak on her behalf. She was nevertheless found guilty and sentenced to six weeks' imprisonment. She had twice been in prison before ; she had not intended to risk arrest as she was in a very delicate state of health, having suffered considerably from her previous imprisonments. She was now in hospital with acute neuritis and a most irritating rash. She had many children at home and was

* This bill, I believe, was passed in Norway, with some alterations.

anxious about them, not having been able to make
adequate arrangements for them owing to her sudden
and unexpected imprisonment.   When I looked into
her suffering face and heard from our whispered conversation that this was her third imprisonment I felt
overcome.   I envied her courage, but felt myself
quite incapable of following her example.

Flowers were provided by the prison authorities,
both in our ward and the one below; sometimes,
too, our friends sent them to us. We were not
allowed to know from whom they came, and they
could not be destined for any particular prisoner,
but flowers are expert ambassadors, and their
messages of good-will from our friends were generally
understood.   They had to be taken out of the ward
at night and returned to the ward in the morning ;
they had to be refreshed, the water changed and
dead leaves picked off. I usurped this office. I
feel ashamed, on looking back, to remember with
what selfish greed I took it over, never giving the
others a choice or chance in the matter. The joy
of handling the flowers seemed like food and rest
rolled into one. All the patients rejoiced in them.
When a new lot were sent in they were handed
round for each prisoner to see them and smell them
at close quarters. Their appearance in prison used
to remind me of Filippino Lippi's Florentine
picture of the Virgin appearing through the sky
with a trail of coloured angels behind her to St.
Bernard in his ascetic and joyless surroundings.
They brought moments of rapture which revitalised
one's spirit and counteracted many of the stunning
effects of prison existence. Some people whom I

told of this have resented the fact that prisoners
should be given the joy of flowers, but unless it be
recognised as part of the punitive system to impose
physical illness, I think the prison hospital authorities are to be congratulated on their wisdom in
this respect ; the flowers did more than the drug-
basket to heal our complaints.

One of the reasons I took on as many housemaiding jobs as I could was that it enabled me to
be let out of the ward for the emptying of slops,
and this afforded a good opportunity for seeing and
occasionally communicating with ordinary prisoners.
They seemed to come and go pretty quickly from
our floor of the hospital, and I seldom saw any of
them more than twice or three times. The prisoner's
dress has a wonderfully disguising and unifying
power, and it was a never-ending interest to try
quickly to diagnose the type of prisoner, so as to
make the most of any possible communication by
whispers. Washing up was done in the bath-room
cell and the door left open. Sometimes the handling
of plates would prove that such work was unaccustomed and uncongenial, others were skilled but
sullen and grudging in their service, some again
would be keen and willing and showed the pathetic
eagerness of a newcomer to inquire as to rules, to
be friendly with her fellow-prisoners, to court the
approval or advice of the wardresses. But such
liveliness was not the fashion and was always
repressed. One could watch the light and spirit of
these human beings wane, as a lamp wanes for want
of oil. Sometimes many days would go by without
opportunity for the smallest communication with

ordinary prisoners, then again there would be
occasions of unexpected good luck. Once when
emptying a basin at the sink a little woman, newcomer, who was dusting the top of the walls and
fittings with a long-handled broom, came close up
behind me. In prison one seems to develop eyes
at the back of one's head and that kind of cunning
which is engendered in human beings and animals
who are much restricted. I realised that no official
eye for the moment was upon us. The splashing of
the tap covered the sound of our low voices ; without
looking round, without changing expression or
gesture so as not to arouse suspicion, the following
conversation took place. *Self :* " The dust collects
quickly here, doesn't it ? " *Prisoner :* " Yes, how
long have you got ? " (The invariable first question
for all prisoners.) *Self :* " A month." *Prisoner :*
" I'm on remand for a week." *Self :* " What is it
for ? " *Prisoner :* " Attempted suicide." *Self :*
" Poor you. Why did you do that ? " *Prisoner :*
" Well, I had a pot of trouble and I thought it was
the quickest way out." *Self :* " I remember feeling
like that too, once, but I don't now." *Prisoner :*
" And nor do I now, life's sweet while it lasts, isn't
it ? " This with a beaming smile. We had meanwhile exchanged furtive glances at each other. She
had a round, rose-like face, with a look of abundant
health and kindliness. Apparently, the " pot of
trouble " had been of no long duration. *Self :* " It
seems odd to send people here for suicide ? "
Prisoner (eagerly) : " Yes, it does indeed. It seems
a shame." Then, with some hesitation, " What
are you in for ? " *Self :* " Suffragette." She

looked at me wonderingly, as if she supposed this to
be the technical term for some form of vice unknown
to her, though her sympathy and respect were not
withdrawn. We were, however, interrupted at this
point and I was summoned to return with my much
scrubbed basin to the ward. I never saw the little
rose-like face again.

Beside the sink there was a tiny sash window about
the level of my head. When this was open I could
catch sight of the yard where remand prisoners
exercised. I was surprised to see that many of
them wore prison dress. This meant either that
they had been made to change their clothes, or that
remand and convicted prisoners were exercising
together. Seeing a great number of prisoners in a
group was a most depressing sight. They were
packed quite close, touching each other as they went
round the narrow asphalt path in single file. They
nearly all of them looked ill. Their faces wore an
expression of extreme dejection ; the lifeless, listless
way they walked, enhanced the look of entire
detachment of one from the other ; in spite of being
so closely herded, each seemed in a world of her own
individual sorrow. Anxiety, suffering, bitterness,
and a harrowing tale of want or degradation was told
by the clothes of those not in prison dress. The
procession was more heartrending than anything
my imagination could have conceived ; it took
away my breath to look at them. Why are they
there ? What has driven these poor wrecks into
this harbour ? What is being done ·for them here
to give them courage, self-reliance, hope, belief in
better possibilities for themselves and their children,

opportunity to mend their own lives, better conditions of work, fairer payment, and above all a
more honourable recognition of their services as
women, of their needs, and of their rights; the
vitality to fight for their own welfare against unjust
handicaps, prejudiced ignorance of their wants
and tyrannous repression of their attempts to cry
out for wider labour markets?

We of the remand hospital No. 2 most often
exercised in this same yard in the afternoon. We
were only about six in number, sometimes only two
or three, but, since seeing the procession of the
morning, their personalities seemed to haunt the
yard. I thought of them as beads of a necklace,
detached, helpless and useless, and wondered how
long it would be before they were threaded together
by means of the women's movement into a great
organised band, self-expressive yet co-ordinated,
and ruled by the bond of mutual service. The test
of a chain's strength is in its weakest link. Where
is our chain weakest? Not in the wretched victims
who daily paced this yard, not in the debtor, the
drunkard, the thief, the hooligan, the prostitute, the
child murderer. These miseries were mostly the
direct outcome of harmful and unjust laws. Amongst
the few that remain of spontaneously criminal type,
their number is insignificant, their influence neg-
ligible; they act as cautions rather than instiga-
tors, although they call for all the remedial forces
which the State or individuals can devote to them.
They themselves are diseased exceptions, but they
belong to groups of women, home workers, wage
earners, skilled craftswomen, who have kept alight

the old traditions of serviceableness, utility, and the powers of women. They have already made many efforts to unite and to preserve their nobility of independence. They, moreover, are quick to respond and eager to serve the modern women's movement. No, the weakest link in the chain of womanhood is the woman of the leisured class. Isolated and detached, she has but little sense of kinship with other women. For her there is no bond of labour, no ties of mutual service ; her whole life is spent in the preservation of appearances, and she seems hardly ever to probe down to the bone of realities. Child-having remains her glory, the one bit of full-livedness in an otherwise most arid desert. This is the one basis on which she feels herself united to other women, and the wrongs and sufferings of child-bearers stand out as the exception on which you can sometimes get her to move on behalf of other women. Until these women can be educated as to the lives of the bulk of women, brought up against the laws with regard to them that now disgrace the statute book, made to feel the horror of custom which still undermines their own existence, and to burst through the gilded bars which hold their own lives in bondage, they act upon the social organism in a way that is almost wholly harmful. Only when their eyes have been opened will their " influence " and " example " bear out a reasonable meaning of those words and their position of privilege make them worthy to lead.

As I had watched the prisoners I saw before me a counter-procession of women of this leisured class, herded as I have so often seen them at ball-rooms and parties, enduring the labours, the penalties, of

futile, superficial, sordidly useless lives, quarrelling
in their marriage market, revelling in their petty
triumphs, concerned continually with money, yield-
ing all opinion to social exigencies, grovelling to those
they consider above them, despising and crushing
those they think beneath them, pretending to be
lovers of art and intellect, but concerned at heart
only with the appearance of being so.   Subservient
to a superficial morality, tested not by the question,
" What has been done ? " but " What is the general
opinion about what has been done ? "   And immediately the procession of Holloway yard seemed
human, dignified, almost enviable by the side of that
other.   It is these leisured women the women's
movement has hitherto cast aside.   They are the
dross, the dead fruit.   All others have responded in
some way, however feeble their power of service,
when they have heard the call ; but these have not.
As I thought of them my pity moved from the procession in Holloway to these other women.   Success
is impossible for a social system that takes no heed
to its outcasts, the pathological victims of national
existence are the symptoms which can lead us to
diagnose its fundamental flaws.   Whether or not
the women alive to-day in the ruling class can be
cured is of comparatively little importance, but
clearly the causes which have brought them forth
must be altered at the root.   The conditions which
go to produce a ruling caste are shifting their ground
throughout the world.   Such things are moulded by
involuntary forces ; they cannot, except in the
immediate future, be foreshadowed or decreed.   But
it is now obvious that, whatever this basis, women

must have a fair and honourable share in it.   Rulers
of the best are not reared by bondwomen.   The
bi-sexual powers must be released at all costs in
those sections of the community which, whether by
intellect, by birth, or by wealth, have the guiding
reins of national life in their hands.   The question
of what that basis shall be is an altogether separate
matter.   Who can turn the force of our women's
movement in that direction, who can be a missionary
to preach war in their peace-bedeadened country ?
The answer that came to me in Holloway, and ever
since it has seemed to me the only answer, was this—
the example of working class organisations, and
above all, of those few splendid women who have
given their lives to lead this movement.   Where
doctrine, precept and example all fail to penetrate,
the spirit of sacrifice, which wakes an echo in all
human hearts, will find a way.

CHAPTER VIII

"A TRACK TO THE WATER'S EDGE."

On March 2, as a result of my pleading to be dismissed from the hospital, I was put to sleep in a separate cell along the passage of our ward. This cell had a floor of unpolished wooden boards, contained a fixed iron bedstead, movable washing stand furnished with tin utensils, a wooden chair, a square plank fixed to the wall near the door as a table, and a corner shelf under the window to hold Bible, prayer and hymn book, prayer card, list of rules, salt cellar, toilet paper, slate and slate pencil. A small basket to contain my clothes was kept under the bed. A bell near the door communicated with the outer passage. The cell was lit by a thickly barred window of small panes of glass, having in the centre a box-like apparatus, with a lid, opened by a rope pulley to let in the air without enabling one to see out, as in church windows. There was a grating ventilator below the window. In the wall of the cell giving on to the passage was a glazed aperture, through which the cell was lighted at night from a gas-jet, as in the "reception" cell. Besides the heavily metalled door, these hospital cells had iron gates, so that the door could be left open when patients had to be watched. At eight o'clock the night wardress went her rounds, lifting the spy hole

and shouting through the door " All right ? " to
which the prisoners have to answer " Yes." If they
are asleep, the question is repeated until they wake
and answer it. The gas was then lowered to a light
by which it would have been difficult to read, but not
extinguished. It was explained to me afterwards
when I pleaded for darkness, that I was an " observation " case on account of my " serious heart disease."
The luxury of privacy after five nights and days of
unrelieved publicity seemed very great, and as soon
as this last " inspection " was over my imagination
conjured up into my presence every friend I have
ever had, including my dog who died twenty years
ago. I held intercourse with them, " dreamed
true," and had a happy time. I then rolled round
and gave myself up to perfect sleep.

After, as it seemed, a very short night, I woke
with a start and a feeling of great horror. I supposed I had had a bad dream, but quickly realised
that the nightmare was on the waking side of my
existence. I sat up in bed. There was a sound of
footsteps which I could not at first locate or interpret.
They came nearer, clear foot-falls and a shuffling
sound in between, as if some of the feet were
reluctant and were being dragged along. Then a
voice in great distress, half shriek, half groan, that
came in broken snatches. The sounds came rapidly
nearer and grew more definite. The massive walls
of the building seemed to become thin and the doors
flimsy with the penetrating noise. I expected that
any moment these night-wanderers might enter my
cell, I supposed it was a case of delirium tremens or
madness. The footsteps stopped. A violent scuffle

was apparently taking place. Then followed a
jangle of keys, the banging of a gate, more turning
of keys, and I realised that a frenzied woman had
been shut into the cell below mine. She immediately
seized hold of the gate and shook it so that it rattled
on its hinges, suggesting almost more than human
strength. The wolf-like barking sounds of her voice
turned into a human yell as she screamed out,
" Nurse ! Nurse ! Let me out." It seemed a most
reasonable remark. The words broke the spell of
horror and woke instead my intensest sympathy.
She was expressing the one desire that is constantly
uppermost in prisoners' minds, the walls echoed it
as a thought most familiar to them. The gate
shivered unceasingly under her onslaught as she
hurled herself against it, and her words came at
intervals, " Nurse ! Nurse ! Open the gate." The
sounds suggested in turn madness, fury, despair. I
strained to interpret and understand, but there was
no clue. I yearned to console her. Presently footsteps came outside my door, a rattling of keys and
locks, my door was burst open and a wardress I had
not seen before put her head in, saying, " I thought
you might be startled." Her face was inflexible and
revealed nothing. I threw out questions, " Was it
a maternity case ? " " Was she ill ? " " Why was
she so wild ? " but the door was slammed to without any answer being given. However, even this
attention was a relief and unfroze my blood a little.
I wondered if the other prisoners, if the poor dis-
tracted woman herself in the cell below, had been
offered as much consolation.

I was kept in bed that morning until after the

rounds of inspection. The Governor was very civil.
He urged me to give the required assurance and bind
myself over " to be of good behaviour," that I might
leave the prison. He asked if I had " considered "
my mother. I have no doubt he thought it his
duty to talk in this way, and probably he was trying
to be kind as well. At the time, however, his
insinuation seemed more like a blow in the face.
The words rushed to my lips : " If you knew my
Mother, if you had seen her only once, you would
know that it was impossible to risk causing her
anxiety without immensely considering it," but I
restrained myself and merely said : " I am not the
only woman here who has a mother." I remembered
that when Mrs. Pankhurst had been imprisoned
she had been punished for exchanging a few words
with her daughter. The Governor then brought out
a stethoscope to examine my heart. This was surprising, as I had not realised that he was a doctor.
He urged tonics, but did not insist. Eventually I
consented to take maltine and a banana after the
mid-day meal, as they were distressed that I was so
thin.

The shrieks and cries from the cell below had
grown less towards morning, but they were renewed
at intervals throughout the day. When I went
into the general ward the horror of the night was
still hanging over my companions. A wardress told
one of us that the woman had killed her child and
been put into the condemned cell after being sentenced to be hanged. After my release it was
officially stated that the woman who had been
sentenced to death for baby-murder had been

perfectly quiet and that the " condemned cell " was in a part of the prison far removed from the remand hospital. The shrieks we had heard were those of a mad woman, under remand for larceny, who had since been removed to a workhouse infirmary. The distressful cries went on intermittently for several days, after which they lapsed into groans like those of the dying. My longing to communicate with her became at moments almost unendurable. I hoped she would die ; she seemed too far gone in distress for any other remedy. One morning before it was light I thought I heard the throaty sound of the death rattle from her cell. After that she was removed, whether dead or alive I could never find out until after my release.

I went into the general ward for the greater part of the day. I made my bed and dusted my cell, but was not allowed to wash the floor or clean the tin utensils because of my " heart disease." The quieter nights enabled me to eat more food, and I think I gained in weight and became generally restored to quite normal health. It was obvious that no ordinary prisoner nor Suffragette prisoner would, in my state of health, have been put in hospital, and that I was being kept there either to give me a soft time or for some other impenetrable reason. I told the Senior Medical Officer that unless I were allowed to the " other side " I should feel obliged to protest by means which he would probably regret when it was too late. He looked very much alarmed, but my threat produced no practical result. I then asked leave to petition the Home Secretary, a right allowed to all prisoners. Blue

official paper, ink and a pen were brought to my
cell, only one sheet of paper being allowed, but it
was a large one. I forget the wording of my letter.
I stated that I had been rather severely knocked
about by the police while on a peaceable Deputation
to the House of Commons to petition that, when the
accepted conditions for which voting rights are
granted have been fulfilled the vote should follow,
in the case of women as of men, a claim which he,
the Home Secretary himself, and a majority of the
Cabinet and House of Commons had recognised as
just. That I therefore was grateful for the privilege
of being placed in hospital during the first few days,
where the careful and kindly treatment of the officials
and excellent food had quickly restored me to my
normal health. I told how I had asked permission
to join my companions in the cells, but hitherto had
asked in vain. I explained that the cell routine of
floor-scrubbing, tin polishing, etc., would be no
exceptional exertion in my case, since I was an
amateur scrubber, having patronised that craft in
much the same spirit in which other unemployed
women took up water-colour drawing or hand-
embroidery. I found that my fellow-prisoners
were kept in the cells when much more seriously ill
than I was, and I was driven reluctantly to the conclusion that the preferential treatment meted out to
me was for no better reason than that I had influential friends whose criticism, if my health should
suffer in prison, was feared by the authorities. I
resented such favouritism on the part of officials,
both as a Liberal in politics, as a believer in the
teachings of Christ, and as a woman, and if the

special treatment of my case continued I should
feel bound on my release to make it known from
every platform of our campaign throughout the
country. I found there was a tradition amongst
prisoners that petitions to the Home Secretary were
always in vain. As I put forward a moderate and
reasonable request, consistent with the prison
regulations, I hoped it would serve as an instance
for proving this tradition to be false. This letter,
perhaps, gave a slightly coloured version of the
hospital *régime*, but I knew that, in spite of their
aims to the contrary, officials are human, and that
if I could express some sort of praise that was fairly
justified, my letter would be more likely to reach
the higher dignitaries and be attended to by them.
Perhaps, I thought, the combination of a very
reasonable request with an allowance of judicious
flattery might even result in the request being
granted.

The following day I noticed a peculiar and welcome
expression on the faces of various officials as of a
smile hidden behind the mask, plainly indicating
that my letter had been read in Holloway, however
much the valentine might be destined for waste
paper basket furniture at the Home Office. I piled
on my good behaviour and ate as much food as I
could, to conciliate the prison authorities. On the
third day following I received a written answer, a
formal statement that my petition had been received,
but that the Home Secretary did not see his way to
granting it. This led to further altercations with
the Governor and doctor. They insisted that the
cell *régime* would be too severe for me. I replied

that unless they allowed me to experience it for
myself I should probably carry away an exaggerated
version of the hardships imposed on my companions.
They pleaded that my exceptional physique and
heart disease required " rest." I answered that
prison was not a " rest cure " and that in the case of
my fellow prisoners, more especially of Miss Lawless
and Mrs. Meredith Macdonald, no such reverend
attention had been paid to their physical needs.
Every day I put forward the request and argued the
point, always in vain. I felt that the time had come
to carry out my threat. My mind brooded on what
form it should take, but for various reasons it had to
be deferred. I had contracted the cold which was
rampant in the ward. The prisoner's handkerchief,
a duster hanging from the waist of the skirt which
did service for a week, was an inevitable conveyer of
infection. This forbidding form of handkerchief
became doubly a trial with a cold in the head. I
used when at exercise to hold it out as I walked, in
the style of a bull-fighting matador, in order to dry
it and shake it out, and I used toilet paper in its
stead whenever opportunity offered, but no efforts
could counteract the disgusting overuse and exposure of the duster. I determined not to press
my request to go to the cells while there was any
rational excuse for keeping me in hospital. When
my cold was wearing off I had the misfortune to
meet with an accident and cut myself with some
broken crockery. This necessitated bandaging, and
again I put off my threat. The days went by
with unvarying monotony. Although I had known
for several weeks of my decision to go on the Deputa-

tion and had full time to prepare for a likely
imprisonment, I was continually remembering some
concern of my home life, the wheels of which would
be getting clogged in my absence. At first these
thoughts were very worrying and kept my mind
continually on the fret at my inability to communicate with the outside world, but the realisation
of one's helplessness gradually subdued these desires.
One day, however, I heard from a more experienced
" gaol-bird " that permission to write a letter was
sometimes granted if " on business." I promptly
determined to try for this privilege, since it had been
granted to other Suffragists. I chose a matter
connected with the village in which I lived, so that
the fact of my being " all right," as the cell inspectors
put it, might be conveyed to my mother. I asked
leave to write to the Rector's wife about a flower
show committee of which I was secretary. Leave was
granted. I was asked to confine myself exclusively
to the " business " for which permission had been
given; the luxury of writing it was nevertheless
very great. Later on I was allowed to write a second
letter to a friend on the Stock Exchange who manages
my money affairs. I wanted some money for a
prisoner friend who was to be released before me.
Cheque books were, of course, not available in prison,
and although a letter to my banker would probably
have been sufficient, I thought a personal friend
would be more likely to let the news of my continued
"all right"-ness filter through to my mother, although
I was not allowed to send a definite message. There
seemed, too, something attractive in addressing a
letter direct from Holloway to the Stock Exchange,

as I did not know my friend's private address. This
letter, of course, required an answer which I was
allowed to receive and keep. The rule for prisoners
is that letters addressed to them by a spontaneous
correspondence from outside are forbidden, but if
permission is granted to a prisoner to write a letter
which requires an answer, that answer can be
received and kept. This answer was about the
money I had asked for, duly enclosed, and contained
also a casual reference to a remote relative. " I
suppose you have heard that X. has been down
with influenza." Evidently the writer assumed that
I had been carrying on my correspondence as usual.
I ungratefully wished that if I was to be allowed
news of the outside world it might have been an
item connected with my more immediate belongings.
But the letter gave me a pleasure difficult to
describe, bringing, as it did, a ventilating whiff of
ordinary human, free existence into prison life. I
clung to every particle of it, envelope and all, and
generally carried it about in my clothes for fear it
should be destroyed while I was out of my cell ; no
love-letter was ever more watchfully guarded by a
girl of sixteen. It, of course, had been opened and
read before it was delivered to me.

I pleaded that as the cell prisoners were allowed a
change of vegetables, cabbage, onions, haricot beans,
succeeding each other in turn at the midday meal,
the hospital patients might be allowed the same,
anyhow the bed patients, to whom the daily cabbage
became extremely distasteful through monotony.
The medical officer who took the inspection rounds
that morning was not favourable to petitions of this

kind. He answered gruffly, " If you were given the variety, depend upon it you'd be petitioning before long to be put back on one kind only," and the daily cabbage continued. But one gets used to snubs in prison and before long I tried again. For three days in succession we had been given salt butter of a rather rancid kind, instead of fresh butter as had been supplied before. I kept a small sample of it in a saucer and showed it to the Senior Medical Officer when he came round. This man, according to my experience, was uniformly obliging, just as if he had been an ordinary man and not a prison official. He did not scoff, but took the saucer in his hands and marched out of the ward with it, saying : " I think I had better see to this myself." We were not given salt butter again. Emboldened by this success when next he came I put the vegetable question before him. He said nothing, but from that time forward we were given a change every day.

One day there was a stir in the atmosphere owing to an unusual event, the fortnightly visit of the Visiting Magistrates was due. This was an opportunity for prisoners to air their grievances. Experience had taught us that, at any rate as regards Suffragettes, prison officials and Visiting Magistrates were one and the same authority, indeed prison officials, Prison Commissioners, Home Office, police, and police Magistrates, all played to the same tune as conducted by the attitude of the Government, and we knew that there was no tribunal of an independent character to which we could make appeal. Nevertheless, as a matter of principle, we left no stone unturned to get injustice redressed by con-

stitutional means. Among the hospital patients
there were several cases of glaring injustice. The
false charge before mentioned on which Mrs. Duval
(Freedom League) had been arrested and sentenced
to six weeks' imprisonment. Mrs. Pethick Lawrence's sentence of two months when other second
offenders in the same Deputation were given only
four weeks and some six, and when Mrs. Despard,
also a prominent leader, had been sentenced to
only one month (second imprisonment) and released
after one week " on medical grounds," her health at
the time being excellent. Finally, the disgraceful
medical diagnosis and treatment of Mrs. Macdonald
after her accident in the yard. Mrs. Macdonald and
Mrs. Duval were unable to leave their beds to appear
before the Magistrates. Mrs. Macdonald decided not
to appeal on her own behalf. The Magistrates were
not medical men and an appeal against the doctor
would have been useless and perhaps would have
aroused fresh prejudice against her. She was
allowed to send a written communication suggesting
some excellent reforms on general lines for prison
management.

That afternoon, when I was locked into my cell, at
an unexpected hour a wardress ushered in a gentleman, apparently an official, whom I had not seen
before. I expected him to order my dress to be
opened and to begin stethoscoping my heart—that
was the usual procedure when a male official appeared. Instead he stood before me and said with
some dignity : " I am Sir Alfred Reynolds." The
name conveyed nothing to me, so I did not answer,
but merely bowed. He went on to ask if I wanted

anything, to say he might be seeing Lord Lytton
soon and did I want any message conveyed to him or
to my home. The sense of bewilderment which
prisoners feel when the unusual happens, breaking
into the monotonous routine of their lives without
explanation, overcame me. I did not know with what
object the stranger put these questions, the wildest
interpretations rushed through my mind—that the
authorities were seeking some fresh excuse to
release me, that my home people had heard some
untrue report and were in a panic, that there was
some underlying purpose connected with my fellow-
prisoners, to which I had no clue. My instinct was
to be on my guard, and to shield myself against
intrusion. I answered coldly that I was " All right,
thank you," and that I had no messages to send.
That evening I was told that this gentleman was one
of the Visiting Magistrates. After my release I
realised that he was a neighbour in our county of
Hertfordshire and knew my brother. It was very
kind of him to visit me in that considerate way and
I much regret that I did not respond to his friendli-
ness at the time.

Mrs. Lawrence put her case, guarded by a wardress,
standing before the seated board of Magistrates.
They had nothing to say in explanation or defence
of her sentence, but offered no redress.

On Friday, March 12, I had an unexpected and
altogether delightful surprise. In the afternoon I
was summoned out of the ward and taken across the
yard. Was I being changed to the other side ? A
deliriously joyful thought suggested itself, could it
be a visitor ? I had already had my due in this

respect, but several visitors were occasionally
allowed to prisoners. Since privileges towards me
were the order of the day it was a possibility. I
was shown into the same " solicitor's " room as
before ; this time it was empty. I was left in charge
of a wardress I had not seen before ; she was very
amiable. I felt quite distraught with the unusual
excitement, and with the torrent of questions that
ramped through my brain. Although I had had no
reason to expect another visitor, I had recently
longed for one with accelerated zest because of the
patient with the injured leg. I had grown daily
more exasperated over the attitude of the authorities towards her case, and felt that the seeming
brutality on their part was probably due to an
official inability to realise all that it entailed to
this suffering woman, that if only one could get the
facts known outside the prison a reconsideration
might bring about the granting of some of the very
moderate requests she had made with regard to her
release, and also by exposure of her treatment
make it unlikely that physically injured prisoners
should be subject to the same hardships in future.
She was a woman of abnormal courage, and in spite
of her crippled condition was planning to go straight
home by rail to Marlow on the day of her release.
She did not keep a servant ; her three children who
had been cared for by friends were to return with
her. It seemed to me she was unfit for her ordinary
life and I was most anxious that she should see a
surgeon before attempting the journey by rail. I
urged her, too, to make some arrangement for being
nursed in her own house or to go for a while to a

" home " or hospital.   For all these matters it was
imperative that she should see her husband and
discuss possible plans with him.   She asked leave
of the Governor to write to him.   This was refused
unless she obtained a permit from the Home Secretary.   It took three days to write to and obtain an
answer from the Home Office.   When the reply
came, permission was granted to write to her husband, but no mention was made as to his visiting her.
The prison authorities would not allow this without
a further permit from the Home Office.   There was
no time to receive and act upon this before her
release.   When I compared such treatment of an
urgently needful situation with my own, the ease
with which I obtained leave direct from the prison
authorities to write two letters, one of them of no
particular importance, and the ease with which two
of my relatives had been allowed to visit me, I felt
exasperated.   The action of the authorities made
no pretence at inflexible, even-handed justice, and
the partiality shown was all on behalf of the prisoner
who needed it least.

After a few minutes, to my surprise and intense
delight, my eldest brother was shown in.   He gave
me good news of those at home.   Before long I was
pouring out to him the facts and my pent-up commentary concerning Mrs. Macdonald, in spite of
frequent protests from the wardress, who exclaimed
from time to time that it was against the rules to
make communications to outsiders about fellow-
prisoners or the prison authorities.   This time I was
careful not to reprove my loved visitor for anything,
and before our all-too-short interview came to an

end I was able to send a message to my sister to make good my regrets about her visit.

The variety of leniency of the different officials, and of the same officials on different days, gave a certain savour of adventure to the dreariness of prison life. Here are two instances of the brighter side. Mrs. Lawrence and I were one afternoon allowed to walk up and down the length of the ward side by side talking in low voices. She told me about the early days of the militant movement and supplemented my book-study of that miraculous fairy tale in which I was now privileged to take part. As I listened and reproached myself continually with the thought, " Women had all this to face and I was not helping them," there seemed a positive charm in the trials of imprisonment—the suffering about my home people, the grim sights and sounds of our surroundings, the rudeness of prison officers, the physical discomforts of unaccustomed clothing, thunder-stuffed pillows, etc. Now that I passed the nights in a cell and came into the ward only for meals and part of the day, I noticed with keener insight how remarkably the atmosphere of leadership clung round Mrs. Pethick Lawrence. Her clothes and the disciplined routine were exactly the same in her case as in ours, she conformed to all the rules and seemed to adapt herself to the life as if it had been of her choice and not imposed upon her. Yet the authority, and above all, the wisdom in her personality seemed to shine out more prominently even than they did in free life when she was controlling the many departments of the office at Clement's Inn for which she was responsible, or of

the public movement from a platform. Everyone
came to her for advice, even the prison officers
seemed instinctively to refer matters to her.   It
was, for once, quite intelligible why they had separated her from the bulk of the Suffragist prisoners
by putting her in hospital. It was obvious that her
control over them would far outweigh the authority
of prison rules and rulers should she choose to exert
it. The reason given, however, was that she too
was suffering from heart disease, but this medical
verdict did not prevent her being sent to the cells,
where the full prison labour of floor washing and
tin polishing was exacted of her, as soon as our
shorter sentences had expired and she was left to
finish her unjustifiably longer term in solitude.

Another unexpected privilege had been carefully
planned so that the joy of it was spread over several
days.   The Freedom League prisoners were soon to
be released.   We schemed a jollification to take place
on the Sunday evening before their departure.   The
Sabbath day reflected national customs in prison as
outside.   The morning was characterised by clean
clothing and an unusual rigidity of behaviour, but
towards the latter half of the afternoon the air of
solemnity wore away, some of the officers had an
afternoon off, bringing back with them an indefinable
sense of the outer world, and the evening hours
sometimes produced an atmosphere almost of
amiability.   Much would depend on whether a
lovable wardress, who often did duty in our ward and
had shown herself invariably friendly towards us,
should be " on " or " off."   The patients, who had
increased to nine, were all of them now out of bed

during part of the day. We were to gather round
the fire, and to tell yarns, stories or poems, as if we
were in camp in the free world. A sense of excitement and expectancy pervaded the ward all day.
I felt as children do before a self-schemed escapade
into the dominions of forbidden joys, my delight
only slightly marred by the prospect of having to
contribute to the recitations, a performance not at
all in my line. I spent the spare moments of the day
trying to remember and write down on my slate
Coventry Patmore's poem " The Toys." Parts of it
had constantly floated into my mind while in Holloway from the striking resemblance between prisoners
and children. I treasured more especially the actual
list of toys which the child, a seven times breaker of
the law, when punished and dismissed " with hard
words and unkiss'd," had put beside his bed :—

> " A box of counters and a red-vein'd stone,
> A piece of glass abraded by the beach,
> And six or seven shells,
> A bottle with bluebells,
> And two French copper coins, ranged there with careful
>   art
> To comfort his sad heart."

When evening came after the supper meal our
little plot developed with unexpected smoothness.
The kindly wardress was in charge, activity and " inspection " in the passage outside subsided altogether
and we were left to our own devices. What chairs
there were we set round the fire and the rest of the
company sat on the floor. An unwonted expression
of happiness beamed from the fire-lit faces of these
prison-clad individuals, drawn together from many
parts of the country and from widely-differing walks

of life. Each one contributed her share to our
spontaneous entertainment. Even the wardress,
completely casting aside her official manner and
addressing herself deferentially to Mrs. Lawrence,
for whom she had a great admiration, told a pathetic
little story with a surprising gift of narration and
concentrated expression. I remember I had dreaded
lest one or two of the company besides myself should
not be " up " to an adequate contribution, and that
our little entertainment would be marred by those
uncomfortable moments of both conscious and
unconscious failure such as are common to " social "
gatherings, no matter where they take place. However, everyone played up. There was great variety
in the different speakers, each in turn adding a new
element to the programme, each was good of its kind
and there was no need for pity anywhere. My friend
with the injured leg contributed a remarkable
political poem of her own making, but far the most
artistic items were given by Mrs. Lawrence. She
told us first an Arab story which she had heard from
a Dragoman sitting round a real camp fire in Egypt.
It was full of the detail dear to the East, which suited
the associations of superfluous time in our then
experience. It was intricate and humorous, lifting
our minds completely out of our present surroundings. She was pressed for " more." She then
repeated Olive Schreiner's " Three Dreams in a
Desert." I had read this allegory many years ago
when it was first published. I remember that the
painter Watts and my father had been enthusiastic
over the poetical beauty of these " Dreams." Their
lyrical force, the imaginative woof and warp of their

parables and the dignified cadence of their language
had impressed me in my youth so that I read them
many times for sheer emotional joy, but their meaning had evidently not penetrated to me. Olive
Schreiner, more than any one other author, has
rightly interpreted the woman's movement and
symbolised and immortalised it by her writings.
Now after even so short an experience of the movement as I had known, this " Dream " seemed
scarcely an allegory. The words hit out a bare
literal description of the pilgrimage of women. It
fell on our ears more like an A B C railway guide to
our journey than a figurative parable, though its
poetic strength was all the greater for that. The
woman wanderer goes forth to seek the Land of
Freedom . . . " ' How am I to get there ? ' The
old man, Reason, answers, ' *There is one way and one
only. Down the banks of Labour, through the water
of suffering. There is no other.*' . . . ' Is there a
track to show where the best fording is ? ' . . . ' *It
has to be made. . . .*' And she threw from her gladly
the mantle of ancient-received opinions she wore, for
it was worn full of holes. And she took the girdle
from her waist that she had treasured so long, and
the moths flew out of it in a cloud. And he said,
' *Take the shoes of dependence off your feet.*' And she
stood there naked but for one white garment that
clung close to her, the garment of Truth, which she
is told to keep. She is given a staff, Reason, ' a
stick that curled.' ' *Take this stick, hold it fast. In
that day when it slips from your hand you are lost. Put
it down before you, where it cannot find a bottom, do not
set your foot.*' The woman having discarded all

to which she had formerly clung cries out : ' For
what do I go to this far land which no one has ever
reached ? I am alone ! I am utterly alone ! '
But soon she hears the sound of feet, ' a thousand
times ten thousand and thousands of thousands and
they beat this way.' . . . ' *They are the feet of those
that shall follow you.*' . . . *Have you seen the locusts
how they cross a stream ? First one comes down to the
water's edge, and it is swept away, and then another
comes and then another, and at last with their bodies
piled up a bridge is built and the rest pass over.*' . . .
And of those that come first some are swept away,
and are heard of no more ; their bodies do not even
build the bridge ? . . . ' *What of that ? They make a
track to the water's edge.*' " And in the last dream she
sees in that land of Freedom where Love is no longer
a child but has grown to a man. " On the hills
walked brave women and brave men, hand in hand.
And they looked into each other's eyes, and they
were not afraid."

We dispersed and went back to our hard beds, to
the thought of our homes, to the depressing surroundings of fellow prisoners, to the groans and cries
of agonised women—content. As I laid my head
on the rattling pillow I surrendered my normal
attitude towards literature, and thought " There is
some point, some purpose in it after all."

Since I had left the general ward there were more
opportunities for the officers to show kindness
without being detected in " favouritism," and I had
come to be on very good terms with several of them.
Even the ward superintendent, who made a special
hobby of outward severity, had relaxed on several

occasions. For instance, she stood in the doorway one morning watching me make my bed. She remarked, with the same outward air of contempt that was habitual to her, but with a kindly look in her eyes : "You're not much used to that, I expect ? " I answered : " Do you think I do it so badly ? " She smiled and seemed distressed that I had interpreted her that way. Her anxiety that I should put on flesh while under her charge made her almost motherly at times. I accounted for my small appetite by explaining that I did not spend myself in prison life. " Don't know about spending yourself, but how about your sensitiveness ? Doesn't that 'spend' you ? " This taunt was because when she renewed the plasters on my cut, which she did very skilfully, I winced a good deal. The sticky plaster adhered closely and the process of removing it generally made me feel faint. I didn't know till she said this that she had even noticed it, but her contempt was softened by a kind smile. I had determined to begin my strike in real earnest the following week if I failed by reasonable pleadings to get sent to the cells. I was anxious that the responsibility of my bad behaviour should not fall on her, and I wished to make very clear that I had no malicious intentions towards her, or anyone else, beyond giving proof to the doctors that I should be better the " other side." She was extremely busy and her visits to me never lasted more than a few seconds. I took the first opportunity to say unconcernedly and not looking at her, but with the hope of arousing her curiosity sufficiently for her consent : " If you should have a spare minute

before Sunday, come in to me when I am in my cell,
I want to ask you something." She looked surprised, but said nothing and avoided me for the rest
of the day.   The following afternoon she looked in
hurriedly, saying in her most official voice : " What
is it you want ? "   I resented the scolding tone
and answered without humility, as one would to a
fellow-being outside, " Come near to me, I want to
speak to you, but only if you can spare the time."   I
was lying on my bed, a privilege I was allowed in the
separate cell.   She came in, pushed the door to,
stood close to my bed-side and said again gruffly,
" What is it ? "   I reached out my hand to take
hers, but meeting with no response I drew it in
again.   I did not want to get angry with the rebuffs
of her officialdom, so I kept my eyes down as I said :
" I like you because you have always treated me the
same as the others, yet you have never really been
unkind to me.   I want to ask you something now,
because by Sunday either I shall have had leave to
go to the other side or I shall have begun my strike
in real earnest and you will be getting more and more
angry with me."   She stooped down and said in a
low voice of extreme tenderness as if I had been a
child : " Why, I have never been angry with you
yet."   I looked up into her eyes.   They were lit
with kindliness and her whole face beamed on me
with genial goodwill.   It was a surprising change.
The personality was the same, but the mask was off
and I realised something of the sacrifice it must be
to this woman continually to conceal her good
nature under so forbidding a manner.   I felt more
than ever how wasteful and unreasonable is a

system which represses the natural powers of good
influence in such a woman and exacts of her, in
their stead, an attitude towards the prisoners of so
much less worth. Her kindness made my determination to carry out my strike at all costs a much
harder job than any amount of her official hardness
and reproof would have done. If it had been for
any less object than a matter of principle I could not
have done it. "No," I answered, "but I haven't
yet begun my strike seriously." I added: "I
don't wish to discuss that now. I want you to tell
me when you could come and see us after I am out.
Mother will wish to thank you for being kind to me,
and to hear about my wicked ways from you. You
must come down to us in the country. We are on
this line and quite near London." Her face grew
serious again, but remained without the official
mask. She shook her head. "That's impossible,"
she said with decision, "it would be against the
rules." "There are no prison rules for me once I
am free again, and you surely have some holidays
when you can do as you like." "No, that would be
quite against the rules." I pleaded afresh and with
determination. She then tried another tack, said
that she had friends of her own to visit in the little
time at her disposal. I answered she must bring
one of these with her and they would spend the day
together with us. But she would have none of it.
I said she, of course, felt obliged to rub in the rules
and regulations while I was prisoner under her
charge and that I respected her for that. It was
obvious, however, that such rules would have nothing
to do with me once I was free again, that I should

write to her after my release, as an ordinary out-
sider, and make fresh suggestions. I had in mind
several instances in which prisoners and warders
had continued friendly after release. I asked her to
give me her home address or, at least, to tell me her
Christian name, for, as several of her sisters were
also prison officers in Holloway, I did not want my
letter to go to them. She, however, would not tell
me any of these things. I asked why it would be
against the rules. She answered, " We are not
allowed to hold communication with ex-prisoners,"
and vouchsafed no further explanation. I said I
thought we Suffragettes might be looked upon as
different from the ordinary ex-prisoners. She
remained adamant. I felt fresh enmity for the
system which continually admitted variation from
its rules on the side of less kindness or for reasons of
snobbish privilege, but which showed itself rigid
and unelastic when it was a case of reasonable,
unharmful good-will. But, of course, I immensely
respected this woman's loyalty to the system she
served and her punctilious adherence to its rules.
She had, nevertheless, let go her own voice and her
own smile just once upon me. They remained
among the joy experiences of Holloway. I wondered
if she had ever shown them to the poor woman who
screamed and groaned in the cell below mine, or to
the yellow-faced patient in the lower ward.

I began my strike gently ; I knocked off all diet
extras, such as the maltine and its accompanying
banana or the pudding at the mid-day meal, and
kept to the food which would be mine the other side,
viz., *Breakfast* : Brown bread, butter, milk. *Mid-*

Lady Constance Lytton, 1908

Left to right: Constance Lytton, Annie Kenney, Emmeline
Pethick Lawrence, Christabel Pankhurst and Sylvia Pankhurst

Constance Lytton (right) takes part in a suffrage march,
London, 23 July 1910

Emmeline Pankhurst carrying a petition from the Third
Women's Parliament to the Prime Minister on 13 February 1908

Constance Lytton in Newcastle shortly before throwing a stone at
Sir Walter Runciman's car, 8 October 1909

Constance Lytton as Jane Warton

A suffragette attempts to break through the police cordon surrounding the House of Commons, 18 November 1910 — known as 'Black Friday' because of the extreme brutality of the police

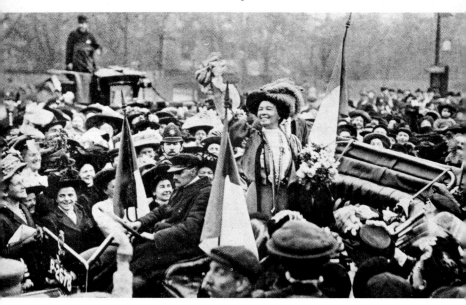

Emmeline Pethick Lawrence receives a rapturous welcome after her release from prison

An artist's impression of forcible feeding, first published in the
Illustrated London News, 27 April 1912

Constance Lytton (right) bids farewell to Emmeline Pankhurst on her visit
to America, 12 October 1912

More than 1,000 suffragettes — carrying silver pennants to
symbolise their prison ordeal — march to the Albert Hall,
London, 17 June 1911

day : Brown bread, potatoes, one vegetable. *Supper* :
Brown bread, butter, milk. Both doctors and
wardresses talked of the plank bed as one of the
hardships likely to be too much for me in the cells,
so I took one of the two mattresses from my bed
and slept with it on the floor. I clambered up on
the furniture and cleaned the windows of my cell to
show I could do some extra housemaiding without
harm. The first night of my floor-bed I was left
undisturbed. The second night, at the time of the
" All right ? " rounds, the hospital superintendent
came in. To my surprise she was not angry, did
not scold. She asked quite gently and interestedly
why I was lying on the floor. " Because the doctors
suggest that I would get ill or die if I laid on a
wooden bed instead of an iron one, so I am just
showing that I can manage it all right ; I am very
comfortable, thanks." But she didn't go away.
The cell, of course, was small, the fixed bedstead
down the centre of it taking up most of the floor-
room, so I had laid the mattress cross-ways under
the bed, my head sticking out on one side, my feet
on the other. The wardress suggested that if I
woke suddenly in the night I might hit and hurt
myself against the bed. I assured her that sleep in
Holloway was not of a kind heavy enough to wake
from it unconsciously. It was true I had enjoyed
such a sleep one night, the first in my private cell,
but the ghastly sounds of human desperation and
suffering by which it had been broken had driven
away sound sleep for the remainder of my imprisonment. At last she went away. The following
night she again came and argued about the bed.

She said she would worry lest harm should happen while she was responsible for me and it would drive away her own rest. I respected her for at last using a sensible form of argument, but for the moment I did not relent. When she had gone, however, I managed by judicious shifting of the movable furniture to find room for the mattress along the wall with my head behind the door. I rang my bell, the night wardress appeared. Peremptory fashion, I sent her with an invitation to the superintendent to come again if she had not yet gone to bed. The wardress positively laughed at my effrontery, but evidently delivered my message, for in a few minutes my friend the superintendent returned. She tried to look severe, but a broad grin enveloped her face when she saw my new contrivance. " However much I jump about now, I can't hurt myself. Will you be able to sleep all right ? " I asked. She said she would try, and left me.

My continued appeals to the authorities to treat me as they did my fellow-prisoners and not keep me in hospital now that I was in normal health, having proved unavailing, I entered upon the last phase of my strike. I had decided to write the words " Votes for Women " on my body, scratching it in my skin with a needle, beginning over the heart and ending it on my face. I proposed to show the first half of the inscription to the doctors, telling them that as I knew how much appearances were respected by officials, I thought it well to warn them that the last letter and a full stop would come upon my cheek, and be still quite fresh and visible on the day of my release. My difficulty was to find suitable tools.

My skin proved much tougher than I had expected
and the small needle supplied to me for sewing
purposes was quite inadequate. I procured another
and stronger one for darning my stockings, but
neither of them produced the required result. I
thought of a hairpin but had only three left of these
precious articles and could not make up my mind to
spare one. I had the good luck, however, while
exercising, to find one, the black enamel of which was
already partially worn off. I cleaned and polished
it with a stone under my cloak as I walked the round.
The next morning before breakfast I set to work in
real earnest and, using each of these implements in
turn, I succeeded in producing a very fine V just over
my heart. This was the work of fully twenty
minutes, and in my zeal I made a deeper impression
than I had intended. The scratch bled to a certain
extent. I had no wish for a blood-poisoning sequel,
and, fearing the contact with the coarse prison
clothes, when the wardress came to fetch me for
breakfast I asked her for a small piece of lint and
plaster. On a previous occasion I had been allowed
these without further inquiry, when the frosty
weather, cold water, and lack of gloves had produced a sore on my hand. But this time the
superintendent herself appeared and refused to
produce the dressing without hearing for what
purpose it was required. I was anxious to proceed
further with my inscription before letting the
authorities know of it, fearing that it was not yet
sufficient to be imposing and that all tools might be
taken from me. However, thanks to our previous
conversations, my friend was suspicious. She

ordered me to show the scratch. She looked very
much startled on seeing it and asked how it had
happened. I explained. She at first did not know
how to take it, but evidently did not think it a laughing matter, to my great relief, for I hoped this meant
the misdeed was grave enough to suggest to the
authorities that I was becoming an awkward cus-
tomer in hospital. She was restrained in manner,
but looked rather angry as she solemnly applied a
large piece of lint and many plasterings which, to my
delight, gave the scratch a quite imposing look, as if
half my chest had been hacked open. So that no
blame should fall on her, I gave her all the information for which she asked and the incriminating tools
were gathered together as if they had been witnesses
in a detective case. After breakfast I was summoned into the presence of the Governor and given
a scolding, but no sentence of punishment was
passed and I remained in doubt as to whether my
evil deed had been sufficiently impressive. Later
on I was taken down to the Senior Medical Officer.
Scolding was not in his line and the official requirements of the occasion were evidently effortful to
him, but his laborious sermon of reproofs was all the
more punitive on that account. As he had invariably been kind to me and civil to all other prisoners,
I was sorry to have to vex him. I reminded him of
the warning I had previously given and how often I
had patiently renewed my request in a reasonable
way before having recourse to these stronger
measures. Of course he had to pretend that he saw
not the remotest connection between his refusal to
let me leave hospital and my " outrageous " conduct

of the morning. He and the ward superintendent, who ushered me into his presence and exposed the scratched " V " for his inspection, were evidently much put out. I felt all a craftsman's satisfaction in my job. The V was very clearly and evenly printed in spite of the varying material of its background, a rib bone forming an awkward bump. As I pointed out to the doctor, it had been placed exactly over the heart, and visibly recorded the pulsation of that organ as clearly as a watch hand, so that he no longer need be put to the trouble of the stethoscope. I also explained how useful the mark would be at the inquest, to which he had alluded, when they wanted quickly to extract the heart in proof that its " serious disease " was responsible for my demise and not the prison regimen. But he was not in a mood for chaff and became more and more distraught as to how to deal with the situation. At last he hit on a brilliant idea and said, " If you go on like this we shall have to dismiss you from the prison altogether." I could have congratulated him with both hands for this really understanding remark. It was obvious that such a sentence wouldn't at all meet with my aims, and would secure my return to good behaviour if anything could. He had effectively checkmated me, at any rate for the moment. I promptly capitulated and capped this suggestion by saying : " I think I had better be sent back to the general ward ; I seem to give a lot of extra trouble in the separate cell." The superintendent wardress exclaimed with gusto, " Yes, you do," and the doctor jumped at the suggestion. As there were now only ten days before

our release I had decided to push through my efforts
to get to the cells regardless of all else, but I was
exceedingly anxious about the patient with the
injured leg. Her release was due, with other members of the Freedom League, the next day (Wednesday, March 17). I had a feeling that I could to a
certain degree watch over her welfare and was to
this extent glad of the opportunity to return to the
hospital. While waiting for the hospital gate to be
unlocked a small gang of ordinary prisoners had for
some reason or another congregated in the passage
and blocked the way. My friend, the superintendent,
took the opportunity to give me a severe scolding
in their presence. Now that the extent of my
criminality had been duly notified and received, as it
were, official recognition, her pent up indignation let
fly and she gave me a regular dressing down. She
did not, of course, allude to the nature of my crime ;
this was left to the imagination of the onlookers, but,
as on all other occasions of the kind that I can recall,
the sympathy of prisoners turns automatically to a
fellow-prisoner, not to the officials. Intercourse by
means of speech being forbidden, the language of the
eyes becomes perfected. Inquiry, interest, fellow-
feeling, loyalty, encouragement, sympathy of the
best, all these emotions are expressed in prisoners'
eyes in a way that outbids the meaning of words and
the intonations of the voice. I respected this superintendent as before, because of the impartiality with
which she treated me, but this example of public
reproof before other prisoners was typical of the
way this sort of prison discipline defeats its own
ends.

Mrs. Macdonald was still suffering acutely. She had been taken out of the ward for the injury to be photographed by X-rays. She was carried up and down the stairs, as before, in a chair with no rest for the feet. She had been told that the photographs had not been distinct and left them " none the wiser," but " Depend upon it," said the doctor, " you had better keep moving about as much as you can." The prison authorities recognised that she was unfit to travel by rail. As she had no home in London and could not afford to rent rooms, they proposed sending her to a hospital. For various reasons, the thought of an ordinary public hospital was extremely repellent to her. The prison officials now discussed the matter with her and seemed to show a certain amount of interest and even kindness towards her.

My wound being the nominal ground on which I had been returned to hospital, it had to be treated with official respect. The ward superintendent told me she would come and inspect it the last thing before she went to bed herself. I looked forward to this opportunity of pacifying her displeasure with me, but when she came she was already in her most benignant mood. My chief concern was to inquire her view as to my chances of ever being sent to the other side. " They'll never send you out of hospital, nothing you can do will make any difference, so what's the use of going on trying ? " In some mysterious way this despairing speech of hers put new mettle into me, and I determined I would renew my attempts. To reassure her with regard to my villainous intentions I told her that the doctor had

hit on a really effective deterrent by threatening to
turn me out of prison. "That's what you deserve,"
she said, severely, but with something of a wink.
"So you think," I retorted.

The hospital atmosphere soon drew my thoughts
away from my strike and its object. Several of the
patients were less restless than when I had last been
amongst them. The night wardress with the hacking cough had been changed. The sick patients had
agreed to make no complaints for fear they should
get her into trouble or perhaps be given a more
disagreeable wardress in her place. But when our
numbers had been increased by a patient who was in
fairly vigorous health but for the most painful
neuritis in her arm, she found the continuous disturbance of her all too precious sleep intolerable and
she reported the wardress's cough to the doctor. We
were then all questioned and had to admit the fact,
whereupon we were given another night wardress.
This one, as had been feared, was more rigid in her
ways and interpreted the absurdly inhuman prison
regulations literally. For instance, one night a
patient who was quite incapable of moving out of
bed had been given medicine which disturbed her
during the night. The wardress at first refused to
wait upon her, but after reluctantly consenting to do
this, she then refused to empty the slops. A fellow-
prisoner volunteered to do this, but was not allowed.
At last, after putting the patient to much distress,
the wardress did the work. On hearing of this the
next morning I was indignant and reported the
matter to the ward superintendent. She answered,
"The officer was quite within her rights. She is not

a nurse and it is no part of her duty to wait on the patients. She was quite right, too, not to allow the other patients to do it." I expostulated as to the brutality of putting a patient who was really ill to such distress and on the unwholesomeness of having slops in the ward all night. "The only thing that can be done in such a case," she replied, " would be to ring the night bell for me." As this woman was on her feet for sixteen hours, from six in the morning to ten at night, the patients would be most reluctant to disturb her, apart from the fact that they would never dream of this being the right thing to do unless they had been specially informed of the regulation.

I found that my poor friend of the injured leg was suffering more than ever. I did my best to ease her pain by rubbing and trying to lift the cruel pressure from the disturbed bones. The wardress did not interfere with me as I had rather expected she would, but the next morning she said, " I must report you for being out of bed half the night." When the doctor came on his rounds he had, I suppose, received the " report," for he shook his head at me reprovingly but with a kind look as if he at least understood the motive of my most recent crime. I felt very despondent all day. The members of the Freedom League were released that morning, all except Mrs. Duval, who had to serve a longer sentence, and Mrs. Macdonald, as the authorities had not yet decided what was to happen to her on release.

In the afternoon the sun shone brightly and the air was full of that indefinable sense of spring. The " spring-running " of the jungle seemed to penetrate

even through prison walls and into the minds of
prison officials.   Whether because of this or for
some less good cause we were accorded exceptional
benefits.   Hospital patients who had not been out
before were allowed to come to exercise and we were
told to walk in couples, arm-in-arm, the healthier
patients supporting the others.   Amazing privilege!
It seemed like a bit of heaven.   We, of course,
discarded the " silence " rule at the same time.
We were exercised in a larger space, not one of
the narrowly-enclosed exercise yards.   The prison
officials passed by—Governor, Matron, doctors—but
they made no comment at the unusual sight, seemed,
on the contrary, quite pleased as we grinned our
pleasure boldly into their faces.

CHAPTER IX

FROM THE CELLS

THE following morning, Thursday, March 18, I was again summoned before the Governor. He looked as if he had an important announcement to make to me. "Do you still wish to leave the hospital?" he asked. I was afraid this might mean my dismissal. "Do you mean going to the other side?" I said. He answered "Yes." 'Rather!" I exclaimed, and could hardly contain myself for surprise and delight. He proceeded to explain: "The weather having changed, the medical officer gives his consent to your being moved to the cells." I should not be allowed to scrub my floor nor do any of the routine "labour," but if my health and behaviour (!) remained good, I might be moved next day.

The weather, of course, had changed many times since we had been in Holloway, varieties of cold or mild, damp or dry succeeding each other day by day, after the familiar fashion of our national climate in February and March. But I was too well content to be sarcastic over the reasons given for the official surrender to my request. I simply said "Thank you very much indeed." I had already announced this decision to several of the ward patients, when the superintendent came on her rounds and I rushed up

to her unceremoniously with, " Have you heard my
good news ? " Her official mood was on and she
ordered me off with a " Hush ! not now." I gathered
from various questions put to me by the Governor
that the authorities hoped I had not told of my
carving-strike to the other patients. It would
never do, of course, to conciliate the wishes of a
striker ! But I was not able to comfort them on
this score, and my triumph was public as well as
complete.

Later in the morning the superintendent took me
before the Senior Medical Officer. With him it was
a real temptation to say, " If now, why not before ? "
to point out how effective had been the behaviour
which two days previously he had professed to find
so incomprehensible, also to draw the analogy
between this little prison episode and the women's
fight for the vote—a reasonable demand, continuously pressed in a reasonable way and with
great patience ; result, blank refusal on the part of
responsible powers. Militant action, by means of
strike and protest ; result, anger, condemnation,
and the request is granted. The vote is not yet
granted to women, but who now doubts that
" they'll get it " before long ; but I restrained
myself and trusted that the lesson would sink home
unassisted. The doctor pointed to a chair by the
side of his desk for me to sit while he sounded me.
In my excitement I forgot all prison decorum and
shook him cordially by the hand. He and the ward
superintendent seemed nearly as pleased as I was
myself. I felt how differently the prison system
would work and with what different results if

the officials were more often allowed to please themselves by pleasing their prisoners.

That afternoon Mrs. Macdonald was released and sent, by arrangement with the Prison Commissioners, to a private hospital. The ward superintendent accompanied her, but on the return of this officer no word escaped her as to how the patient had stood the transit, nor as to the result of the further radiograph which had been taken the day before. As soon as I was released, I heard that her leg was broken and had been from the first. A committee was formed for her care and her redress. The Home Secretary, Mr. Gladstone, was sure that the leg had been broken before and refused to read our statement. It was not till 1910, when Mr. Winston Churchill was made Home Secretary, that he read the case and paid her £500 compensation. She was taken to another hospital and had a serious operation to her leg. Had it been treated at once, the fractured bone would have been restored to its own length, but after about eighteen days of her being in prison, when nothing was done for it, the bone had overlapped and the muscles hardened round it. This, of course, inevitably shortened the bone. The operation was successful, but she is lame for life.

The only item in the cell-life routine to which I looked forward with considerable misgiving was discarding the hospital slippers and having to wear the hard shoes continuously all day. I felt quite absurdly pleased with the reward of my efforts. At the mid-day meal I drank, or rather ate, the doctor's health in rice pudding and insisted that the wardress

in charge should do the same. That day there
happened to be on duty one of the outwardly least
human of her kind, but my good spirits were
irrepressible, and these being so rarely seen in prison,
they gave me a certain air of authority, I suppose,
for her severity melted and she ate the rice pudding,
as ordered, with even the flicker of a smile.

The luxury of a bath was allowed once a week, my
turn was due that evening. The superintendent
said : " If I let you have it, will you promise me not
to cut yourself about or any nonsense of that kind ? "
I answered : " Is it likely now that I've achieved all
that I've been struggling for ? " That evening,
when she came to my bed for a last inspection, I said,
" You see, they have given way after all." " Yes,"
she answered ; " I never thought they would, but
there, you never can tell what is happening behind
the scenes." I cordially agreed with this last
sentiment. " That is why," I answered, " one
should never grow disheartened when things seem
to be impossible."

The next morning, while dusting the ward, the
little 3rd Division cleaner came up to me and,
without looking at me after the manner of prisoners,
said in a low voice, " I shall miss you." I took her
to mean that my housemaiding had to a certain
extent lightened her labours, and I was filled with
pride ; I have seldom received praise that gave me
more pleasure. I redoubled my energies and turned
over and dusted the beds that were unoccupied.
The superintendent passed and said, " What are you
doing there ? " I explained. " Oh ! " she answered,
" That's good of you." It's wonderful how luck,

good or bad, never comes singly. Everything
seemed to win approval that day.

In the afternoon I was sewing a new stripe on to
Mrs. Duval's sleeve, a good conduct badge that had
been dealt out to her, as the first month of her
sentence had been served (she was in for six weeks),
when a stranger wardress came into the ward and
summoned me to " bring your things and come with
me." This meant the other side at last ! Now that
the long-fought privilege was actually mine I felt
self-reproachful at leaving Mrs. Pethick Lawrence,
but she thought I had done right to try and join
the others. No time was allowed for goodbyes. As
I retreated through the gate I waved the hated
shoes at my companions, in token of my good wishes.
I was made to change all my clothes. The wardress
was reluctant to allow me to wear my nightdress, as
I had done from the first in the day time. I insisted,
fearing that I might catch cold without it, and I
promised the doctor to care for my health in every
way if allowed out of hospital. She relented, but
told me I must inform the matron about it. I was
taken over to the new building " D X," and shown
to a cell on the third floor, No. 10. It was very
clean, had no bars on the window and no gate, and
was in every respect much brighter looking and
without so much of the death's-head element as the
hospital cell I had just left in the older part of the
prison. It had a hot pipe and, to my surprise,
was considerably warmer than the hospital cell or
general ward, so that the official excuse about the
change of weather seemed less to the point than ever.
After depositing the sheets, towel, soap, etc., which

I had brought with me, I was taken to join the others, who were sitting at associated labour on the ground floor passage. The building had a strange appearance, as of an enormous bird cage. The cells are ranged on either side of a barrack-like hall giving on to narrow galleries with iron rails. The different storeys are reached by a small iron stairway in the centre. These and the balconies are covered over with wire netting for the prevention of suicide, a precaution in every way most characteristic of the prison system, a symbol of the suicide of its own success. The wire netting gives the building an abnormal appearance; newcomers question " Why is it there ? " The explanation fills the mind with horror and revolt. A deeper investigation into prison life brings to light the fact that nothing is done to prevent or counteract the desire for suicide in prisoners, the evil is only met by artificial prevention of its consequences when the mutilation of all spontaneous wishes, human instincts and reasonable paths of self-interest have engendered the passionate longing to cease existing.

The moment of joining my companions was most exhilarating. They were sitting on chairs placed in regular rows, knitting stockings or sewing women's underclothes and men's shirts. I was put into a vacant place about six rows from the front. Patients who had returned to the cells from hospital had spread the news of my continued but vain attempts to rejoin the bulk of my fellow-prisoners, so that my appearance among them caused great surprise. Some of them were almost unrecognisably changed by the prison dress, others I was distressed to see

looked extremely ill, but, as the news spread amongst
them of my presence, they looked my way in turn
and gave me a welcoming smile that momentarily
changed prison into paradise. I quickly understood that the right we had claimed to talk with one
another at associated labour had been effectively
maintained, but for the sake of not getting the
wardresses into trouble we talked only in low voices
or whispers to our immediate neighbours. The
greatest eagerness, of course, was for news of Mrs.
Lawrence. She had sent a special message of
thanks to Mrs. Corbett and to Miss Carling, news
having reached the hospital that these two had
been particularly active in maintaining the rights
and decencies that had been won by our prede-
cessors through much hardship, also in their efforts
to secure fresh reforms of the same kind. These
were mostly connected with ordinary prison routine
and affected the welfare of all prisoners besides ourselves. They were, amongst others—the use of an
earthenware mug for drinking purposes instead of a
tin ; permission to empty slops more frequently ;
a chair with a back to it had been substituted for
the stool ; a better standard of food, cooking and
clothing through complaint whenever these were
amiss ; the right to appeal direct to the Governor—
previously the applications to see the Governor had
frequently not been delivered, this being, of course,
more especially the case when it was suspected that
complaint would be made about any of the officers ;
protest whenever prisoners were unjustly punished
for offences they had not committed ; the right to
speak to each other at associated labour.

The prisoners near me were eager to point out these two valiant women and cordially endorsed the report of their splendid persistency. They were sitting near the front, and it was several days before I achieved getting a place near enough to convey to them Mrs. Lawrence's message. They were immensely pleased. One of the reforms for which they had asked most continuously, but always in vain, was for alteration in the lavatory doors. These, which we nick-named " the cowsheds," were only about three feet in depth and left a space of one foot from the ground, there was no lock or bolt or catch of any kind and they could not be fastened. As the lavatories occupied a position next door to the sink and in the very centre of the gallery, there was no sense of privacy whatever. Both feet and head of the occupant could be seen from the passage, and in the hurried passing to and fro of prisoners to the sink to draw water or empty slops the lavatory door was frequently flung open. The excuse given for this arrangement was that it was in the interests of cleanliness and because of the tendency amongst prisoners to commit suicide. If they were invisible or could lock themselves in, it was stated that besides foul behaviour they would seize the opportunity to kill themselves. Obviously neither of these precautions were necessary in the case of Suffragettes, and we pleaded that when our numbers exceeded sixteen, the number of cells to which a lavatory was provided, one might be set apart for our use. With the W.S.P.U. and Freedom League together the Suffragette prisoners during my time amounted to about forty. We asked that a bolt should be put on the inside of the door, and a curtain hung from the top of the doorway. This would have been easy and inexpensive, and the wardress in charge could, at any time necessary, draw the curtain and open the bolt from outside the door. It is difficult to see how this arrangement would be harmful even to the ordinary prisoner. The modern cells are fitted with electric light, the lamps of which have glass shades. The prisoners are locked into these cells and pass the night without inspection. If they intended suicide nothing would be easier than to break the glass and open a vein with it. The lavatories contain no such easy implements for suicide. The almost unanimous experience of our prisoners, and of many ordinary prisoners with whom I have compared notes since my release, is that prison life disorganises digestion. The unaccustomed food, the many hours of sitting still, the want of air, the inability to leave the cell except at stated times, and the great depression of spirit, are all of them certain to produce digestive disorders. Bread is the staple food of prisoners. The prison brown bread is excellent in quality and in nutritive properties to those who can digest it, but to most moderns, of whatever class or sex, it is an unaccustomed food. To some people it is too coarse and acts as an irritant, while producing the opposite effect on others. The white bread of the hospital, also excellent of its kind, though not so irritating, is also not easily digested because of the stagnant life and small quantity of vegetables or butter allowed. The part played by the drug-basket in prison routine, and the surprise of its attendant if purgatives were not required, is proof sufficient that prison conditions in this matter are abnormal. The cells are supplied with tin chambers fitted with a lid which can be used in an emergency, but the close atmosphere of the cells makes this extremely undesirable to people trained in any sense of cleanliness. Every cell has an electric bell for summoning a wardress, but frequently no notice is taken of such a summons, and the bells are often out of order and do not work. Many of our Suffrage prisoners have had their health permanently impaired, some have had to undergo operations, as a result of the prison life in these respects. From the writings of ordinary prisoners and from what I have heard from them direct, digestive disorders seem to be common to most prisoners. My own comparative immunity I ascribe to the following precautions : Doing physical exercises twice or three times a day, saving potatoes from the midday dinner so that I had some vegetable food at every meal ; keeping my allowance of bread until it was stale ; the extra milk and butter allowed to vegetarians ; the freedom from drug taking made possible by these precautions ; the privileges extended to me in the way of occasional permission to leave my cell out of the drill routine limitations.

After we had returned to our cells the Matron came to visit me. I reported the fact that I was wearing my nightgown under my day clothes. She said I could not be allowed to do this without special permission from the medical officer. I accordingly put in " an application " to see him the next day.

I think there must be something of Asiatic origin

in me, for, contrary to Western customs, I never feel
that meals are a suitable time for conviviality, but,
on the contrary, that eating should be in solitude. I
enjoyed the change to the cell routine in this respect.
It was good to have always the same drinking mug,
the cleaning of which I had done myself, and I was
glad to be rid of the hospital tablecloth, for this was
changed only once a week, and the over-filled dishes
of fish and vegetables, as well as tea and milk, left
their mark upon it abundantly, so that during the
last days of the week it presented anything but
an appetising appearance. In the cells, milk was
poured into my own pint mug, vegetables were
served in an unpolished tin which looked very dirty
and sometimes smelt objectionably, but the potatoes
were in their skins and I ate of the vegetables only
that part which did not touch the tin. A tin plate
and spoon were provided in the cells, and a curious
piece of tin, oblong in shape, doubled over up one
side to make a rounded surface and corrugated on
the other to make an uneven saw-like edge, was
handed in with the meal to serve as knife. This I
used as it was put out again with the empty tins, but
I soon learned that if the plate and spoon were
greased with food it was very difficult to get them
clean again, as they can only be washed in cold
water. The pail of water allowed to stand in the cell
quickly became greasy itself, and there was no time,
when let out to the tap to draw water, to wash up these
things at the sink. I therefore used some of the freely
supplied brown toilet paper to cover my plate and
helped myself with my fingers instead of the spoon as
they were much easier to wash. We were allowed a

small supply of hot water at the same time that supper, consisting of hot milk and bread, was brought round. It was rather a trial that under conditions where luxuries were scarce, two should be supplied together in a way to make the full enjoyment of them both impossible. I preferred a hot wash to a hot supper and performed my ablutions first.

I had hoped that having left hospital I should be allowed to sleep in the dark, but it was a disappointment to find I was still an " observation case " because of my " heart disease." I did not sleep much and when morning came I felt strangely tired, but supposed it was due to the unusual excitement of rejoining my companions and of having at last attained to "the other side." One of the hospital patients had kindly given me elaborate instructions as to the mysterious and dexterous craft of bed-rolling in the cells. As the failure to achieve this correctly was a frequent cause of reproof and as the instructions given by wardresses were often inadequate I was very grateful for this special training. I remember that the patient, Mrs. Manson, of the Freedom League, was reading George Elliot's " Mill on the Floss," and it was on the cover of this book that she elaborated to me the furniture of the cell, where each thing should be placed and how the bedding was to be folded, then rolled into a kind of Swiss-roll coil. In the cells the mattress is stuffed with some kind of chaff, a not uncomfortable form of bedding if not stuffed too full. But mine was a new one, it seemed filled to its utmost capacity, so that it was as hard as a pincushion to lie upon, and it was only after repeated efforts, requiring my utmost strength for about fifteen minutes, that I succeeded at last in curling it up and buttoning it together in the required fashion. I was sufficiently exhausted after doing this to necessitate a long pause before I started afresh on the folding of the sheets and blankets which had to be done with minute exactness. Much more prolonged physical labours in hospital had never produced this effect upon me even during the first days when my heart was in an actively disturbed state. I wondered whether there was some health-maiming condition in this much-yearned-after " other side " which had really justified my retention in hospital. I then remembered the ventilation system of the cells against which Suffragette prisoners had made such a determined stand. The Governor and doctors had never once mentioned this lack of air in the cells as among their reasons for keeping me out of them, but now I became convinced that this was the cause of my faintness. Beyond a general feeling of what might be described as extreme slackness I did not notice anything peculiar until I exerted myself, but then the absolutely stagnant quality of the atmosphere seemed to overwhelm me. The window had no opening of any kind, the sixteen small panes of glass in their wooden framework were hermetically sealed. There were three ventilators in all, but on placing my hand upon them there was no feeling whatever of a current of air. The window was not fogged, so proving that the air was not yet vitiated to that degree, but whatever the scientific diagnosis of the results of this ventilation, there could be no doubt to an occupant of the cell that it was difficult to

breathe in it after the eleven or twelve hours of close
confinement.*

During the morning, following on my " application," I was visited by the medical officer. I put
the request, as ordered by the Matron, of wearing
my nightgown in the day time. He turned to the
wardress and said, " What an extraordinary request
to put before a doctor. That has nothing to do
with me." I explained that the leaving off of
this garment would probably affect my health
injuriously, but as it was contrary to prison discipline a doctor's permit was required. He made
some contemptuous remarks, but, when pressed,
reluctantly gave his consent. This seems a very
trifling incident as I record it here, but I vividly
remember how it seemed another link in the chain
of degradation which is forged afresh continuously
around every prisoner. Some exceptional treatment becomes necessary, one is ordered to apply for
it through some particular channel, on application
the prisoner is refused, reproved or laughed at, as if
this were a fresh instance of misdeed or foolishness.
In this instance I reminded the doctor that the
authorities were anxious that my health should be
good at my release, and that in making this request
I was assisting them, otherwise I should prefer to go

---

* In the Report of the Commissioners of Prisons for the
year ending March 31, 1911 (Part I.), the Surveyor of
Prisons tells that : " The provision of opening panes and
clear glass in cell windows has been continued . . . another
two years' work (if funds are forthcoming) should complete
the prisons." Two years to wait—and for want of money
from the richest exchequer in the world ! But they would
have waited much longer if it had not been for the
Suffragettes.

without a privilege which would not be extended
equally to all prisoners under like conditions. I had
intended bringing forward the question of ventilation, but felt that it would be useless to appeal to
this particular official, who had invariably treated
all my requests as unreasonable. On looking back
after my release on this man's conduct, it has
occurred to me that possibly he adopted his attitude
towards me from a righteous indignation at the
orders for specially favourable treatment which
were ordered for my case from headquarters. I
have heard from other Suffragette prisoners and
also from ordinary prisoners of his considerate kindness to them on several occasions. I afterwards
told the Chief Medical Officer about the airlessness
of these cells, I think with some effect.

We were exercised in the morning, not in the
afternoon as from the hospital. It was a moment
of great delight to see my companions in the yard,
where I had a better view of them than at associated
labour. We were exercised in sections of about
sixteen at a time for an hour, in the central yard
of the prison, as it seemed, a triangular yard
flanked by high walls of the oldest blocks of cells
and adjoining the high central tower, which enables
Holloway prison to stand as a landmark for many
miles distant. It can be seen from the Great
Northern Railway on the line between Holloway
and Finsbury Park Stations. I never look at it
without recalling the sensations that gripped my
soul and checked my breath when I first set eyes on
this inner yard. It seemed the quintessence of
prison, the very heart of it. The length of each side

of the rough, triangular formation is, I should think, about twenty-four feet. The walls facing south-west and east are very high, so that a deep shadow lies across the yard at all hours ; on the right, as we entered from D X, is a low walled building used apparently, for cooking and laundry purposes and facing south. This seems to be a more modern erection, and from its low, single-storey construction is responsible for most of the sunlight allowed to enter the enclosure. The remarkable feature of the yard, which caused the first feeling of horror that has remained a nightmare in my mind ever since, is the tier upon tier of cell shutters, they could not be called windows, in the two high walls giving on to the yard. They are designed to let in the very minimum of light or air, the shuttered layers of wood are, moreover, coated with refuse of the pigeons which fly freely about the yard, and are in every other respect a great delight to prisoners. The prison from here looks like a great hive of human creeping things impelled to their joyless labours and unwilling seclusion by some hidden force, the very reverse of natural, and which has in it no element of organic life, cohesion, or self-sufficing reason. A hive of hideous purpose from which flows back day by day into the surrounding city a stream of evil honey, blackened in the making and poisonous in result. The high central tower seemed to me a jam pot, indicative of the foul preserve that seethed within this factory for potting human souls.

Sometimes, in momentary reaction from the pent-up feelings of indignation and revolt, which

were chronic with me during my imprisonments, I
could have laughed out loud at the imbecility and
pathos of human fallibility, that civilised (?) educated beings could continue such processes by way
of ridding themselves from the dangers and active
harmfulness of crime.   Wardresses stood at different
points of the yard.   Whenever in our march round
there was a tendency for the single file to draw
closer together, the wardresses would say nothing,
but catch hold of one of us by the arm until
the spacing was again correct.   This handling of
prisoners instead of appealing to their ordinary
intelligence was typical of the mistaken routine,
as in hospital, imposed upon prison officials.

Once, to my delight, I recognised among these
superintending wardresses one who had been with us,
and exceptionally kind, in hospital.   I hoped that
she would manage somehow to give me news of Mrs.
Pethick Lawrence and possibly also of my friend
with the injured leg, whose fate I thought must
surely have filtered through to the wardresses.   For
some days no opportunity occurred, although this
officer smiled at me once or twice with a friendly
recognition that was quite unofficial, but only at
carefully chosen moments, showing that such a
smile would not be allowed by higher authorities.
At last, when I purposely crowded up rather near to
the prisoner ahead of me, she took the opportunity
to check my progress by putting her arm in front of
me in the recognised fashion, meanwhile telling me
in a hasty whisper and without looking at me, just
as prisoners communicate, that Mrs. Lawrence was
well, but that Mrs. Macdonald had been found to

have a fractured hip-joint and would have to stay
in hospital a long while.

Although my cell was considerably warmer than
that in the hospital, I still had not grown accustomed
to the insufficiency of my underclothing, and as now
there was no worse condition of things ahead of me I
put into use the strip of flannel that had been given
me for knee-binders. I found that either they
slipped off immediately or had to be bound so tight
that they impeded circulation and the free use of the
limbs. As one had to be constantly kneeling down
for bed making, etc., this device proved quite
impracticable. Fearing lest fresh suggestion on my
part would have to be passed by a series of officials
and finally submitted to the judgment of a doctor
who might, as in the nightgown question, satiri-
cally exclaim that this was a point not suitable to
put to him, I took advantage of the light that was
left on all night, and during the uninspected hours
sewed the strips of flannel on to the flannel drawers ;
this enabled me to tuck them into the stockings
knickerbocker-wise.

The chaplain kindly came to visit me and
remained for quite a long talk. He is the only male
prison official who visits the prisoners without an
attendant, the Governor and Deputy Governor being
accompanied generally by the Matron, and the
medical officer by a hospital attendant or wardress.
He told me that many prisoners after release wrote
to him with gratitude for his kindness and help ;
nevertheless he seemed to me to have but little
fellow-feeling for the flocks he shepherded in
Holloway. I appealed to him, in a way I had not

been able to do within hearing of the other patients in the hospital, about the case of Mrs. Macdonald. I told how it seemed to me an instance of the way in which prison officials left to themselves could not possibly have shown such brutality and neglect as was actually the case, had not the tradition of the prison system exacted a lower standard of conduct than was natural. I summed up the special grievances—her being made to walk across the yard, to walk up the three flights of stairs, being left a whole day in her cell before being conveyed to hospital, the refusal of the doctors to use the X-rays for investigation in the first instance, the contempt with which they had ignored the suggestions of this unusually intelligent woman, the refusal to allow her to see a doctor from outside when she was dissatisfied with their diagnosis, in spite of the fact that she could not in any sense be regarded as a criminal, having been charged for " obstruction " only when on a perfectly peaceable deputation to the House of Commons. The difficulties put in the way of her communication with her husband relative to her release. The cruel, needless physical suffering as well as mental worry which such treatment had entailed, perhaps resulting in maiming her for life. He had no word of sympathy to offer in connection with this case, and when I compared the treatment with that meted out to myself, when much greater consideration was shown with much less need, he took the official line that all that was done by officials must be right, and that his own wife had had a similar fall, some friends had advised X-rays, others had said they would be useless. Nothing was done, the

injury turned out to be slight and her recovery had
been complete. At the time he was using such
arguments to me, it was already known that in
Mrs. Macdonald's case the hip-joint had been
fractured.

I know that it is a very serious matter to tell
of these things in a published book. I shall be
reminded that officials are unable to answer back
or to defend themselves in public. It must, however, be remembered that prisoners are in a yet
more defenceless position, and that having personally witnessed and experienced the effect on prisoners
of certain kinds of official infallibility, it is a matter
of conscience to speak out. But in all these
instances it is the bad tradition, the wrong standard
of conduct exacted, not the personal character of
officials, that has to be attacked. This chaplain,
given ordinary surroundings, would no doubt be
according to his light a well-meaning, and according
to his powers a well-doing man. If his work were
in a West End parish or in a rural district among
people whom he genuinely revered, I can conceive
that his sympathy and understanding would be
considerable. The blame of his attitude towards
prisoners should rest on those who selected him for
a prison job and on the many elements responsible
for a system which instils contempt for the prisoner
as a fundamental tenet of the prison official. I was
told by a fellow-prisoner, a Suffragette, who on
admission had entered her religious beliefs under the
title " atheist," that this chaplain several times discussed religious matters with her in a spirit of
tolerant reverence for points of view differing from

his own. The combination of the two offices, priest
and prison official, seem to be almost incompatible,
anyhow while the prison system rests upon its
present basis. It would be more suitable if religious
and moral teachers could come into the prison solely
as representatives of the ethical bodies they represent. They could then offer their spiritual guidance
and consolations to the unfortunate inmates, as
they would to free individuals, without in any way
compromising the "system" or the officials who
have to carry it out.

On Sunday we were allowed to go to Holy Com-
munion. This impressed one very strangely. An
attempt was made to treat one more freely, combined
with many of the same restrictions as at other times.
There were about ten or twelve women altogether,
of whom about six were Suffragettes. To our great
delight Mrs. Lawrence was one of them. It seemed
ages since I had left her, and I was delighted to see
her again. The beautiful words of the service were
almost more than one could bear, and every one of
them seemed to contain freedom. It seemed as if
we must be holding it privately among ourselves.
"Drink ye all of this, for this is My Blood of the New
Testament, which is shed for you and for many for
the remission of sins : Do this as oft as ye shall drink
it, in remembrance of Me." Yet there was the
wardress with her face from which neither good nor
bad could be told, neither kind nor unkind, and the
face of the parson which seemed of the very nature of
officialdom. After the service we left the chapel by
different doors, Mrs. Lawrence's batch and ours, and
we did not see each other again.

The next morning when we were returning, through
the many halls of the building, single file, our huge
boots ringing out on the stone floor, at one door a
hospital superintendent stood and said to each one
as she passed : " Any application for the doctor ? "
When it came to my turn, I saw that it was my friend
from the hospital, but no look of recognition betrayed
itself in her face. She put out her arm to stop me
and wheeled me round to the back. When several
others had passed her she turned to me, began
quickly undoing my dress and said rapidly, but with
still no look of recognition : " Well, have you been
all right ? "   " Oh, yes," I said, " but surely you are
not going to look at it here ? " She made no
answer, but began to inspect me even more quickly.
I insisted on turning my back on the long file which
seemed never to end. She asked kindly questions,
and said she would come and see the other wound
that afternoon. She did not come, however, but
sent one of the younger superintendents. She came
once in the early morning, and it was very nice to
see her again ; it was the last time.

On one of the latter days a girl was wrongfully
accused of laughing in chapel, and confined to her
cell in consequence the following day. It is possible
that someone was guilty of this. The severity which
some of the wardresses used at chapel seated above
the prisoners, one at every two or three rows, their
backs to the altar and their attention completely
taken up with the prisoners, gave one a strange
sensation in church ; it took away all reverence of
the usual kind, and made one nervous and possibly
inclined to laugh. But, as it happened, the girl

punished for this offence was far removed from the
possibility of laughing. She was one of those I had
noticed with particularly long hair ; it must have
reached below her knees. We had come away together once from an Albert Hall meeting in a four-
wheel cab when I had been lucky in securing it, and a
wet evening made me invite strangers who were
anxious to get away. She was particularly deferential and modest in her ways, her manner in chapel
was irreproachable, and that she was picked out for
punishment was most singularly ill-judged. We
volunteered punishment of the same order as hers,
and neither chapel, exercise, nor concerted labour
had the benefit of us during the day.

The last days were spent in burning excitement.
Nothing that I can say will explain the feeling I had
that I was going to be free once more.   The food, the
clothes, the getting up at 5.30 a.m., these were bad
enough, but they were as nothing compared to the
incessant brutal treatment of the official manner, as
with Mrs. Macdonald more especially, but also with
Mrs. Duval, Miss Lawless, and others ; in the constantly being ordered about and spoken to as if one
had no feelings or perceptions, there was nothing but
an extreme severity of manner without the smallest
variation. On the third or fourth day before our
last, someone had a visitor while we were at associated labour. On her return along the line she said
to me : " A speech is expected of you ; they hope
great things of you at the feast." My heart gave one
bound. This meant release without a doubt, but a
speech ! How was it such a thing was expected of
me ? " I'll simply tell some of the things that

take place here," I thought, and I felt that this was necessary.

The morning of March 24 we were released. My excitement was great, I had not slept, and from 4.30 onwards it was impossible to keep quiet. At 5.30 we were called in the regulation way and towards 7 we were taken down to other cells. I was put into one with a stranger whom I had not seen before. She was a servant, a lady's maid, who had left her last place, or, rather, they had left her, because of her opinions. She had determined to go in for the Deputation, although probably it would mean that she got no place again.* The cell where we were was dirty and smelt horribly, but I said nothing, hoping that my companion would not notice it. She soon did, however, for the smell nearly made her faint. I was given a packet of letters—a large heap from friends and strangers all the world over. At the head of the telegrams was a two-sheet one from our baker in the country, sent off the moment I was a prisoner, addressed to "The Castle where Suffragettes are confined, Holloway," most anxious about my food, and might he send the special bread he always made for me! I read my mother's letter again and again; it was all kindness, and I could hardly wait to see her. We were arranged in a long, close file, in the same order in which we had been ushered in, and put to stand in the big gateway. I never knew what it was that kept us, but there we stood for nearly an hour. A wardress or two were watching us, and we were not allowed to move. At

* I heard afterwards that the married daughter of the lady she was last with had taken her gladly and at once.

last the big doors were unbolted, we were half pushed
from where we stood, we were out in the open—
we were free. My sister and her eldest girl and boy
had somehow gained permission to come within the
outer gates. I saw them and forgot all else. There
was no release-breakfast feast ; we were told that
we were to meet that evening at the Inns of Court
Hotel and make our speeches there.

Some days had passed when I went back to the
prison. I thought I should be glad to get within
reach of the ordinary prisoner, I in no way dreaded
it. I had more to find out about X., the 3rd
Division prisoner of the hospital. But, strangely
enough, when I saw the big tower of Holloway, that
looked quite different from anything else, and which
brought back the inevitable picture of the women
that go in, are kept in durance, and let out again to
a life more horribly unnatural, I felt my legs begin
to shake, and by the time I was shown in to the
Governor, who kindly saw me, it was all I could do
to walk upstairs. I could not see X.; they said
that someone else had been to visit her that month.
I got in touch with her case through the Prisoners'
Aid Society but they said that she was being
" attended to " by another lady.

I went again to Holloway the morning that X.
was to be released. Her freedom was due at 8 a.m.
Two women and her little boy were waiting for her,
they had kept the boy from all harm during the long
months of her imprisonment. They didn't know
where she was going to live, or what she would do,
they had heard nothing from her. Soon after eight
the great doors swung open, and the prisoners for

that morning were let out, but there was no X, among them. I inquired at the door, but they would give no information there. After waiting another three-quarters of an hour I put in an appeal to see the Governor. The little boy of four years old had waited more than an hour outside, I had petitioned for him and one of the women to wait inside, but in vain. I was shown up to the Governor, who kindly saw me and made inquiries for me about X.'s case. She was booked to go out that morning, but was waiting for her uncle, a well-to-do man, to take her away. I said her little boy was there, might he not spend the time with her, as she would be taking him away. The answer was "No." The Governor said it was a case in which the Chaplain and a lady visitor had taken a special interest, that he knew very little about it. He asked me very kindly to wait in his room, but as he had nothing more to tell me I went back to the women outside. They told me more fully about X. She seems to have been in every way a good and hard-working woman. She had killed her child, knowing that it would be impossible to keep it alive. The man, the father, lived in the same street, but now he had gone, they did not know where. They hoped that she would come back and live where she had been before, but they feared the rich uncle, a publican. X. had been to live with him and her aunt when quite a young girl, but they had insisted that she must tout the men for them, and engage in illegal intercourse as an attraction. She had run away, and would not live with them. At her trial the uncle had been called in, and he, being a Citizen of

London, had kindly managed that she should be tried
only for concealment of birth. He had done well
for her at the trial, but now they feared he would
get hold of her again. My feelings were indeed torn
when I had to tell them the Governor's news. They
had kept the child without help from anybody,
sometimes it was a very hard thing, but they had
always kept it in good health. Presently a tall man
came by and went into the prison. About a quarter
of an hour after he came out. X. was with him.
She walked head down, her face in tears. Scarcely
knowing what she did, she advanced towards her
little boy, stretched out both arms and gave him a
passionate embrace. He had rushed towards her
calling out "Mother!" Then, sobbing as if her
heart would break, she followed the man to the
public-house opposite. The two women made as if
they would follow her, and I slipped into her hand
a letter I had written in case I did not see her.
The man then rounded on the women, and driving
them away with his hand, said : "Keep away, we
don't want you—your money shall be paid you
all right," and he fled along the pavement, taking
X. by the arm. We went and had some belated
breakfast at a shop. I took the address of the women
and the little boy, but I unfortunately lost it when I
was abroad. I had given them mine, but I have
never heard of them from that day.

I went abroad with my mother, and in the meanwhile things happened apace in England. The
deputations, in ever-increasing numbers, succeeded
one another with imprisonments of two or three
months. The officials treated all the deputations

with the utmost indifference. Miss Wallace Dunlop wrote up on the walls of the House of Commons: "Women's Deputation, June 29. Bill of Rights. It is the right of all subjects to petition the King. All commitments and prosecutions for such petitioning are illegal." This is one of the most fundamental laws of Great Britain, but the vote has rendered it unnecessary for men. For this she was given one month's imprisonment, and she it was who began the hunger strike, and was let free after four days. For several months succeeding prisoners followed Miss Dunlop's fine example, and the Home Secretary, Mr. Herbert Gladstone, let them out after four or five days, some of them were kept five or six days. When they were let out they were released unconditionally. Towards the middle of September, Mr. Gladstone thought that he would make another move and, instead of releasing them, he had them fed by force in the prisons. The horror this created was at first small, for there were but few people who realised what it meant. I shall never forget the impression that it made on me.

CHAPTER X

NEWCASTLE : POLICE STATION CELL

I WAS at Birmingham in October, 1909, and I had
two meetings with Mrs. Pankhurst. Whenever this
happened one felt most singularly useless beside that
great woman. I was overcome by the sense of being
superfluous, and oppressed at having to go through
the same ordeal in the evening. After the first
meeting she took me with her to a nursing home to
see the girl who had been the first to be released
after the hunger-strike and forcible feeding. It was
a fine evening, and a beautiful red light lit up the
window as we came in ; against it was merely the
shadow of a girl, sitting in an arm-chair. She did
not look ill in an ordinary way, but young and fresh,
only so absolutely thin and wasted, it would not
have surprised us if life had gone out. She told her
story very simply, just the bare facts and nothing
more. She had been fed for a month. Mrs.
Pankhurst, in cross-questioning her, elicited some of
the horrors. She had resisted the gag as long as
possible, then, with the increasing weakness, she had
not the strength to resist much. Yes, the tube was
a long one, pushed down the throat, in spite of all
attempts to prevent it, and into the stomach. The
feeling was that the tube was absolutely choking
you, and when it was withdrawn that it dragged
after it the whole of your inside.

She looked absolutely ethereal as she smiled at us
and said " Good-bye." For several days her face
haunted me, it was startlingly like something. Then
I remembered the paintings of Fra Angelico in the
Chapel of St. Mark's at Florence. I bought one of
the little sixpenny editions of his pictures. There
it was, the thing I had seen lately, the look of
spiritual strength shining through physical weakness.
I looked through the book to choose one specially
like the girl at Birmingham ; there were several
that reminded me of her. I had looked at these
pictures in my younger days, and their great beauty
had given me joy, but I had felt annoyed with the
man for painting beings so inhuman, women that
were ethereal but so little real, a look of purity that
no living creature has. Now I had longed for them,
having seen the thing portrayed in life. As I
looked through the book, I turned over suddenly
on a picture that was quite different. There was a
crowd of women, real women, doing battle with men.
One hit out at a soldier—the men were soldiers—
another thrust out her arm, and with her hand over
his face, kept him away with all the strength she
could, a third had been thrown to the ground, but,
with a face of raging despair was thrusting out in
every direction. The soldiers were simply carrying
out their duty, an order had gone forth and they
obeyed it ; in the arms of the women were little
babies, they had been told to kill them, and they did
as they were told. In a seat above, looking on quite
calmly, was Herod. It was the Massacre of the
Innocents. The picture made a deep impression upon
me, yet it all seemed so small compared with the

unnecessary death rates of now. I was, just then, reading some facts that dealt with the death rate of infants. I found in one of the booklets by J. Johnston, Esq., M.D., 1909, this passage : " The first big fact which faces us upon this subject is that while the death rate for England and Wales for 1906 was 15.4, the infantile mortality—the death rate of children under twelve months—was 132. This means that one in eight of the children born in this country dies before its first birthday—a death roll of 339 per day—a massacre of the innocents greater than that of King Herod at Bethlehem. And this wholesale slaughter of young life goes on, not for one day, as did that historic butchery, but is repeated every day, every week, every month, year in and year out, until in the year 1906 the army of baby martyrs reached a grand total of 123,895. Well might the African monarch, King Khama, say, " You English take great care of your goods, but you throw away your children."

I left that room in Birmingham in a maze of feelings. An angel had been in my presence and I, who agreed with all she did, had left her and many others to go through with this alone. My mind was made up. I would take the very next opportunity of making my protest with a stone.

. . . . . .

On Friday, October 8, Christabel Pankhurst and I were on our way to Newcastle. We were seated opposite to each other in the midst of a crowded third-class carriage. It was on this occasion that I realised, as I had not yet done, the wonderful

character, the imperturable good temper, the
brilliant intellect of my companion. As we could
not talk in this crowded train, I showed her some
letters and papers on which I wanted her advice,
or which I wanted her to know about. Whether
they were print, typewritten, or manuscript, she
had read them all in a moment, so as to discuss
them with me afterwards. When we arrived at
Newcastle we found that we had accompanied
Mr. Lloyd George ; there was a small crowd that
welcomed him and that cheered half-heartedly.
We went, after depositing our things at an hotel,
to join an outdoor meeting. Christabel spoke. I
sold *Votes for Women* in the crowd, which, though a
large one, was mostly composed of out-of-work men,
who took little interest in what was said. We
drove round the town in honour of Miss New, who
had just come out of prison, and went to a tea in
her honour in an hotel where some fifty or sixty
women were assembled. After this there was a
strange meeting in the ground-floor room of a
lodging-house. There were twelve women ; we were
all intending stone-throwers, and Christabel was there
to hearten us up and to go into details about the
way in which we were to do it. Mrs. Brailsford
was there, whose husband was lately on the staff of
the *Daily News ;* he and Mr. Nevinson had resigned
their posts because of the shameful way in which
that paper and the Liberal Government had for-
saken the women.

I had made up my mind that I was going to
throw a stone—that was as sure as death, but the
manner of it was going to be my own ; I was equally

sure of that. I was not sure of "the stone-throwers."
I had vaguely felt that they would have different
reasons from mine for this errand, that perhaps,
though they could not be more certain than myself,
they would mind it less. I had not been in the
room with them five minutes before I realised that I
was mistaken. I was the "hooligan," if there were
one amongst them. One I specially remember.
She was pretty, with a great deal of fair hair. She
had not, I thought, the look of determination, of
silent, unhesitating determination, which gave an
air of inflexibility to the others. She leaned forward
and asked many questions : the wardresses, would
they, too, be disagreeable, would they pull down her
hair and tear out the tortoise-shell combs ? One
somehow knew by her voice that she was not ready,
she asked her questions as if something of a nightmare was in her mind ; they were asked quite
simply, but seemed to say, "Oh ! save me from
this !" I asked Christabel, when alone with her
at the hotel, if I might tell her there was no need for
her to do it, that I thought she was not quite prepared. "Of course," she answered, "if she does
not feel up to it, let her stand aside. One cannot
tell how one is going to feel, she has never done
anything before." Not long ago Mrs. Pethick
Lawrence had met her, it was at a bazaar. She
wore a big hat and looked as remote as it is possible
to look from stone throwing. She expressed the
greatest admiration for the militants. "There is
only one thing," she said, "which I cannot think
worth while—that they should go to prison." I
was to get her out of it the next morning, the

day of Lloyd George's meetings and of our militancy.

That evening there was an immense meeting at the drill hall where Christabel was to speak, but before she began a gang of about forty students howled and threw squibs, so that nothing could be heard. When she got up for a moment the applause drowned everything, but it soon was again impossible to hear her. The students broke up the seats and threw everything about. Then some ten of them charged the platform. A row of stewards hastily ranged themselves and tried to check their advance, but their arms were wrenched apart, until the husband of one of them took his turn and gave it to one of the students, whereupon the other men turned tail and ran. At this man coming forward the police interfered, they had been appealed to in vain by some of the stewards. It was most difficult not to help them, but I had sworn to keep myself till the next day. The row made by the other students went on unabated. Meanwhile, Christabel remained perfectly good-tempered. For the first quarter of an hour she spoke up, but as it was impossible for her voice to carry above the noise she lowered her voice and spoke only to reporters. The next day her speech appeared in full in all the local press.

The next morning, October 9, we were to meet early at the same lodging-house. The morning papers were full of Mr. Lloyd George, and in biographical sketches emphasised the glory of his having been militant, and successfully militant, through several questions that he cared about in his

early days. It was different in the lodging-house
from the night before. All was hurry and determination. Two of the women had gone already to
deliver their stony messages. The organiser, a
very straightforward and reasonable woman, was
sending each one to a different place. She said,
" There is a stone wants to be put through the door
of the Palace Theatre in the Haymarket. It must
be done at once or the gang of detectives will have
become too thick." A firm voice said : " I'll go."
It was the young girl with fair hair who had asked
so many questions the night before, and whom I was
going to set free. " Oh, no," said the organiser,
" this job will have to be done alone—two would be
detected at once." " I'll go." It was like a force
of nature that reiterated this, and there was something of adamant at the back of the voice. She
picked up two or three papers to sell, and was out
in the street before we any of us knew what she was
doing. I dashed after her. I couldn't believe that
there was so much change in her since the night
before. I moved quickly, but it was only down the
street that led out of the lodging-house street that I
caught her up. " I had thought of getting you out
of it, because you seemed too young to do the work,"
I said. " That was last night ; to-day all is quite
different." " But let me try and say what I have
in my mind. You are going to throw a stone.
Think, as you lift your arm to do it, of the majority
in the House of Commons who for years have said
they are for Votes for Women, who over and over
again for twenty years have voted for the second
reading of a Woman's Bill, and were quite content

that it should stop there. Think of the nearly total Cabinet for Woman Suffrage when the Liberals came in, under a Suffrage Prime Minister, but all attempts to pass a Bill were treated as futile. Think of the women who work with a sweated wage, who have not the energy to rebel, who are cloaked with poverty ; the thousands who, stricken with poverty more hideous than we can think of on one side, and tempted with money on the other, sink into a life of shame, which is endured for five or six years, till death releases them. Think of Lloyd George, whose speech is always fair but who carefully prevents anything being done for women. Think of the women who have been sent to prison for their protest against these things, who have hunger-struck as a fresh protest and who now have been fed by force. Then throw your stone and make it do its work."

"Thank you," she said, "thank you." I looked up at her, as I had not liked to do till that minute. A changed being stood before me. I had noticed that she had changed from the night before, she had changed unbelievably at this minute, and all that strength, determination, complete forgetfulness of self could give her, were with her now.

We parted. I went back to the others. The next thing I heard of her was in the other office, where we provided ourselves with stones. A little girl of about sixteen, who kept on running messages for us, came rapidly into the room. "Miss X.," she said, "has thrown her stone, broken her window, and been arrested." Then she went out. From that moment I knew that all was well. Miss X. got through the two days in the police-court, the trial, the hunger strike, and the forcible feeding that followed for the space of fourteen days, as did the others. Her body was weakness, but her soul was strength.

No particular job was given to me. Miss Emily Davison and I were to keep together. It was still early, and first we had to make sure of our stones. We went to the other office to get them. I was doing up mine in brown paper, double thick. " You will not be able to throw those," said the organiser, " if there is the least bit of wind, it will get inside and send them you don't know where." That was true. I found some much thinner paper which kept closely round the stone. I took four or five. On each one I wrote a different thing, I think they were all taken from Mr. Lloyd George's recent speech. I put them into my pockets and went out. Miss Davison had been speaking from every part of the town during the last week. I recommended her to buy another hat for partial disguise. We went into a hat shop and did so. In the shop there was a fascinating little black kitten which it was hard to leave. Then we went into an eating shop, thinking it was as well to have some luncheon. The shop was overpoweringly stuffy and hot. I had not met Miss Davison before, and it was most interesting to hear her experiences. Still, we could neither of us speak nor listen with anything but effort. We decided to go and see what it was like at the Haymarket, a large, open space, where the car with Mr. Lloyd George would probably pass. There was

still more than an hour before he could come. The
crowd was already considerable. Nearly every
woman that I saw looked friendly ; this was probably my imagination, but it did me good. The
Suffragettes were greatly thought of that day. The
place, we found, was divided in two by a hoarding
of about ten feet in height ; there was a space,
guarded by police, that could be opened to let a
carriage through. We looked round at the windows
of all the adjacent buildings, but they were not of an
official or of a sufficiently conspicuous character for
our stones. Presently a man in front of us—the
crowd now was pretty thick—was twirling round
one of his cards in his hands which were folded
behind him. He then held it up, so that we could
see there was writing on it. At last his signals
grew more desperate. One of us took the card
from him. On it was written his deferential
greeting, that he knew what we were out for, could
he help us in any way, run messages for us or anything ? We answered, writing on the other side,
that we thanked him cordially, but as we had no
particular job, it was best for him to " wait and see."
He had a kindly face and looked the right sort, but
we thought it was just as well that this was the true
answer. There was a monument to the soldiers
who had died in the war in the midst of the open
space. Their names were written on it, and the
little boys were clambering up the monument to see
above the crowd. They had died for their country,
that was the one fact which seemed to stand out
very clearly from the monument. Yes, nobly, and in
a good fight, they had died—where is the statue

to the women who had given their lives to the nation ?

We heard cheering in the distance, it was the arrival of Mr. Lloyd George at the theatre, he having driven by another way. My companion began to think that our chance was over until the evening. A feeling came over me that I could not wait any longer, and that somehow or other I must throw my stone. As it would anyhow be but symbolical, it seemed to me one could find an occasion as well here as elsewhere. One thing, however, I was determined upon—it must be more zealously done, more deliberate in its character than the stone-throwing at ordinary windows, which had been done lately. I was determined that when they had me in court my act should inevitably be worse than that of other women. At this moment there was a hurry in the crowd, the police were making a clearing and opening the carriage entrance for a motor-car. We found ourselves on the very edge of the crowd. As the motor appeared, I whispered to Miss Davison : " Is this any good ? " " Not the least in the world," was her reply, " just one of the motors coming back." I knew this, of course, but the instinct was too much for me. To throw a stone against the car as it ran along the side was dangerous, as there were two men in the front. I stepped out into the road, stood straight in front of the car, shouted out " How can you, who say you back the women's cause, stay on in a Government which refuses them the vote, and is persecuting them for asking it," and threw a stone at the car, but very low down. I thought I had thrown it too low, so

that it would not hit the car. I was going on, in
the space of time which seemed infinitely long, to
tell the car to turn back and get their answer from
Mr. Lloyd George, then call to the people to come
through the gap and hear his answer. I had time
to think out all this. Miss Davison came to my
side, and I saw someone take hold of her before she
could throw her stone. Then two plain-clothes
detectives caught hold of me, but what was my
intense surprise, without any violence whatever.
They simply led me back through the crowd which
surged around on every side. I had thought there
were no actual friends where we stood, but I at once
saw one or two ready to come and help me if I
wanted it. So I was still and said not a word. My
part was finished, and I saw that anything said
might easily cause a tremendous disturbance at
those close quarters. Miss Davison was arrested
at the same time, though she had done nothing,
and we were led away together. It was a business
getting through the crowd. When we had left the
Haymarket the crush was very much less, and the
two detectives in plain clothes who were responsible
for me walked on either side without touching me.
This went rather strangely with the newspaper contention that I was " very excitable." Another incident which got put into the papers was, that when
we were going down a main street, two tramcars,
going different ways, were about to meet. This
pressed the crowd that followed us and pushed us
all together. We were walking, of course, in the
roadway. A little girl with a baby in a perambulator
and a small boy on foot had got on to the island

and were wishing to pass to the pavement, being afraid of the two trams. I realised that I was the policeman of that show. I stopped and just held out my hand to the detective on my right. We let the baby and its leaders pass, then we moved on.

We were taken to the central police station of the town. The police here were most civil, and, indeed, kind. We gave our names and addresses, and then we waited in the main room. Poor Miss Davison was very distressed at doing nothing. Her heroism had to wait for another day.* Mrs. Baines came into the police court and spoke to us. I was filled with disappointment that I had not been able to do more. She told me that she was quite content, that I had thrown my stone straight, and, she believed, hit the car. She was delightfully encouraging, and made one think one had done well. Presently Mrs. Brailsford joined us, she had done exactly what she meant to do, and with a hatchet had hit one of the barricades.

* Soon after this Miss Davison was forcibly fed in Manchester Prison, and, on barricading her cell, the hose-pipe was played upon her from the window, a process of force that caused her infinite pain. She fainted, and it was many days before she recovered. She owed her life probably to being released from prison, and to the fact that she was a great swimmer, used to the shock of cold water and to with-standing its force. In 1913 she met her death with the most heroic courage at the Derby race. It was her opportunity of proclaiming to the whole world, perhaps heedless till then, that women claim citizenship and human rights. She stood in front of the race and was knocked down by the King's horse Anmer, rendered unconscious, and died the following Sunday, June 8. Millions of people, not only in our own but other countries, knew, from this act, that there are women who care so passionately for the vote and all it means that they are willing to die for it.

I noticed in this central police station a large
iron cage. It was empty, and we wondered what
purpose it could serve. On one of the benches a
little boy was sitting, of about seven or eight years
old. He had on ragged clothes, but seemed quite
happy with a cup of soup which he had been given.
It seemed odd though to bring small children to such
a place, with nothing but policemen, although
several of these were good-natured.

After we had been here a considerable time and
were joined by some of our companions, we heard
that it was unlikely they would allow us bail, and
we were taken off to the cells. Who could have
believed that in the central police station of a place
like Newcastle they could be so dirty ? Mine was
No. 2. It was on the left side of a broad gangway,
which could be shut off by an iron gate. It was
October and inclined to be dark, and when I was
first put into the cell it was impossible to see what
it was like or what it contained. It was rather high,
the very small window opposite the doorway was
either of foggy glass or grimed with dirt, it scarcely
lit up anything but itself. To the right was a plank,
rather wide and long, and with a kind of bolster
made of wood. This was all for seat or bed. When
the evening light was lit above the door, where it
was barred with iron on the side of the cell, I saw
that the wood was filthy. There was a plenitude
of fleas, but no lice. Under the window to the
right was a lavatory, it was extremely dirty, the
water could only be turned on from outside. There
was a ledge about three feet high, which sheltered
the seat. Under the window, but this I could not

see till the second day, was a men's urinal, there was a gutter in the floor for this, but no water. The cleanliness of the wall can be imagined. The smell in the cell was continuously foul.* I was very tired, but only liked to sit, not lie, on the bed.

After what seemed a very long time, a policeman summoned me, and said we were all to have food together in the wardresses' room. As I was let out I noticed seven of the others being let out too—Winifred Jones, Ellen Wines Pitman, Kathleen Brown, Kitty Marion, Dorothy Pethick and Emily Davison. Mrs. Brailsford was the only one I did not see. The four others—Violet Bryant, Ellen Pitfield, Lily Asquith and Dorothy Shallard—had all done their work the previous evening, and had been sentenced on this, Saturday, morning to two weeks' imprisonment. It was, of course, a joy to see them. It seemed so very long since that morning. When we had passed the central police office, and were ushered into the wardresses' room, it appeared that Mrs. Brailsford was shut into the wardresses' bedroom—whether for a more honourable imprisonment, she being a woman whose public work none could call deficient in selflessness and courage, or whether because she was a "dangerous criminal," having used a hatchet in making her mark on the barricade, we did not know. I remember catching sight of her as the door was opened to let in a cup of tea. There she sat, calm and erect, and Mr. Brailsford, who had been let in to see her, in piteous

* I have been in police station cells in several other places—a variety in London and two in Liverpool—but never have I seen anything like this. The other cells were scrupulously clean.

trouble, having the one thought—" Will my wife
be fed by force—how can they dare to do it ?
How will she be able to bear it ? "

Most of the others I had not seen before, yet
I felt exuberant delight at being with them.
One only I knew well, and that was Miss Ellen
Pitman. She was in the Deputation of February
and, after being in prison some ten days, she was
brought to the hospital for neuralgic pains in
her leg. She was a trained nurse, we had got
to know each other well, and her fine face will
always be very dear to me. We now got to know
the wardresses—they were as kind to us as possible.
I was so tired I could scarcely see, and after a time
we retired to rest. There was a deafening noise ;
the cells were filled mostly with drunkards, for it
was Saturday. Thundering blows on the doors,
accompanied by a string of oaths, went on all
through the night. The police were very kind to
them, bringing them fresh water to drink, chaffing
them and coaxing them. No bedding of any kind
or rugs were provided by the police, but our friends
outside were most wonderfully good to us, and,
when they found we were not to be bailed out, they
were busy collecting rugs and blankets. At about
12 they sent me in a rug and a sort of air-cushion
bed, which would have been most delightful, but I
tried every end in vain, I didn't know how to put
air into it. I was stiff for several days from my
rest on the plank, but I owed it to the friends that
I did not have two nights of it. On Sunday they
brought a mattress instead of the air bed, and my
flannel sheets which gave me a restful night.

On Sunday I sent for the district visitor, supposing she would be a woman, but was told there was no district visitor; a police-court missionary? not one either; finally, I sent for the doctor. My complaint was that no toilet paper was provided, and no sanitary towels for the women. Prisoners are kept from Saturday afternoon until Monday. I said, were not these people the same as those who go to prison, they have these necessaries there? " I don't know about a prison, I'm sure they would never use them in Police Station cells." Exactly the same remark was made about the prisons, but all the same these things were instituted and now used by prisoners. I begged that, at least, they might be kept in charge of the wardress.

Not long after I had seen the doctor, I was summoned out to see someone else. To my great delight it was Mrs. Pankhurst. She was all sympathy, and it was delightful seeing her.

I was had out of my cell yet another time, for my name, age, etc., to be " taken down " by a policeman in a book. I was able to look over the book as he wrote, and I saw, to my intense surprise, that the law brought three charges against me, first, of assault on Sir Walter Runciman, who was in the car; secondly, of malicious injury to the car at £4; thirdly, of disorderly behaviour in a public place. I felt very exalted to think I had done so much, and thought that three months was the least they could give me. I could not help being pleased to think that the car had contained the host of Mr. Lloyd George, not merely the chauffeur. But what pleased me most was the £4 damage. How

I could have done it was indeed a mystery, but I was
glad to know that the stone had not gone on the
ground, as I had feared. As I went through the
central room on one of these occasions, the cage which
I had seen before, to my astonishment, was inhabited
—by a man, I expected to see some fierce brute, but
he was small, frail and miserably degraded, without
power to do anyone an injury, with marks of abnormal weakness in his face. When I saw him, the
feeling came over me with a great tide, that I should
throw myself at his feet and try to bear something
of his burden, because if I had done my duty, and
if my contemporary women and those who went
before had done their duty, we should have given
him another life, by securing better, more human
conditions, for himself and for his mother who gave
him birth. He had lived in that terrible state of
things which make it hardly possible to survive.
Here, at any rate, was a man intensely feeble in his
body, and he was put in an iron cage as the only
suitable place !

We were called out and made to stand at the doors
of our cells.   Presently, the plain-clothes police came
to " learn our faces," and after looking at us stead-
fastly for some minutes, we were put back again.

The food was brought for us by our friends from
outside, who provided for us deliciously, and we had
our meals all together in the wardresses' room. Only
Mrs. Brailsford never appeared, being shut in the
inner room, but we sent her some of our food.
On Sunday night, the wardress had brought us a
little basin with some warm water to our cells,
which was indeed a boon.

That Sunday night the police were most kind,
they allowed me to sit at a table outside my cell and
write. My cell was much too dark for writing.
To-night the place was more full of noise than it had
been before. The wild yells, and blows on the
doors, made my hand shake so that at first I could
not write, but by holding the pencil, lent to me
by the police, over the paper, it came sufficiently
legibly at last. I wrote to my mother and my sister.
I also wrote to the *Times* the following letter; from
the eleven * who were imprisoned :—

" SIR,—We ask you to give us our last opportunity, before we go through the ordeal awaiting us
in Newcastle Prison, of explaining to the public the
action which we are now about to take.

" We want to make it known that we shall carry
on our protest in our prison cells. We shall put
before the Government by means of the hunger-
strike four alternatives : To release us in a few days ;
to inflict violence upon our bodies ; to add death to
the champions of our cause by leaving us to starve ;
or, and this is the best and only wise alternative, to
give women the vote.

" We appeal to the Government to yield, not to
the violence of our protest, but to the reasonableness
of our demand, and to grant the vote to the duly
qualified women of the country. We shall then
serve our full sentence quietly and obediently and
without complaint. Our protest is against the
action of the Government in opposing Woman

* I handed this letter to a friend on Monday morning.
At the trial Miss Davison was dismissed, so her name was
taken from the signatures.

Suffrage, and against that alone. We have no
quarrel with those who may be ordered to maltreat
us.

" Yours sincerely,

" LILY ASQUITH.   WINIFRED JONES.
" JANE E. BRAILSFORD.   CONSTANCE LYTTON.
" KATHLEEN BROWN.   KITTY MARION.
" VIOLET BRYANT.   DOROTHY PETHICK.
" ELLEN PITFIELD.   ELLEN W. PITMAN.
" DOROTHY SHALLARD.

" CENTRAL POLICE STATION,
    " NEWCASTLE,
        " *October* 10, 1909."

I wrote on the wall of my cell my name and
the words which rung in my head over and over
again, from the Book of Joshua : " Only be thou
strong and very courageous."

I received a letter in the police cell, saying that I
had thrown my stone not far from a family residence
of relatives of ours—did I not feel it hence a double
disgrace ? In answer to this I had thought some time.
Who were those for whom we fought ? I seemed
to hear them in my cell, the defenceless ones who
had no one to speak for their hungry need. The
sweated workers, the mothers widowed with little
children, the women on the streets, and I saw that
their backs were bent, their eyes grown sorrowful,
their hearts dead without hope. And they were not
a few, but thousands upon thousands. Side by side
I considered what they could do, what they had done,
where women had the vote. The wife has half her
husband's wages, by law, and when he does not give

it, she can have the amount paid direct to her. She
is given money for her children by the State when
her husband dies. When she is not married, if she
has a child she is paid for it, not by the father direct,
but through the public authority, and she has not to
apply to the father for her money. I thought of
all these helpless women, of the Parliament that
had given its theoretic consent for over twenty
years, but refused to pass a Bill, and I thought what
are my relations ? I do not know, but if anything,
they are for us, and if they are still asleep, in the fog
of the " don't know and don't care," am I bound to
consider their dreaming ?

I wrote on the wall :—

> " To defend the oppressed,
> To fight for the defenceless,
> Not counting the cost."

CHAPTER XI

NEWCASTLE PRISON : MY SECOND IMPRISONMENT

THE next morning, Monday, October 11, we got up early, with a sense of excitement that we were to be " tried." We were allowed to wash in a basin arrangement all together. The water was cold, but clean and fresh. The roll towel was horrible, I have never seen anything so dirty—blood had freely been wiped upon it. Nothing could surpass the kindness and civility of the wardresses. One, who thought only of the hunger-strike, cried as we left. We were then led off to the cells upstairs, which were rather cleaner and much lighter. A man came to mend something outside my window ; it was open and I could see out by two or three square inches. He looked in at me with great curiosity, but without ill-will. I had the policeman's pencil still, and wrote on a paper to hand up to him that he should not be afraid of the Suffragettes, but help them to get the vote. I was still thinking about it when the police began to rattle the keys, so I refrained, although it was some time before they came to fetch me.

They led us forth to the other side of the building where the court was. We waited in a passage underneath it, and were led up in turns to the prisoner's

box. The others, who had done nothing but
break glass, were sentenced to the 3rd Division
and hard labour for fourteen days, and some a
month, without any option. Mrs. Brailsford and
I were both given the alternative of being bound
in money sureties for a year. In reality, this
offered us no alternative, but in the estimation of the
magistrate, I, who had done deliberately most
harm, was given the option of going free, while the
others, who were many of them younger than I was,
first offenders and all had done much less damage
than I had, were prisoners beyond their recall.

When it was my turn, I was prepared for the
three charges I had seen on the paper the day
before. First came the charge of assault on Sir
Walter Runciman. I said that I did not know it
was Sir Walter Runciman in the car, and that I
threw the stone low down, so that it should not hit
the chauffeur or anyone. They did not take up
this charge. Then came the charge of damage, at
which I was well pleased. But the man facing the
magistrate, the clerk, who conducts most of the
affairs in several courts I have been into, would not
let this charge come on. He said that I had
evidently not intended the damage to the car, and
that part of the case was dismissed. I tried to tell
him that I had no concern for the motor-car, and,
though I didn't know how a stone so small could
have done so much harm, I was not in the least
concerned over the £4 worth of damage, but he
would not let me speak and passed on to the third
charge, " disorderly behaviour in a public place."
I put in, with a loud voice, " My disorderly behaviour

of throwing a stone with violence in a public place
was deliberate and intentional." After this, they
could not but go on with it, since the whole court had
heard what I had said. They apparently treated
me as a lunatic, and began to ask if it was through
not knowing what I was doing that I had thrown a
stone ? " If I had not known what I was about to
do, I should not have held a stone in my hand," I
answered.

I had made up my mind, at one time of the trial,
that I would deny the tales that had circulated
about the Suffragettes and Mr. Lloyd George's
children. It had been said that we tried to kidnap
them, that we had wished for their illness, and all
kinds of invented evil. Who are the Suffragettes
that they should make war on children ? If the
child of Mr. Lloyd George were ill or in any way
suffering, we were sorry, we were sympathetic, as
with every other child, and we were sad for him as
the loving father of that child. I tried to speak, when
I first was called on, and repeatedly afterwards,
but I was always stopped and could get no innings.
Finally, the magistrates convicted me of " disorderly behaviour with intent to disturb the peace,"
and bound me over, myself in the sum of £50 and
two sureties of £25 each, to be enforced for twelve
months ; in default, one month's imprisonment in
the 2nd Division. I, of course, had no option of
finding sureties for twelve months, and was sentenced
to the month's imprisonment. My companion,
Miss Davison, was dismissed, as she had literally
done nothing.

Mrs. Brailsford, who had struck at the barricade

with an axe, was also given the option of being
bound over, which she, of course, refused, with the
alternative of a month's imprisonment in the
2nd Division. She had not, as I had, committed
any offence before. She was a splendid woman
who had gone out to help with the Macedonian
relief fund in 1903. She had fed the hungry and
nursed the sick and wounded until she contracted
typhus fever. The whole " trial " was unworthy
of the name—it was a device whereby Mrs. Brailsford and I should be separated from the others and
treated with more respect, I having been the only
one to do a glaring act and an, apparently, harmful
or greatly risky one. The others, without exception,
were treated to the 3rd Division.

We were put again into a van, but had only a
short way to drive. We were shown into a passage
of the prison where the governor came and spoke
to us. He was very civil, and begged us not to go
on the hunger-strike. Then the Matron came, a
charming and very refined woman, who walked with
a stick, being lame. Miss Davison had headed our
little band of twelve ; when she was dismissed, Miss
Dorothy Pethick, Mrs. Pethick Lawrence's youngest
sister, was our head and spoke for us. Her face had
all the beauty that freshness, youth and grace could
give it, and with it all for her age—she was twenty-
seven—there was a wonderful strength about it.
She spoke civilly to the Governor, but in a very
determined way. He could not do enough for us.
" Don't break your windows—please don't break
your windows." " We will not break them if they
can open. You must understand that we have

come here, not to please ourselves ; we have pleaded
for windows to open in the cells through two years
in vain. Now we break the glass to make more
sure. It is for the poor things who are shut up in
these little cells for weeks and months at a time.
Whether they know it or not, their bodies know it—
it is all that is bad for them to sleep and live in a
room supposed to be ventilated, without a window,
and to be given a book telling them elaborately how
a window may be kept open in all weathers by
placing a board in front of it on a slant, will not
make things any better. And what is more, if you
feed us by force, we shall break every window we
can lay hands on." " Very well," said the Governor,
" choose your own cells ; come round and see."
Then, with the Governor and Matron, we went
round. Several cells were shown to us. We were
left in some that were small but new—the windows
did not open. Finally, Mrs. Brailsford and I were
taken to different cells on the ground floor where we
were separated completely from the others. We
were allowed to have our doors open all the time,
and some iron gates only shut us in. Compared with
Holloway, their good manners made a great difference, but the kindness about the cells was mostly
put on ; at least, they had not windows that opened,
so they could do little. Mrs. Brailsford and I had
cells next door to each other, we spoke together
frequently all day. The wardresses were dear
northern women, affectionate in their ways. The
Matron we found to be even more charming than she
looked. She took Mrs. Brailsford and me for
exercise, and we talked to her nearly the whole

time. She was quite a Suffragette and understood
our rebellion.

There was no attempt to put us into prison
clothes ; we had small packages of things with us.
My underclothes were not all that one could wish
after two days and nights in the police-station cells.
They were amongst other things covered with fleas,
and I had at my trial, and on various occasions,
become exceedingly hot, which, now that the hunger-
strike had begun, was exchanged for extreme cold.
The prospect of a month in them as they were was
extremely undesirable. I wrote to the Home Secretary, as I was told this was the only means, but I
knew that anything I asked for from him might as
well be let alone.

The first day, Tuesday, was fairly fine. At
exercise in the morning we looked around and we
noticed some broken glass windows. We shouted
" Votes for Women, Hurrah ! Hurrah ! " but were
not sure of any response. They had put our companions, of two days before us, into the punishment
cells. We were scarcely back in our cells before
there were hasty footsteps ; they slammed our
doors shut, we could only dimly hear the steps as
they passed our cells and then above. Soon after
we heard shrieks, always coming from the same
direction. It seemed as if the others were being fed
by force. During about half an hour the sounds
were terrible. Then the doctors, two of them, came
to us. They had on white jackets, as if they had just
come from an operation, as indeed they had. I said
to them, " You have been feeding our friends by
force ? " One of them answered, " Well, yes, we

were bound to have a food trial with one or two of
them." They felt my pulse, first one, then the
other ; they felt it over again, then they went out.
Mrs. Brailsford and I discussed the feeding of our
friends, which had sounded most awful; we did not
know what to do. We had, of course, not touched
any food since our breakfast in the police-station cells.
We ourselves had met with nothing but kindness.

The knotting in my stomach from lack of food
was fairly painful by the second night. Whenever
I fell asleep I woke with my knees curled under my
chin. I had also a great aching in my back, probably through fatigue and the plank bed in the police-
station. The night wardress was very kind to me. I
asked once if she couldn't come in and rub my back
just a little. "Why, my dear, the gate's locked
and I have nae got the key." Mrs. Brailsford said
she felt well in every way, save that she could do
nothing but think of the other prisoners who were
being fed by force. When we walked round the
exercise yard on Wednesday morning it was snowing
hard. It made me think of Robert Buchanan's
poem, " The Ballade of Judas Iscariot."

> " 'Twas the wedding guests cried out within,
>   And their eyes were fierce and bright—
> ' Scourge the soul of Judas Iscariot
>   Away into the night ! '

> " The Bridegroom stood in the open door,
>   And he waved hands still and slow,
> And the third time that he waved his hands
>   The air was thick with snow.

> " And of every flake of falling snow
>   Before it touched the ground,
> There came a dove, and a thousand doves
>   Made sweet doves' sound.

' 'Twas the body of Judas Iscariot
    Floated away full fleet,
And the wings of the dove that bore it off
    Were like its winding-sheet.

" 'Twas the Bridegroom stood at the open door
    And beckon'd, smiling sweet ;
'Twas the soul of Judas Iscariot
    Stole in, and fell at his feet."

As I looked upon that dreary scene I saw the
prison walls, the cell windows, looking more like
tiny shutters, the infinitesimal small windows of the
punishment cells in the ground below where we
were. The Matron stood on a ledge above us. She
was considerate and kind in all her ways. We were
either alone and quite unguarded or else she was
with us. One evening, when a wardress was letting
me back into my cell, I heard the most melancholy
sound of a woman calling out to herself again and
again, in a tone of uttermost misery. As always,
I thought, in a prison, no one answered her, no one
said anything. Presently there came the Matron's
consoling voice. Very gently I heard it on the floor
above ours, it sounded almost like a mother's voice :
" Oh ! there is that poor woman again. Can't you
some of you go and comfort her ? " And some
one did, for all was quiet after that. I watched
at my gate all day, and was pleased to notice that
the prisoners who worked outside the cells moved
happily, ran about with a springing step and
seemed like ordinary servants about their work.
How different this was from Holloway !

The first morning the Chaplain came to visit me.
He was a pleasant-looking man, with a fine beard.
He laughed as he told me he was the father of

fifteen children; he said this as he left. I longed
to tell him I hoped that he had had at least two
wives to bring them into the world!

The second morning, Wednesday, October 13,
when the doctors came, I stood in the corner of my
cell with my arms crossed and my fingers caught in
my nostrils and my mouth. It was the best position
I knew of for them not to be able to feed me by
nose or mouth without having first a considerable
struggle. They came, and after I saw that they had
no tube I came out from my corner and let them
both look at my heart. They thumped, each of
them in turn, and felt my pulse as well. Then they
appeared to be agreed and went out. I said to
them, "You seemed to be puzzled by my heart; I
can tell you about it if you like." But they had
made up their minds about something, and did not
want any help from me. Later in the day they came
in again with another man in their company. I was
again in the corner, my hands in my mouth and nose,
but they brought no feeding things. At first I
thought the third man was another prison official;
but soon, from the way they talked to him, I
gathered that he was an outside doctor, apparently
from London. He was very civil. He tapped my
heart repeatedly and then brought out a tube,
which at first I thought was a feeding tube, but it was
only another way of testing the heart. He was
about a quarter of an hour or twenty minutes over
the whole thing, then they went out.

As I had no answer from the Home Office, though
I had written on the Monday of my arrival in the
prison, I thought I would begin to wash some of my

things, as the doctors would not come back unless to
feed me, and that would be nearer six o'clock. I
washed my brush and a few other things in the large
pail of my cell, then asked if I might empty it, and,
as I did this, I held the things some seconds under
the tap. It was only cold water, of course, but I was
glad of even that. I then put them on the chair to
dry as best they might, and lay down on my plank
bed, for the pain in my back was terrible, when a
wardress came in and announced that I was released,
because of the state of my heart! Though this was
fairly evident from the visit of the outside doctor, I
had not realised it. I gathered my things together
and went out. I called to Mrs. Brailsford; she was
released too. We were put to wait in the Governor's
room; he was not there. We wondered if we were
the only two to be released, and if so, why not the
others? How about the heart of Nurse Pitman,
who was close on sixty, or of Miss Brown, who had
only just been released from a recent hunger-
strike! Mrs. Brailsford had seen a doctor before
she came on this expedition to Newcastle, and he
had declared her absolutely sound in every way, so
we did not know why she was released, except for
the fact that she was, through her husband, closely
connected with Liberal journalism and herself
had the noblest reputation for public service in
Macedonia. I had heart disease, though only
slightly; it had been marked in me since the
Deputation on which I had been to the House of
Commons, at the beginning of this year. But I was
not in so bad a condition as either Nurse Pitman or
Miss Brown. After a time the news came that we

were the only two released!   Poor Mrs. Brailsford
was so overcome at this news that she was unable
to drink the glass of hot milk that was given to us
before we were let out.   The Governor came back to
his room.   He had always told us how keen he was
for the vote, and he seemed very glad for us that we
were to be released.   The cab was ready and we
drove away, I think at about 3.30 in the afternoon.
It seemed appalling to go and to leave the others in
prison, to the hunger-strike and to forcible feeding.

Nurse Pitman and Miss Brown were released the
next day.   It was not possible to understand for
what reason they should have been kept twenty-four
hours longer on hunger-strike than Mrs. Brailsford
and myself ; the only reason that we could see was
that our names were known, theirs were not!

The only thing which made an impression on me,
not told in the above, was that once the wardress
led me out to one of the lavatories.   Just in front
of it a woman had been sick, and I was taken away
to another.   It showed the great loneliness of
prison life.   There, in rows thickly set all around
me, were the cells, in each a prisoner.   One had been
taken out immediately before I had, but she was put
back and all the cells were locked before I came.
The mystery was intense, the silence, the loneliness
as great as they could be.

My sister, Betty Balfour, came from Scotland to
see if she could do anything to help me when she
heard that I was in prison.   She was convinced that
I should not be forcibly fed because of the state of my
heart, but that I should be let out after a day or two
of hunger-strike.   It was delightful to be with her,

and the next day we travelled south together to my
home.

In December I went to speak at Glasgow, and
Dr. Marion Gilchrist listened to my heart. This
was her verdict : " I have examined Lady Constance
Lytton's heart and find she has a chronic valvular
lesion, but it is acting well in spite of the fact that
she has just undergone great exertion." She said
it was easily understood why I had been let out of
Newcastle Prison.

CHAPTER XII

JANE WARTON

"Under a Government which imprisons any unjustly,
the true place for a just man (or woman) is also a prison."

I was sent to Liverpool and Manchester to join
in working an Anti-Government campaign during
a General Election in January, 1910. Just before
I went, there came the news of the barbarous
ill-treatment of Miss Selina Martin and Miss Leslie
Hall, while on remand in Walton Gaol. They had
been refused bail, and, while awaiting their trial,
their friends were not allowed to communicate with
them. This is contrary to law and precedent for
prisoners on remand. As a protest they had started
a hunger-strike. They were fed by force, in answer
to which they broke the windows of their cells.
They were put in irons for days and nights together,
and one of them was frog-marched in the most
brutal fashion to and from the room where the
forcible feeding was performed. These facts they
made known to their friends at the police court on
the day of their trial.

I heard, too, of another prisoner in Liverpool,
Miss Bertha Brewster, who had been re-arrested
after her release from prison, and charged with
breaking the windows of her prison cell, which
she had done as a protest against being fed by

force. She had been punished for this offence while in prison. She did not respond to the summons, and when arrested on a warrant, three and a half months later, she was sentenced to six weeks' hard labour for this offence.

I felt a great wish to be in Liverpool, if possible, to get public opinion in that town to protest against such treatment of women political prisoners. If I failed in this, I determined myself to share the fate of these women.

When I was in Manchester, Mary Gawthorpe was ill with the internal complaint which has since obliged her to give up work. She saw me in her room one day. We had been distressed beyond words to hear of the sufferings of Selina Martin and Leslie Hall. Mary Gawthorpe said, with tears in her eyes, as she threw her arms round me : " Oh, and these are women quite unknown—nobody knows or cares about them except their own friends. They go to prison again and again to be treated like this, until it kills them ! " That was enough. My mind was made up. The altogether shameless way I had been preferred against the others at Newcastle, except Mrs. Brailsford who shared with me the special treatment, made me determine to try whether they would recognise my need for exceptional favours without my name.

Our meetings were always crowded and enthusiastic, especially in Manchester. This was my first experience of meetings in a really poverty-stricken district. I never shall forget one in the Salford Division of Manchester. A small room was packed as close as it would hold of the poorest working

women. How eagerly and intelligently they listened,
and what a wonderful light came into their eyes as
the hope dawned in their minds : " Can it be that
Parliament would really begin to think of *us* and
attend to *our* interests ? "   All their questions were
to the point and practical.   How different was
the atmosphere from that of the typical drawing-
room meeting, where many women came together
with the remark : " I am all for *propertied* women
having the vote," but their fear is lest the electorate
should be flooded with working women voters.   I
have never yet been asked by a working-class
woman whether our Bill, to give votes to women for
the same reason as men have it, would not give
undue power to propertied women.   That is a man's
question, though often taken over by women of the
leisured or professional class who identify themselves with the objections of theoretic politicians.
To the working-class women the matter presents
itself easily and naturally, as it actually is—a
woman's question, not a class question.   To have
their right to labour unrestricted, their protection
controlled by themselves, their economic position
independent and on the straightforward footing of
being judged by its value and by that alone ; their
property, earnings, and their persons to be defended
by law, and their right over their children to be
acknowledged by law.   In fact, their freedom as
human beings, their full recognition as equal
members of the community with men—that is how
the Votes-for-Women question appeals to them.
They see it neither as a party question nor as a
class question.

Suddenly I had my opportunity.   The Press and
the people in each different constituency were entirely
engrossed with the elections.   Up till now, protest
meetings were being held by our Union every week
outside Walton Gaol, Liverpool.   These were not
held during the elections, but I told the Liverpool
organiser, Miss Flatman, and the general organiser,
Mrs. Jennie Baines, that if they would have one
more of these protest meetings on Friday, January 14,
it was my intention to go in disguise, call upon the
crowd to follow me to the Governor's house, and
insist upon the release of the Suffrage prisoners
who had been tortured by forcible feeding.   It was
not our wont to do any militancy or to hold any
protest meetings during election time, that being a
time, as it were, when no Government is in, but it
seemed to me that this was the opportunity to make
the Governor of the prison responsible.   It was a
case of nothing less than cruelty and did not specially
concern, unless they chose to back it up, the Government.

I joined the W.S.P.U. again, filling up the
membership card as Miss Jane Warton.   The
choice of a name had been easy.   When I came out
of Holloway Prison, a distant relative, by name
Mr. F. Warburton, wrote me an appreciative letter,
thanking me for having been a prisoner in this
cause.   I determined that if it were necessary to go
to prison under another name, I should take the
name of Warburton.   When I went to Newcastle,
my family raised no objection.   Now nobody was
to know of my disguise, but Warburton was too
distinguished a name ; that would at once attract

attention. I must leave out the " bur " and make
it " Warton." " Jane " was the name of Joan of
Arc (for Jeanne is more often translated into
" Jane " than " Joan ") and would bring me comfort in distress. A family sympathetic to our cause,
who lived in the suburb near Walton Gaol, were
informed that a keen member, Miss Warton, would
call at their house in the afternoon before the
protest meeting, to investigate the outside of the
gaol and the Governor's house by daylight, and that
she was ready to be arrested if she could not obtain
the release of the prisoners.

I spent the previous day and night in Manchester
where no one knew of my intentions. In the afternoon, at a drawing-room meeting, I was introduced,
after I had spoken, to a woman who was a factory
inspector. She had very often to attend in the
police courts. She said to me : " I think it is
impossible to attend these cases, and hear the other
cases while you wait, and not be a convert to votes
for women if you were not one before. The other
day a man and two women were had up before the
magistrate. They had been found in the street, the
man and one woman had been cohabiting together,
the other woman mounted guard. The case was
quite clear, and the facts were not denied, the man
had bribed the women. The man was let free, the
two women were sent to prison. If women had the
vote such things could not be ; in those countries
where women have the vote they get altered in less
than a year."

In the evening we went to a meeting in a large
hall. It was full of working men and working

women ; it looked as if there were not room to move, so crowded were the seats and gangways. They were tremendously enthusiastic, many of them shook me by the hand, and the thought of them remained for a long time in my heart.

The next morning I took leave of my two kind hostesses. Their last injunction to me was, the agitation of my impending task having affected my appetite, " You should eat more ; mind you eat more."

I accomplished my disguise in Manchester, going to a different shop for every part of it, for safety's sake. I had noticed several times while I was in prison that prisoners of unprepossessing appearance obtained least favour, so I was determined to put ugliness to the test. I had my hair cut short and parted, in early Victorian fashion, in smooth bands down the side of my face. This, combined with the resentful bristles of my newly-cut back hair, produced a curious effect. I wished to bleach my hair as well, but the hairdresser refused point-blank to do this, and the stuff that I bought for the purpose at a chemist's proved quite ineffective. A tweed hat, a long green cloth coat, which I purchased for 8s. 6d., a woollen scarf and woollen gloves, a white silk neck-kerchief, a pair of pince-nez spectacles, a purse, a net-bag to contain some of my papers, and my costume was complete. I had removed my own initials from my underclothing, and bought the ready-made initials " J. W." to sew on in their stead, but to my regret I had not time to achieve this finishing touch.

All this sounds simple enough, but I suppose it

was due to my preoccupation of mind that I have
never known a day's shopping fraught with such
complications and difficulties. At the frowzy little
hairdresser's shop, the only one that seemed to me
inconspicuous enough for so important a part of my
disguise, the attendant was busy, and I had to
return in an hour's time. I told him that I was
going a journey and wanted the hair short, since
that would be less trouble. He cut it off. Then I
wanted what remained to be worn in a parting, with
the hair falling straight on either side. This part
of the process was most absurd, for that way
of wearing my hair was obviously disfiguring to
me. " Ah ! now that looks very becoming," said
the hairdresser, and with that I left the shop in
haste.

The eye-glasses I had first bought made me feel
giddy from the quality of the lens. I had to take
them back and have the glasses changed to the
weakest possible. At the first place, in spite of all
my protests, the shopman insisted on elaborately
testing my sight, afterwards requiring me to wait
for half an hour or so while he fitted up the glasses.
So I went to another shop, and in self-defence
invented the story that the glasses were for stage
purposes, for a friend of mine who had very good
sight, and that if she was not to trip up in her part
the glasses must be as nearly plain as possible.
This time I was more successful with the lens, but
the grip of the folders was still galling to the very
large bridge of my nose.

When I had finished this errand I was startled
to see walking along the street one of my kind

hostesses, whom I had parted from early that morning, professedly to return to Liverpool without delay. I took refuge down a side-street until she had passed by. Then I had strayed into the more opulent quarters of Manchester, in my search for another spectacle shop. All the shops were of a high-class order, and Jane Warton could find nothing to her requirements. On inquiry for a " cheap " draper, three different people recommended me to a certain shop named " Lewis." A sale was on there and Jane found that it was the very place for her. So many Miss Wartons were of the same mind that the street was blocked with customers for some distance down ; but I was obliged to wait, for no other shop was of the same description. The hat was a special difficulty ; every article of millinery was of the fashionable order, warranted to cover half the body as well as the head. This did not suit Jane. Finally she succeeded in getting the right one of stitched cloth, with a plait of cloth round the crown. Before leaving Manchester I realised that my ugly disguise was a success. I was an object of the greatest derision to street-boys, and shop-girls could hardly keep their countenances while serving me.

I had done my shopping at last, and hurried off to the station. I took out my box, put in it my own hat and jacket, put on the label " Miss Jane Warton, Cloak Room," and left it there. In the refreshment room, where I went to take a last hurried meal, a delightful big, brown dog, a mongrel, came and talked to me. He was with a party of two men and a woman, who sat at a distant

corner of the room. The dog came up to me at
once ; he put his head on my lap and was most
dear.

After this I got into the train. I finished a letter
to my mother, telling her of yesterday's meetings
and that I might not write to her for some little
time because of being so busy with the elections.

Arrived at Liverpool, and not knowing my way
to Walton, I took a cab and drove out for nearly
an hour before reaching my destination. I was
already racing hard with daylight and, thanks to a
damp fog, it was already quite dark when I arrived
there.

The house to which I had been directed was
in a new quarter and nowhere to be found. We
drove up and down the roads and inquired at shops
and post offices. Presently I spotted the familiar
sight of a woman stooping to chalk on the pavement
some announcement—it was our protest meeting.
I felt happy again, it was like seeing a friend. She
turned out to be one of the daughters of the very
house I was seeking. There were three daughters
who lived with their mother. The daughters were
zealots and welcomed Jane without a sign of
criticism. I saw the mother gasp a little when I
entered her drawing-room, but she was nevertheless
most courteous and kind.

I was escorted to the gaol and took my bearings.
To anyone who has been in prison, few things, I
think, are more exasperating than the unrevealing
face of the outer walls. On this occasion I felt an
overmastering longing to inquire after the prisoners
who had stirred me to my coming deed. What was

the degree of their suffering and exhaustion ? What should I be able to do for their release ? If by some miracle I obtained it, would it be too late to help them ? I thought more especially of Miss Selina Martin. I had seen her in Birmingham a fortnight after her release from the weeks that she had been fed in the prison there. She was in the nursing home, together with Mrs. Leigh, that splendid fighter for the women's cause and most heroic woman. Their look of illness haunted me still. The idea that Selina Martin was again, perhaps at that very moment, undergoing the same cruel treatment exasperated me. I felt so feeble, had so little faith in the utility of what I was about to do, yet I was athirst to do it, and the strength of my wish that it should be effective made me feel, at moments, capable of anything. But to all this the prison walls had nothing to say. They revealed nothing. They looked angry with all the world, angry above all because of an uneasy conscience.

I returned to the house of my friends, selected from their garden small, flat stones in case of need, which I wrapped in paper, and snatched a hasty meal. My kind hostess had heard that I was a vegetarian, and had provided a most appetising dish of stewed white pears. My mouth was parched with the weary work of the day and the thought of what lay before me, but I had no time except to taste the pears ; the memory of them during the hunger-strike filled my dreams.

Again we set out for the prison. All through the day I had been dogged by the nightmare thought that I should be too late for the meeting, or for some other reason should be prevented from achieving my purpose. As we neared the place, a crowd of between two and three hundred men and women were following the carriage in which were our speakers. It had been agreed that I should mix with the crowd, not join with the speakers, but at the end of the meeting should have my say from below. I passed the carriage to report myself to the organisers. Many of our members were standing around, but I think most of them did not recognise me, except from my voice later on.

Miss Flatman, Miss Patricia Woodlock and Mrs. Baines made stirring speeches, but the crowd had mostly gathered out of curiosity and were not many of them likely to listen to my coming appeal. I was afraid lest they should disperse before I had my chance, so I rudely interrupted Mrs. Baines and spoke from the outer rim of the crowd, on the side of the Governor's house.

I reminded the audience of how the men of Dundee, when forcible feeding of Suffrage prisoners was threatened in that town, had assembled to the number of two thousand and protested against it. How thereupon the hunger-strikers had been released and no forcible feeding to our women had been inflicted in Scotland. Could not Englishmen have done the same ? Let the men of Liverpool be the first to wipe out the stain that had been tolerated up till now. We were outside the gaol where these and other barbarities were actually going on. The Home Secretary had denied responsibility and asserted that it rested with the prison officials. Let us put this to the test and call upon the Governor of the prison to release these women. No violence was needed, but let us go to his house, insist upon his replying to our request and refuse to be dispersed until he had released these women. " If there are no men in Liverpool who will stand up for these prisoners, let the women do their part—I call on you all to follow me to the Governor's house." With this I turned towards the house, a separate building surrounded by a little garden. To my surprise, the crowd began to follow me. Again I shouted out to them—" No violence, remember, but call for the Governor and refuse to be dispersed till you have secured the release of the prisoners."

A policeman began leisurely to follow me; there were only two or three of them about. I took to running and urged on the crowd. The police then took hold of me. As for once it was my object above all else to get arrested and imprisoned, I began discharging my stones, not throwing them, but limply dropping them over the hedge into the Governor's garden. One of them just touched the shoulder of a man who had rushed up on seeing me arrested. I apologised to him. Two policemen then held me fast by the arms and marched me off to the police station. The crowd followed excitedly, and our members gathered round me, appealing for my release and saying that I had done nothing.

It had been agreed with the organisers that I should be the only one arrested. As I have said, militant tactics were in abeyance because

of the elections, the less disturbance was made,
therefore, the better ; as it was, I feared lest my
action, being out of the straight course, should be
displeasing to the leaders. I said to the other
members : " I am all right, don't bother about me,
but take the crowd back to the Governor's house."
I did not wish to be recognised.

As they marched me off at a great pace, the
police, who were very civil and considerate, questioned me : " What was you a-doin' ? You
weren't in the carriage with the others, were you ?
What was that you was sayin' ? " They knew
they would have to make up a charge against me,
and wisely thought the best plan was to ask me
direct for information ! I told them that I made
towards the Governor's house, appealed to the
crowd to follow, and refused to desist when called
upon by the police. I feared that this might not be
enough to achieve a conviction. I was thinking,
" Was there nothing else ? " when the man appeared
whose shoulder had been touched by my stone ; he
carried the missile in his hand, still wrapped in the
purple hand-bill announcing this very meeting,
no doubt a most evil-looking document in the
eyes of the authorities. I knew then that I
was safe.

Presently, two others who had been arrested were
brought in. It was a most unlooked-for consolation
to have their company through the night, though I
hoped, of course, that they would be let off and not
share the rest of the ordeal with me. Two of the
members, on hearing my voice, determined that I
should not be alone, so they returned, and one of

them poked a flag through a window in the Governor's house, breaking the glass ; the other mounted guard while she did this. They were both arrested. One was Miss Elsie Howey, a valiant as well as most dear one of our members ; the other was a local member, who gave the name of Mrs. Nugent. I had twice stayed with her and her husband when at Liverpool. She was not only most charming, but also of attractive appearance, which awoke a great deal of curiosity in the police as to her identity, and luckily drew off all possible suspicions from me.

We all played up to the situation ; Elsie Howey and I treated her with deference, as a person of great importance ; we nicknamed her " the Princess."

The police were exceptionally friendly to us, although they were punctilious as to the regulations. For instance, Miss Howey and I were suffering from bad colds and had eucalyptus inhalers in our pockets. We were not allowed to keep these ; they were removed with other things, such as a purse, stylo pen, brooches, watch, etc. We were all three allowed to be together and away from other prisoners, locked into a cell of the usual police-station description—that is, unfurnished but for the bare plank, serving as seat or bed, along the wall, and about one and a-half feet from the ground, terminating in a lavatory accommodation under a high-barred window, but now lighted by an electric light in the wall above the door. This cell was scrupulously clean and blankets were supplied to us. Our friends sent us some sandwiches and fruit, and

the police themselves provided us with an evening
newspaper.

We had been arrested at about 8 o'clock; the
police station was some distance from Walton, so it
was getting on for 9 o'clock when we were at last
shut up after the charges were reported and entered,
and we had been stripped by a wardress of our
small belongings.

The quick walk from the scene of our arrest,
hurried along between two policemen, had been a
warming process, after which the cold in the cell
seemed intense.   The bench being wider than most
in police-station cells, Mrs. Nugent lay down at
one end, while Elsie Howey and I lay side by side
under the same blanket and warmed each other.
Mrs. Nugent and Elsie kept up an animated conversation.   Elsie told anecdotes of her former
imprisonments and those of the fellow-prisoners.   I
was short of breath and fearfully tired, so I rolled
round and kept quite quiet.

At about 12 o'clock the husband of Mrs.
Nugent had heard of her arrest, and came off
to the police station to see her.   He came to the
door of our cell and was greatly distressed.   It
was ever so nice to see him.   His visit had
caused a great deal of concern amongst the
police, who recognised him as one of the magistrates.   He put himself out to do what he could,
and we offered him the comforting news that we
were almost sure that his wife would get off, as she
had done nothing at all.   With that, as his wife was
kept standing at the little window so long as he was
there, he felt obliged to leave us,

Towards about 3 a.m. we were taken out of the
cell and ranged along a seat by the wall of a large
room ; at the other end was a desk with a policeman
sitting at it. We went up in turn to give our
names, ages, etc., that is, about seven or eight other
prisoners, all females, and our three selves. It was
the turn of Jane Warton. She walked across to the
policeman, one shoulder hitched slightly above the
other, her hair sticking out straight behind and
worn in slick bandeaus on either side of her face, her
hat trailing in a melancholy way on her head. The
large, grey woollen gloves were drawn up over
the too short sleeves of her coat ; on the collar of
it were worn portraits of Mrs. Pankhurst, Mrs.
Lawrence and Christabel, in small china brooches ;
her hat had a bit of tape with " Votes for Women "
written on it, interlaced with the cloth plait that
went round it, and eye-glasses were fixed on her
nose. Her standing out in the room was the signal
for a convulsed titter from the other prisoners.
" It's a shame to laugh at one of your fellow-
prisoners," said the policeman behind the desk, and
the tittering was hushed. It was all I could do not
to laugh, and I thought to myself " Is the *Punch*
version of a Suffragette overdone ? " As I got back
to my companions they too were laughing, but I
thought it wonderfully kind of the policeman to
have spoken on my behalf.

When this process was finished, we three Suffragettes were taken to the policemen's room, where
there was a good fire, to wait for our Black Maria.
The other prisoners had disappeared. The police
sat round and spoke quite pleasantly ; there were

two or three of them at times. We discussed the
chances of women getting the vote, they seemed
quite in favour. Elsie Howey and Mrs. Nugent did
most of the talking. I warmed myself and saw the
police looking at me from time to time, wondering
why I did not talk too.

At about 3.30 a.m. or 4 o'clock, Black Maria
came and we were put in. This was different from
the prison vans I had hitherto seen; it was not
broken up into separate cell-like compartments,
but was in the form of a double omnibus, one side
for men and the other for women, divided by a thin
wooden partition, each side having two seats facing
each other and extending the length of the carriage.
There were no windows; the light filtered in only
through the grated ventilators. When we got into
this Black Maria there was no one but us three,
but we were told to sit near the door, so Mrs.
Nugent sat first, then Elsie Howey, and then
myself. The jolting of the van is excessive and
suggests a complete absence of springs, the noise of
its passage through the streets is terrific, to the
point of excluding all other sounds—a noise of
thundering wheels, of jolts and jars and bumps.
I have not yet made out the reason why 3.30 a.m.
was selected, none was given at the time to the
prisoners.

Our destination was the Bridewell Police Station,
but we called on our way at the other police stations
in the town, picking up whatever unfortunates they
had netted during the night. We called at four
different stations, if I remember right. The drive in
all took about an hour, and seemed a very long one.

We had not gone far before the rumbling and jolting ceased, the door was thrown open with a sound of keys and great rattling, a shaft of light fell along the 'bus, and lit up momentarily ourselves and those who were thrown in to add to our number. These were the only moments when the occupants had a chance of seeing each other. The door then hastily closed again, darkness, jolting and noise reasserted their grim influence. Drunken voices, the smell of the gin palace, an occasional query and reply shouted through the thin wall to the men on the other side, that was all. Knee to knee, and breath to breath we sat, companions of this world of darkness, fellow-sisters of the order of the outcasts. Before we had finished, we had taken up six women in all.

At the first stop, two Irish girls were let in ; some men were put into the other side. The girls were only sufficiently drunk to make them intensely cheerful ; they laughed and talked gaily at first and shouted lustily to their companions on the other side. But the effect of the pitch darkness was depressing, and after a time their communications ceased. They sat opposite to us near the door, and whenever there was a gleam of light I watched them, for they gave me immense pleasure. They were quite young, with beautiful arms, which one could see as their sleeves were rolled up ; they had shawls on, and their faces were fresh and strong, and pretty, too, had it not been for the effect of the drink ; they were as far removed as possible from the degraded town type, in every way they were healthy specimens, fresh from an Irish fishing

village. They spoke to us several times, and there
was a delightful feeling that disguise or no disguise
did not matter with them, but it was difficult to
hear what they said in the fearful noise of the Black
Maria, and we felt that our answers were mostly
lost on them. They put the question in a friendly
way : " What did you get taken up for ? " " We're
Suffragettes," was the all-sufficient reply. This was
very interesting, and they had to try to tell the men
on the other side, with many a laugh, as a tremendous bit of news.

At another stop, a little woman got in with fair
hair, a fluttering white boa, and in a white dress.
She was dead drunk, but whereas the others
smelt of cheap drink, her breath was of good
brandy. She laughed, and now and then gave vent
to a half sentence or two that rolled in and out
of her sleep.

At the next stop, two were shot in who
seemed really deformed with poverty, their com-
plexions yellow, their hands gnarled and worn,
their faces of utmost sadness. They said something to each other as they got in—something to
give comfort, but their sentences were full of oaths
of a senseless kind, and their speech, too, was broken
with drink.

Finally, it was another type altogether who was
let in. A woman who looked any age, her face of
utmost melancholy had yet the appearance of
having drunk heavily ; she had all the hang of an
" habitual," her clothes were the dregs of clothes
and tumbling off her. When the door was opened
for her to be put in, she murmured a few broken

words to the effect that her salvation didn't lie in prison.

The Irish girls and the little woman with the white boa were young, the others looked old and worn out.

I think I shall never forget the self-reproach that stung through my whole being when I had thought my intervention necessary between one prisoner and another. On passing some unusual light in the street, which momentarily lit up our van, not enough to see our faces but only to distinguish the outlines of forms, I noticed that the prisoner opposite to Elsie Howey, my neighbour, was leaning forward and bent towards her. The momentary flash of light was too short-lived to judge whether this was a rapid movement perhaps, as I thought, of assault or drunken affection, or whether it was that the position of physical weariness could find no rest from leaning back on the walls of the jolting van. I was unable to see Elsie, but I imagined that she too might be scared by the attention of the prisoner opposite. As the darkness closed in upon us, I thrust my hand into hers ; it was welcomed, but quite unnecessary. Before the end of our drive two things were clear—the prisoners might be evil-minded towards all the rest of the world, they might be blind drunk or raging with misery at their own plight, but the one thing impossible to them would have been to hurt a fellow-prisoner. Every one of those pathetic human wrecks, deformed by drink, so that one could not tell if they were guilty of crime besides, overtaken at a moment when their self-respect was lowest, and captured by a punitive system which would do its utmost to dissolve

what remained of it, as they were thrust into the
black cavity of the van, made a vigorous appeal to
their own courage and met with instant response
from their unknown companions. It might be only
some drunken joke, it was almost invariably accompanied by a laugh, but for each one it had a call on
their inmost strength, and it made its appeal to
those in the van. Issuing from different spheres of
existence, each one representing lives the most
remote from one another, scarcely any two alike in
a single respect as to detail, their one point of
similarity being poverty and that they had given
way to drink, the instinct of our first contact,
doubtless to each one of us, was repulsion, mistrust,
fear of one another. But it lasted for less than the
flash of a moment, less than the inhaling of one
breath. Our differences were there, but for the
time unimportant, whereas the all-embracing fact
was our similarity of fate. No need for social laws
to bind that company, no rules of the club were
necessary, the code of instinct, expediency and
honour were all one and spontaneous to us. " We
are all of one blood," may be a great tie, but " We
are all of one fate " is, while it lasts, a better ; the
bond of the outcast needs no seal.

We arrived for the fifth time in a courtyard,
with a deal of jolting and din ; it was the Bridewell
Police Station, and we all got out. The little
woman in the white dress and fur boa tumbled from
the van into the arms of a policeman—she assured
us that she loved him on finding herself thus closely
against him ; he remained stalwart as a piece of
wood.

We Suffragettes were put into a cell by ourselves, it was perfectly clean. We had not been
there very long before the door was opened with a
clang and another woman was thrust in. She was
reassuring to look at, smartly dressed with fashion-
ably-shaped brown furs draped round her neck. She
had come from Ireland that night and was terribly
cold. We gave her the blankets that had been
given to us ; nothing, however, did much good. She
had come over with another woman, who on landing
had been taken as " wanted by the police." This
woman had been arrested, too, as " her friend," but
she said she was quite sure of getting off, as she had
only known the other woman quite a short time,
and had no idea that she was in any way " suspected." The concern of this woman to get free
was natural enough, but she seemed to care not at
all for the other one, for whom my heart welled over
with sympathy. I thought of her with a more
or less deceitful face, but I loved her because
she was " wanted by the police," and this woman
who was with us I wanted to get off, of course,
but that was all ; I could not feel any sympathy
towards her.

We waited in this cell until it was dawning light.
It was not a place for sleep, and the cold was terrible.
As it was getting towards morning, we were taken
out of the cell and led off to wash our hands and faces
in another part of the prison. It was fearfully dark
in one part, with only a light occasionally here and
there, so that one could not see where one was going.
On a bench, some ten or twelve little boys were
sitting.

It was the first time I thought of children as
prisoners. At Newcastle, it was true, I had seen
one little boy in the police court, but he was enjoying
himself over a cup of soup in the central room with
the police, and he was much too small to be convicted, whatever his offences ; possibly, if his
parents were hopeless, he would have been sent to
a reformatory school. That, of course, was bad
enough ; one knew that for half of the money that
would have to be expended there was many a
woman in the country who would have cared for
him with motherly tenderness. But with these boys,
who looked about nine years to fifteen or sixteen
years old, it was another matter. The place where
they sat, though public, for it was a gangway, was
terrible, it was just where the passages seemed to
go underground ; they were extremely dark, on one
side they abutted into a regular network of cells, with
small communicating alleys in between. There the
boys sat and gazed at the grown-up criminals who
appeared from time to time ; they looked at us with
the greatest curiosity. It was horrible to see them
in a place so profoundly ill-suited to children.

The Liverpool organiser, Miss Flatman, and Miss
Maude Joachim came to us with the daylight of
Saturday, January 15. It was a most unexpected
joy to see them—not alone, for that was not allowed,
but in one of the many passages near a window with
a policeman standing by. I was able to write a
little scrap of a letter to Mrs. Pethick Lawrence in
the name of " Jane Warton." This made me very
happy. I believe we were offered breakfast, or
should have been able to get it had we asked for it,

but, in any case, those surroundings were so wretched that we almost as soon went without, and I was eager to begin the hunger-strike.

As the time of the assembling of the court, 10 o'clock, drew near we waited in different parts of a large and rambling building. At last we were conveyed, through what seemed an underground court, to the foot of a staircase that led right up into the prisoner's dock.

I was the first of the Suffragettes to be taken up. Mr. Shepherd Little was the magistrate; he seemed to be thoroughly out of temper. They took only two or three minutes convicting me. When the policeman had done his work of charging me with urging the crowd to follow me to the Governor's house, with refusing to desist when called upon by the police, and with throwing a "missile" (small stone wrapped in paper), I put in, " I had three stones upon me which I let fall in the Governor's garden. A man in the crowd ran past me just as I was letting go the third—it fell on his shoulder; I apologised to him."

On the strength of its being my first imprisonment, I was sentenced to a fortnight. 3rd Division, with option of a fine. Just when I had left the court I was called back. The magistrate thought I ought to have a longer sentence, thanks to my having thrown stones, but the clerk thought not, and in the little altercation he got the best of it.

The women of last night were waiting on the stairs. "How long have you got?" they all said to me. "Ah! well, buck up," they added on hearing of fourteen days. Miss Elsie Howey, with the admission of her former imprisonments, got six weeks, and Mrs. Nugent was, to our great joy, released. The policeman downstairs told me that hard labour always accompanied the 3rd Division sentences, unless stated to the contrary.

CHAPTER XIII

WALTON GAOL, LIVERPOOL : MY THIRD
IMPRISONMENT

ELSIE HOWEY and I waited together at the Bridewell Police Station for the greater part of that day
(Saturday, January 15). Towards evening they
took us away in a partition van, alone, to Walton
Green Gaol, we arrived at about 7 o'clock at
night. The other prisoners must have journeyed
here when we did, though by a different van, for
we were all together again when we were to give our
names, vocation, etc., to the prison warders. We
stood up by a wall, all in a row, and waited our turn.
The prisoner with the white boa and the apparently
white gown, I was able to see closely and by a high
light. The boa was in imitation fur and extremely
dirty, the white dress was of some thin cotton,
nearly transparent ; it was open on her chest and
she seemed to have hardly any clothes underneath.
I did not like to think what she must have suffered
this wintry day, in and out of the icy cold police
station cells. The effect of the drink was wearing
off, and she waved her head about as though she
had a very bad headache ; all her cheerfulness had
gone. Poor little thing, I felt extremely sorry for
her, she had been given plenty of the best brandy
and she had done what was wanted of her ; the
next day she found herself in prison. When her
imprisonment was over, in all probability, to go the

same road of drunkenness and prostitution would seem the only one open to her.

There were several other prisoners besides those we had seen before. Some were so familiar with the place that they reeled off their age, religion, birthplace, calling, without waiting to be asked, and then walked through into a large hall in which were the waiting cubicles. Suddenly I felt awed, a feeling of supremest pity almost took my breath away. Passing in front of me into the larger hall was a woman of great beauty, her features were intensely refined, and in every part of her there seemed to be some great determination, not in respect of the prison she was in now, that was only part of it, but with regard to her life of shame that went before; the whole face and figure were virtuous and good. The other woman who had come over from Ireland was not there, but this was the one, I felt quite sure, who was " wanted by the police." I had not heard her tell anything to the officer, I had not seen her till that moment, and I never saw her again, but I shall never forget her face which will rest always on my memory, beautiful, commanding, and of an absorbing sadness.

It was our turn at last. We gave the required details, and then Elsie Howey said that we should refuse all food and all the prison rules. " We are sorry if it will give trouble; we shall give as little as possible; but our fast is against the Government, and we shall fight them with our lives, not hurting anyone else." The wardress gave no answer, but with a wave of her hand showed us towards the cubicles. Before we went in there we were

separated ; we had to part, and I never saw Elsie
again till long after I came out. A wardress came
and showed me to a room with two other officers, the
place where I was to undress. I said that I did not
bow to the imprisonment and so would not undress
myself, whereupon a wardress began to pull my
things off, but I showed them this was not from
disagreeableness but only through the prison strike.
On taking out of my pocket a clean handkerchief I
noticed that it had the initials " C. L." still upon it,
and when next there came a reel of cotton with the
name " Lytton " written quite distinctly round the
top, I felt overwhelmed with horror. Scarcely
knowing what I was about, I seized them both in
my hand and put them on the fire which burnt in a
stove near where I was standing. The next moment
I thought I had done wrong and that the attention
of the officers would inevitably be called to my
action, but they seemed not to have noticed and
never said anything, so I thanked my stars that I
was safe. The look of Jane Warton was still comic
in the extreme, the two wardresses laughed as they
undressed her. Her glasses were the subject of
excessive care and she was allowed to keep them
with her. I would most gladly have given them up,
for they hurt the bridge of my nose which was far
too wide for them, but it was good, of course, to
help the disguise for some while longer. I had my
bath, and was put into a 3rd Division dress of coarse,
brown serge, and my cap and apron were tied on.
I was put before a large basket of worn boots, not in
pairs, and told to pick out two for myself. I chose
the largest I saw, but they were not nearly big

enough, and it was only after a tremendous effort
that I got my feet into them. I was then taken to
the large hall and put into a cubicle. These were
like cupboards, without ceiling, giving on to the
hall for light and air, so that they had not the
stuffiness of the cells. By this time I was dropping
with fatigue, the seat seemed there for me to sleep
on, and being alone was immensely restful. But
the sounds of the other prisoners made it too painful
for rest ; one of them sobbed all the time, and soon
I saw we were here only to be inspected. The door
opened and a wardress put in a pair of sheets for
me to take to the cell. Then the Matron came, a
capable-looking woman, but severe. She spoke to
me of the hunger-strike, and of how very wrong it
was. I said that of course without an object it was
very wrong, but the Government had been petitioned
in every other way, we thought they would not like
hunger-strikes for ever, that now there were still
comparatively few, but later there would, if necessary,
be many more ; that feeding by force was horrible,
besides it did not meet the difficulty of keeping
the women in prison. When one saw what the
wrongs of women were to redress, it seemed a little
thing that some women should die for the sake of the
others. She did not stay to prolong the discussion.

The next to come was a young doctor accompanied by a female officer. He called me out, and
the ordinary questions were put to me. I said that
I was free from any infectious disease, but that I
could not answer any other questions. He seemed
to have expected me to say this, and told the officer
to put it down in the book she carried with her.

I had decided, as on the occasion of my previous hunger-strike, to refuse to answer medical questions, but not to resist medical inspection. However, to my great relief, it was not attempted. This was the same at Newcastle, so seemed to me nothing extraordinary.

At last the longed-for moment had arrived, and I was taken off to my cell. To my joy there was a window which opened a little bit; at night it was lit by a gas jet that was set in the depth of the wall behind the door, the passage side, and covered in by a thick glass. I was ever so tired—I laid down and slept.

The next day was Sunday (January 16), but they did not ask us to go to chapel. For several days I did not wear my cap and apron in my cell, but did not in other ways continue my protest against the clothes. The cold seemed to me intense, and I wore the skirt of my dress fastened round my neck for warmth. The Governor, accompanied by the Matron, came to see me, but he was in a temper about our having broken his windows, so I said nothing. He was in a fury at the way I had fastened my skirt. I answered that it was for warmth and that I would gladly put on more clothes and warmer ones if he gave them to me. Later on the Senior Medical Officer came in. He was a short, fat, little man, with a long waxed moustache. I should have said he disliked being unkind; he liked to chaff over things; but as I looked at him I thought I would rather be forcibly fed by anyone in the world than by him, the coarse doctors at Newcastle and the cross little doctor I had seen the night before. I said I had not asked to see him, but he made no examination and asked no questions.

I lay in my bed most of the day, for they did not disturb me, and I tried to keep warm, as I felt the cold fearfully. They brought me all my meals the same as usual, porridge in the morning at 7, meat and potatoes mid-day at 12, porridge at 4.30. When they were hot I fed on the smell of them, which seemed quite delicious; I said "I don't want any, thank you," to each meal, as they brought it in. I had made up my mind that this time I would not drink any water, and would only rinse out my mouth morning and evening without swallowing any. I wrote on the walls of my cell with my slate pencil and soap mixed with the dirt of the floor for ink, "Votes for Women," and the saying from Thoreau's *Duty of Civil Disobedience*—"Under a Government which imprisons any unjustly, the true place for a just man (or woman) is also a prison"; on the wall opposite my bed I wrote the text from Joshua, "Only be thou strong and very courageous." That night I dreamt of fruits, melons, peaches and nectarines, and of a moonlit balcony that was hung with sweetest smelling flowers, honeysuckle and jessamine, apple-blossom and sweet scented verbena; there was only the sound of night birds throbbing over the hills that ranged themselves below the balcony. On it there slept my sister-in-law, and on the balustrade, but making no noise, was a figure awake and alert, which was my brother. My dream was of a land which was seen by my father in his poem of "King Poppy," where the princess and the shepherd boy are the types etherealised. I woke suddenly. I could sleep a little in detached moments, but this dream had made the prison cell beautiful to me ; it had a way out.

The strain was great of having to put on my shoes, which were too small, every time I was taken out of my cell to empty slops or to see the Governor. The Matron was shocked that I did not put the right heel in at all and every day I was given another pair, but they were all alike in being too small for my right foot.

The next day, Monday (January 17), the wardress took my bed and bedding away because I would not make it up, but lay on it in the day-time. I told her if she wished she must roll me off, but that I did not intend voluntarily to give it up. She was quite amiable, but rolled me towards the wall and took the bed and bedding from underneath me. There was a little table in my cell which was not fastened to the wall. I turned it upside down and was able to sit in it with my body resting against one of the legs. It was very uncomfortable, but I felt too ill to sit up in the chair, and the concrete floor was much too cold without the bed. Every now and then I got up and walked backwards and forwards in the cell to get a little warmth into me. The Chaplain came in for a moment. He was a tall, good-looking man, of the burly, healthy sort. It seemed to me, from his talk, that he would be very well suited to be a cricket match or football parson, if there were such a thing, but he was totally unsuited to be the Chaplain of a prison, or anyhow of a woman's prison. He thought it wise to speak to me as a " Suffragette." " Look here, it's no good your thinking that there's anything to be done with the women here—the men sometimes are not such bad fellows, and there are many who write to me after they've left here, but the women, they're all as bad as bad can be, there's absolutely no good in them." I did not answer, but I felt inclined to say " Then good-bye to you, since you say you can do no good with the women here."

Presently an officer came and led me out. The manner of nearly all the officers was severe ; one or two were friends but most of them treated me like dirt. I was shown along the gangway of the ward, which seemed to me very large, much larger than the D X at Holloway, and went in various directions like a star. I was shown into the Governor's room, which lay at the end of the gangway. It was warm, there were hot pipes against which I was made to stand with my back to the wall, and for a moment, as I put my feet to rest on the pipes, I could think of nothing else but the delight of their heat. The Governor was very cross. I had decided not to do the needlework which constituted the hard labour, for this he gave me three days on bread and water. He would not let me speak to him at all and I was led out, but, before I had got to my cell, I was called back into his presence. " I hear you are refusing to take your food, so it's three days in a special cell." I was taken out and down a staircase till we reached the ground floor. I think my cell was two stories above, but I am not sure ; then down again and into a short passage that looked as if it was underground, with a window at the top seemingly only just level with the ground. The door of a cell was opened, I was put inside and the door locked. It was larger than the cell upstairs, and the jug, basin, etc., were all made of black guttapercha, not of tin, placed on the floor. This would have been bad for the ordinary prisoner, as it was quite impossible to tell whether the eating things were clean or not and, in any case, it smelt fairly strong of guttapercha ; but as the rule for me was neither to eat nor drink, I was able to put up with it well. The bed was wider than an ordinary plank bed and nailed to the ground, so that I was able to lie on it without being disturbed. Best of all was the fact that it was nearer to the heating apparatus and so seemed quite warm when I was led in. I did not notice at first that the window did not open, but when I had been there six or seven hours it became wonderfully airless. I only left my cell for minutes at a time, when I was allowed to draw water, and the air of the corridor then seemed fresh as mountain air by comparison. I had an idea that Elsie Howey or some of the others would have been put into a punishment cell too. I called, but in vain, my voice had grown weak and my tongue and throat felt thick as a carpet, probably from not drinking anything. I tried signalling with raps on the wall, " No surrender—no surrender," Mrs. Leigh's favourite motto, but I was never sure of corresponding raps, though sometimes I thought I heard them. I could not sleep for more than about an hour at a time, my legs drew up into a cramped position whenever I went off and the choking thickness in my mouth woke me.

Tuesday, January 18, I was visited again by the

Senior Medical Officer, who asked me how long I had
been without food.   I said I had eaten a buttered
scone and a banana sent in by friends to the police
station on Friday at about midnight. He said,
" Oh, then, this is the fourth day ; that is too long,
I shall have to feed you, I must feed you at once,"
but he went out and nothing happened till about
6 o'clock in the evening, when he returned with,
I think, five wardresses and the feeding apparatus.
He urged me to take food voluntarily.   I told him
that was absolutely out of the question, that when
our legislators ceased to resist enfranchising women
then I should cease to resist taking food in prison.
He did not examine my heart nor feel my pulse ; he
did not ask to do so, nor did I say anything which
could possibly induce him to think I would refuse to
be examined.   I offered no resistance to being placed
in position, but lay down voluntarily on the plank
bed.   Two of the wardresses took hold of my arms,
one held my head and one my feet.   One wardress
helped to pour the food.   The doctor leant on my
knees as he stooped over my chest to get at my
mouth.   I shut my mouth and clenched my teeth.
I had looked forward to this moment with so much
anxiety lest my identity should be discovered
beforehand, that I felt positively glad when the
time had come.   The sense of being overpowered
by more force than I could possibly resist was complete, but I resisted nothing except with my mouth.
The doctor offered me the choice of a wooden or
steel gag ; he explained elaborately, as he did on
most subsequent occasions, that the steel gag would
hurt and the wooden one not, and he urged me not

to force him to use the steel gag. But I did not speak nor open my mouth, so that after playing about for a moment or two with the wooden one he finally had recourse to the steel. He seemed annoyed at my resistance and he broke into a temper as he plied my teeth with the steel implement. He found that on either side at the back I had false teeth mounted on a bridge which did not take out. The superintending wardress asked if I had any false teeth, if so, that they must be taken out ; I made no answer and the process went on. He dug his instrument down on to the sham tooth, it pressed fearfully on the gum. He said if I resisted so much with my teeth, he would have to feed me through the nose. The pain of it was intense and at last I must have given way for he got the gag between my teeth, when he proceeded to turn it much more than necessary until my jaws were fastened wide apart, far more than they could go naturally. Then he put down my throat a tube which seemed to me much too wide and was something like four feet in length. The irritation of the tube was excessive. I choked the moment it touched my throat until it had got down. Then the food was poured in quickly ; it made me sick a few seconds after it was down and the action of the sickness made my body and legs double up, but the wardresses instantly pressed back my head and the doctor leant on my knees. The horror of it was more than I can describe. I was sick over the doctor and wardresses, and it seemed a long time before they took the tube out. As the doctor left he gave me a slap on the cheek, not violently, but, as it were, to express his contemptuous disapproval, and he seemed to take for granted that my distress was assumed. At first it seemed such an utterly contemptible thing to have done that I could only laugh in my mind. Then suddenly I saw Jane Warton lying before me, and it seemed as if I were outside of her. She was the most despised, ignorant and helpless prisoner that I had seen. When she had served her time and was out of the prison, no one would believe anything she said, and the doctor when he had fed her by force and tortured her body, struck her on the cheek to show how he despised her ! That was Jane Warton, and I had come to help her.

When the doctor had gone out of the cell, I lay quite helpless. The wardresses were kind and knelt round to comfort me, but there was nothing to be done, I could not move, and remained there in what, under different conditions, would have been an intolerable mess. I had been sick over my hair, which, though short, hung on either side of my face, all over the wall near my bed, and my clothes seemed saturated with it, but the wardresses told me they could not get me a change that night as it was too late, the office was shut. I lay quite motionless, it seemed paradise to be without the suffocating tube, without the liquid food going in and out of my body and without the gag between my teeth. Presently the wardresses all left me, they had orders to go, which were carried out with the usual promptness. Before long I heard the sounds of the forced feeding in the next cell to mine. It was almost more than I could bear, it was Elsie Howey, I was sure. When the ghastly process was over and all quiet, I tapped on the wall and called out at the top of my voice, which wasn't much just then, " No surrender," and there came the answer past any doubt in Elsie's voice, " No surrender." After this I fell back and lay as I fell. It was not very long before the wardress came and announced that I was to go back upstairs as, because of the feeding, my time in the punishment cell was over. I was taken into the same cell which I had before; the long hours till morning were a nightmare of agonised dread for a repetition of the process.

The next day, Wednesday, January 19, they brought me clean clothes. When the wardresses were away at breakfast I determined to break the thick glass of my gas jet to show what I thought of the forcible feeding, it seemed the last time that I should have the strength required. I took one of my shoes, which always lay at my side except when I moved from my cell, let it get a good swing by holding it at the back of my shoulder and then hurled it against the glass with all the strength that I had. The glass broke in pieces with a great smashing sound. The two wardresses, who were in charge of the whole ward while the others were away, came into my cell together ; I was already back in my bed. They were young, new to the work, and looked rather frightened. I told them I had done it with a shoe, and why. " But that is enough," I said, " I am not going to do any more now." This reassured them and they both laughed. They took away the shoes as " dangerous," and brought me slippers instead, and, to my intense relief, I never saw them again. As the morning wore on, one

after the other of the officials proclaimed that I had
done a shameful thing. On being changed to the
cell next door, one of the head wardresses—I never
made out exactly who she was—was in a great
temper. I had told her, as I did every one of the
officials, why I had broken my gas jet. " Broken
it, yes, I should just think you had, indeed. And all
that writing scribbled over your cell ; can't keep the
place decent." " I'm so sorry," I said ; " I assure
you there was nothing indecent in what I wrote
on the wall." " No, not indecent, but——" she
hesitated and, as the words would not come to her
assistance, the remark remained unfinished.

I had not been long in the other cell before the
doctor and four or five wardresses appeared. He
was apparently angry because I had broken the jet
glass ; he seized one of the tin vessels and began
waving it about. " I suppose you want to smash
me with one of these ? " he exclaimed. I said to
him, so that all the wardresses with him could hear,
" Unless you consider it part of your duty, would
you please not strike me when you have finished
your odious job " (or I may have said " slap me,"
I do not remember). He did not answer, but, after
a little pause, he signed to me to lie down on the bed.
Again the choice of the wooden or steel implement,
again the force, which after a time I could not with-
stand, in the same place as yesterday where the gum
was sore and aching. Then the feeling of the
suffocating tube thrust down and the gate of life
seemed shut. The tube was pressed down much
too far, it seemed to me, causing me at times great
pain in my side. The sickness was worse than the

time before. As the tube was removed I was unavoidably sick over the doctor. He flew away from me and out of the cell, exclaiming angrily, " If you do that again next time I shall feed you twice." I had removed my serge jacket and taken several precautions for my bed, but I am afraid one or two of the officers and the floor and wall were drenched. I shut my eyes and lay back quite helpless for a while. They presently brought in fresh clothes, and a woman, another prisoner, came and washed the floor. It seemed terrible that another prisoner should do this, it was altogether a revolting business. Two wardresses came and over-looked her work, one of them said, in a voice of displeased authority: " Look at her ! Just look at her ! The *way* she's doing it ! " The woman washed on and took no notice ; her face was intensely sad. I roused myself and said, " Well, at any rate, she's doing what I should be doing myself and I am very grateful to her." The wardresses looked surprised at me, but they said nothing.

The Governor came in for a moment to see me. To my surprise his anger had cooled a little. He had before spoken to me in a rage and, if I asked ques-tions which implied a complaint, had told me they were not proper questions for me to ask, or that I must not argue or raise discussions. After failing to get a definite answer as to under whose authority the forcible feeding was done, I said it surely could not be right for him to allow such a thing in the prison over which he had jurisdiction, unless he had seen it and at least fully realised what it entailed. With apparently some reluctance, he admitted that

he had witnessed it.   I asked, " And after that you
sanction and approve of such a thing being done to
prisoners who have committed *only nominal crimes
with no criminal object and in defence of a claim
which they have no recognised constitutional means
to enforce ? " *   The last italicised part of this
remark remained unheard, for the Governor interrupted me with " That is not a fitting question for
you to ask."   Later, I was had up before him in his
room and was severely reprimanded for breaking the
glass of the gas-box and " inspection " glass, and
for defacing the walls of my cell, but I was dismissed
with a caution for glass breaking, and my punishment was reserved for the Visiting Magistrates.

When it was evening the light was lit and the
doctor and wardresses came again to feed me.   I
asked if I could not sit up in a chair and the doctor
said " Yes."   I told him that I was a small eater,
that the capacity of my body was very limited and
if only he would give less quantities the result might
be better.   I also begged that he would not press
the tube so far down into my body.   He treated the
request with contempt, saying that anyhow my
stomach must be longer than his, since I was taller
than he was.   This third time, though I was continually sick, the doctor pressed the tube down
firmly into my body and continued to pour food
in.   At last this produced a sort of shivering fit
and my teeth chattered when the gag was removed ;
I suppose that every vestige of colour must have
left my face, for the doctor seemed surprised
and alarmed.   He removed the tube and told the
wardresses to lay me on the floor-bed and lower

my head. He then came and lay over my chest
and seemed very sorry for what he had done. I
told him I should not faint, that I was not liable
to this or any form of collapse ; I did not mention
the slight chronic debility of heart from which I
suffered. He called in the junior medical officer,
who happened to be passing at the time, to test my
heart. The junior doctor, who was in a jovial mood,
stooped down and listened to my heart through the
stethoscope for barely the space of a second—he
could not have heard two beats—and exclaimed,
" Oh, ripping, splendid heart ! You can go on with
her " ; with that he left the cell. But the senior
doctor seemed not to be reassured and he was kind
to me for the first time. He tried to feed me
with a spoon, but I was still able to clench my teeth
and no food got down. He then pleaded with me,
saying in a beseeching voice, " I do beg of you—I
appeal to you, not as a prison doctor but as a man—
to give over. You are a delicate woman, you are
not fit for this sort of thing." I answered, " Is anybody fit for it ? And I beg of you—I appeal to you,
not as a prisoner but as a woman—to give over and
refuse to continue this inhuman treatment." After
I had lain quiet for some time I managed to clean
the cell myself. I took out two pails to the sink,
but had only strength to carry them a few yards.
As I was journeying like this, getting on very slowly,
a wardress told me to take only one at a time ; her
sympathy was moved to this extent, but no further.
I took one pail back to my cell, went on with the
other, and then came back for the first. When I
had finished this business of washing up—which I

was glad to do myself, even if it took half the day, that it might not be given to another prisoner, and also for the better cleaning of the hideous mess—I fell on my bed and lay there till evening ; they now left me both bed and bedding, which was a tremendous blessing.

I lay facing the window, which was high up, and very little light seemed to come from it. As the sun went down I saw the shadow of the wooden mouldings fall across the glass,—three crosses, and they were the shape of the three familiar crosses at the scene of Calvary, one in the centre and one on either side. It looked different from any of the pictures I had seen. The cross of Christ, the cross of the repentant thief, and the cross of the sinner who had not repented—that cross looked blacker than the others, and behind it was an immense crowd. The light from the other two crosses seemed to shine on this one, and the Christ was crucified that He might undo all the harm that was done. I saw amongst the crowd the poor little doctor and the Governor, and all that helped to torture these women in prison, but they were nothing compared to the men in the Cabinet who wielded their force over them. There were the upholders of vice and the men who support the thousand injustices to women, some knowingly and some unconscious of the harm and cruelty entailed. Then the room grew dark and I fell asleep. When the doctor came again with his apparatus he had bovril and brandy, and the tube was left for only one second in my body. The next morning, Thursday, January 20, I told him that the brandy, which at first had the effect of warming me, left me freezing cold after about two hours, and I thought it was no use. As for the bovril, I had the strongest objection to it of a vegetarian kind, and I begged him not to give it to me again ; he said he would not. It was only when I was sick that I knew what were the ingredients put down my body. That morning it was again milk and plasmon that was given me, and I was horribly sick. The doctor said to me, " You are absolutely not fit for this kind of thing. How could your Union send a woman like you to do a thing of this kind ? It is like sending a wisp of wind to fight against a—— " I did not hear the end of the sentence, but I think he said " a rock." I was not able to answer, but the next time he came I said to him, " Our Union does not send anyone ; service of this kind is absolutely voluntary. In my case not one of the leaders even knew of my action. I did it entirely off my own bat and only told the local organisers."

From the third feeding, when the junior doctor had felt my heart on Wednesday evening, the senior doctor had been much kinder to me ; in fact I noticed a change in the way I was treated generally, so much so that I concluded my identity had been discovered or was at least suspected. I left off wearing my hair in a parting, as it was almost impossible to keep it away when I was sick. I brushed it back and did it up in a towel every time when I was fed. I left off wearing my glasses, which were too uncomfortable to be tolerated now that the necessity for them had worn off and they were forcibly feeding me quite happily. I then decided to take the utmost advantage of any

privilege, in order to bring the officials to act
reasonably, to check their recklessness as much as
possible, and to bring them to strain the regulations
so far as might be—not, as heretofore, in the direction
of brutality, but in the direction of hygiene, if not
of humanity. I pleaded afresh with the doctor to
try the experiment of giving me less quantity of
food, of putting less of the tube into the body, of
using less glycerine, which greatly irritated my
throat the moment the tube touched it, or to use oil
instead of glycerine. He listened to what I said,
and though except as to the glycerine—he wiped the
tube almost free of it, and called my attention to
the fact—there was not much difference in what he
did, yet his manner of doing it was different.

When I was at the sink on Thursday morning, two
or three other prisoners were there, and they hastily
whispered to me, " It *is* your friend next to you,
No. 21." The kindness which beamed from all
their faces did my heart good, but I could never
hear or see Elsie Howey next door, and eventually
I imagined that they must have mistaken me for her
when I threw back my hair after the third feeding.

That day I thought I would clean my window,
through which I had seen such a wonderful vision
the evening before. Though the day was generally
spent in loneliness, I knew that I might be visited
at any hour, so I put off till about 3.30, when the
ward was generally quiet for a time. All the furniture
in the cell was movable, so I placed the table in
front of the window and the chair on the top, then
I climbed up. Through the small part of the window
that opened I looked down, and in a beautiful red

glow of the sinking sun I saw a sight that filled my very soul with joy. In the gloaming light—it was an exercise ground that I looked down upon—I saw walking round, all alone, a woman in her prisoner's dress, and in her arms she carried another little prisoner, a baby done up in a blanket. I was too high up to hear her, but I could see distinctly that she cooed and laughed to her little companion, and perhaps she sang to it too. I never saw maternal love more naturally displayed. The words of the Chaplain came back to my mind—"The women, they're all as bad as bad can be, there's absolutely no good in them." No good in them! and yet amongst them there was this little woman who, at least, loved her child and played with it as only a mother-heart can!

I got down and put the table and chair in their place ; I felt amazed, having seen a sight as beautiful as the most beautiful picture in the world.

The wardress who came most often to my cell was kind to me. I said to her, " Oh ! if you only knew what a nightmare it is, the feeding. I have never been any good at bearing pain, and each time it comes I feel as if I simply couldn't endure it." " Oh ! well," she answered, " it gets better, you'll see." She said this in a comforting voice, but the vistas of experience it gave of other prisoners who had gone through the process made it anything but a comfort to me. Most of them had been let out half dead before the end of their time, and I had but very little faith in the assurance that it would " get better." I asked her after the other Suffrage prisoners, but she could tell me nothing of them.

This wardress came back to my cell rather late one
day and said to me hurriedly : " I am going away
to the other side of the prison. Will you write to
me when you get out ? " I told her that I was
afraid my letters might get her into trouble, for I
felt sure it would not be allowed. She said she
was quite sure it would be all right, if I sent it
to her name, Miss ——. I said, " Very well, then,
I will."

I was filled with terror in the morning when the
gas-jet was put out and in the evening when it was
lighted again ; within about half an hour of these
changes in the light came the doctor and wardresses,
the gag and all the fiendish consequences. I
walked up and down my cell in a fever of fear,
stopping now and then and looking up at the window,
from which all good things had seemed to come. I
said, " Oh, God, help me ! Oh, God, help me ! "

After, I think, the sixth meal, I complained to the
doctor that the processes of digestion were absolutely
stagnant. I suggested to him that he should leave
out one meal, with a view to allowing the natural
forces of the body to readjust themselves, unhampered
by the kind of paralysing cramp and arresting of the
natural functions which resulted from fear. I also
suggested that instead of brandy—he had given me
another meal of bovril and brandy—fruit juice or
the water in which a pear or apple had been stewed
should be added to my food.   He did not answer me,
but turned to the head assistant, whom he had
already assured me was a fully-trained nurse, and in
a half-insolent, half-contemptuous tone of voice,
said : " Do you understand her ? I don't. Does

she mean that she is constipated ? If so, you see
about it."   Very likely I had spoken unintelligibly.
I seldom had interviewed a doctor on my own
behalf, and am not versed in their technical language.
Whenever I spoke to this doctor it was either
immediately before or after the feeding, so that my
nerves were unstrung. Moreover, prisoners are
made to feel in the presence of nearly every prison
official that they are the scum of the earth, suspected of deceit, prejudged and found wanting ;
this has a paralysing effect on a prisoner's powers of
expression.   The chief assistant was the woman who
took me daily to the weighing machine. She was
kind and refined in her ways. I explained to her
what I wanted, I reminded her several times about
this ; once I spoke again to the doctor of it, but I was
never given either a drug, or, so far as I know, the
fruit juice in my food.

I asked the doctor if a smaller tube could not be
used for the feeding. He answered, " If I fed you
through the nose it would be with a smaller tube."
I suggested that the smaller tube should be used
through the mouth, if he thought that process the
easiest. He said, " Well, that might be," but the
tube was never changed to a smaller one. As to my
suggestion about omitting a meal, he also seemed to
think it plausible, but he promised nothing, and fed
me in the evening, saying that I had again lost
weight, so that he could not leave me without food.
Of course, this quite ignored my argument that until
I began to keep down the food I could not profit by
it or gain in weight.

My limbs, hands and feet, were stiff with cold at

all times.   I was allowed flannel underclothes and an
extra blanket.   In spite of continued reproof from
the wardresses I kept on my nightdress in the day
time, the only under-garment with long sleeves, and
I passed the night in all my day-clothes.   At last I
was able to do this without comment from the
authorities.   They also, as a great favour, allowed
me yet another blanket when I asked for it after some
days ;   I then had three.   I was allowed to keep the
cape, usually only for out-door use, in my cell.   But
it was like trying to warm a stone by clothing it.
Hot water was allowed in a pail once a day after the
evening feeding.

Most of my friends had been fed by the doctor
standing at the back of the patient, whereas this
doctor adjusted the tube and fed me from the front,
a process which he carried out by sitting across my
knees.   By this time I could not feel my legs and
arms, except just by the joints where I felt the pain
of the cold.   At night I used to get up and walk
from time to time to prevent them from becoming
useless.   But on Thursday night, my sixth in
prison, I fell really asleep and when I awoke I had
an unexpected feeling of ease and freedom from pain
or fear.   I was unconscious of my nearly rigid
limbs, the beat of my heart was scarcely perceptible ;
I supposed I had only a little while to live.   The
prospect of release was inexpressibly welcome.
Presently I heard, as distinctly as if the wall of my
cell had a mouth and had spoken, the words which
Mrs. Leigh has made glorious in connection with our
cause :   " No surrender."   They beat upon my
brain with a new meaning ; not only to a repressive

Government, not only to heedless laws and their attendant punishments, but to the temptations of our inabilities, no surrender. What was I about, to abdicate my job in this ease-loving way ? I rubbed the painful life back into my feet, hands and limbs, and forced myself to walk up and down my cell. Pictures succeeded each other rapidly in my mind of our fellow-prisoners in the " Black Maria," of all undefended women, of children's blighted lives, of down-trodden men and women, undeveloped or ill of body or mind, whose fate women, through their abject surrender of the woman's part in the world's jurisdiction, must to a certain extent have laid at their door. How misplaced, unrighteous and un-womanly did non-resistance appear to me then. With every throb of my returning pulses I seemed to feel the rhythm of the world's soul calling to us women to uncramp our powers from the thraldom of long disuse. My whole being responded and I yearned to hand on the message as I myself had in spirit received it—" Women, you are wanted. Women, as women, because you are women, come out in all your womanliness, and whether or not victory is for your day, at least each one of you make sure that the one course impossible to you is sur-render of your share in the struggle." To you, dear, faithful Suffragettes at heart, whatever the handcuffs of circumstance which may limit your powers of visible service, I pass on this message.

I had been told that the Visiting Magistrates were due to come to the prison on Friday (January 21), and that my offences would be judged by them. On Wednesday morning I asked if I could be allowed to go to chapel, as on Thursday, probably, I should move with difficulty and after that I would not have a chance, as they would have me put in irons for breaking the glass of my gas-jet—they had put my friends in irons for less than that. The wardress seemed to think this improbable, but she gave her consent to my going to chapel. That morning at 10 o'clock, I was taken downstairs and put in a long row of waiting prisoners, we were close enough to be touching each other, all perfectly silent. They changed me about, putting me in a different place each time, for no apparent reason. We had waited about a quarter of an hour, when the order came to move along, and we went through several buildings to the chapel. The men, who were much the most numerous, were seated below, the women in a gallery above with a screen of wood jutting out, so that nothing could be seen by one of the other. I was shunted several times from my place, and at last was put in a row by myself. I looked in vain for any of my companions, they were not there. The service was short and with several hymns, in which, as in Holloway, the prisoners joined heartily. Then the Chaplain got up into the pulpit and preached a sermon with a great deal of energy. He told of a wreck, evidently a quite recent one, in which the lifeboat men had behaved splendidly. Many were saved, and they gave thanks to God and to the lifeboat men. Then he went on to describe how we were born, helpless and ignorant, in the world. As we thought of it, we must give thanks to God. I listened with interest, but nothing further was said. There was apparently no mother to thank, who through nine months had tended the little one in her body, and through pain, sometimes excruciating, brought it to birth. These were entirely forgotten. Was it because the women were " as bad as bad can be " ?

The next day, Thursday, January 20, I asked if I could go out. The longing for more air than I could get in the cell was intense, though the window of this one opened just enough to let in some air. I found that I could walk all right, although it seemed as if my legs were painful things attached to my body. The wardress told me I might go that afternoon. As I was taken out of my cell that morning to be weighed, I passed a little girl prisoner. She was not more than a child. For aught I knew she may have been taken straight from the life of the streets the night before, but she had at that moment the face of an angel, and she looked down on me from the steps that she was cleaning above with a smile which you can never see out of prison. Her whole face seemed lit up with it and it touched my very soul. I never saw her again, but I felt that all my resentment and anger were gone. In a way my physical courage was no greater than before, but at least I should go on ; I knew that I should last out.

In the afternoon the wardress came to let me go out. I saw none of my companions on the way, and I was put in an exercise yard quite alone. A pain in my side had by this time grown acutely. I rested against the wall, but nothing did it any good. The sight of the grey, frosty sky and the feel of air were a delight, but I could not bear the cold nor hold myself up, and after a little while I asked to come in.

The next day, Friday, January 21, as I was being fed—the wardresses had given up holding me—the pain of the tube in my body was more than I could bear ; I seized hold of it and pulled it up. The wardresses reproved me for interfering, but they did not put the tube in again ; the doctor said nothing. I was overwhelmed with the horror of the process, and for the first time I was convulsed with sobs. The doctor was kind to me. I said that I only cried from having no strength to resist, but that I meant to live out my sentence if I could.

This was the day the Visiting Magistrates were due. Later in the morning they came to my cell with the Governor, who said, " Have you any complaint ? If only about the forcible feeding, you will have the opportunity later on in my room ; don't talk of that now." I answered, " I have complaints to make not only about being fed by force, but as to the manner in which it was done." He said, " Your opportunity for that also will come later on." I think it was now, in the presence of the Visiting Magistrates, that I said to the Governor, " I shall be saying several things when I am out of prison, and it seems to me more fair and square to tell you of them now while I am still in your hands, and you can refute them if you like." He allowed me to proceed, so I went on : " About the Governor, I shall say that while he was shocked at the great wickedness of breaking glass as a protest against forcible feeding, he sanctioned and approved of the violence and brutality of the forcible feeding itself." He almost smiled, and replied hastily that he had never said anything of the kind. I began to ask which part of my statement he denied—his condemnation of glass-breaking or approval of the forced feeding, but he stopped me and would not allow any further remarks on that point.

Soon afterwards, when summoned before the Magistrates in the Governor's room, I was allowed, in replying to the charge of glass-breaking, to which I pleaded guilty, to make my protest against the forcible feeding. I said I had been unable to ascertain on whose authority it was done; if by the order of an individual it seemed to me cruel and abominable, but if by order of the departmental authority, and in the name of law, I thought it much worse; then it was sheer barbarism, for under cover of such an order, kindly and well-meaning subordinates were made to assist, for the sake of duty, in the performance of many things which they would never tolerate under different circumstances. As a protest, I owned a feeble one, against this barbarism I had actually been guilty of defacing the walls of my cell with inscriptions and of breaking a valuable piece of glass. The latter part of my remarks, I think, were scarcely heard, for the Magistrates had begun to interrupt me. My breath gave out; I looked round at the Magistrates, at the Governor, at the Matron. They had ordinary faces, neither kind nor unkind; they were displeased with what I said, they looked angry—that was all. Then I asked if I might now lodge my complaint against various points as to the manner in which I had been forcibly fed. The Governor replied, "No,

not now. You will have another opportunity for
that later on." After a lengthy and severe repri-
mand for my prison offences and condemnatory
remarks on the subject of the behaviour of Suffragettes outside, the Magistrates waived the matter of
the wall inscriptions as having been already dealt
with by the Governor, and with regard to the broken
glass they deferred judgment *sine die*.

When back in my cell, the Governor presently
visited me. I said I had understood I was to have an
opportunity of seeing the Magistrates again to lodge
my further complaint against the manner of feeding.
The Governor said, " You will not see the Magistrates
again ; but now is your time, I have come on purpose
to hear your complaints." I had the impression,
probably not uncommon to all prisoners, that the
higher the authority the less likelihood would there
be of an appeal to them taking effect. Certainly
there had been nothing in the manner and remarks
of the Visiting Magistrates to alter this impression.
I was therefore well pleased to make my complaint
to the Governor alone. It is no part of the prison
protest to plead for merciful or even rational treatment, and though I had deliberately decided upon
a different course, I was haunted by the fear of
breaking our policy and proving disloyal to my
comrades then in prison. The Matron was present,
as always when the Governor visits prisoners in their
cells, and he allowed me to remain on my bed. For
the first time he listened to all I had to say without
attempting to interrupt me, or to curtail or change
the drift of my remarks. I reported to him having
been forcibly fed without my heart having been

tested or the doctor even feeling my pulse. I said I
mentioned this in no spirit of personal complaint,
for, though suffering from slight chronic heart
disease, my heart happened to have great resisting
and recuperative power; but I didn't suppose it was
possible to diagnose this fact merely from looking
at me, and that on general medical grounds, as a
matter of principle, I thought the heart ought most
carefully to be tested before any prisoner who had
been on hunger-strike was forcibly fed, since both
these processes were theoretically believed to tax
the heart.

I said, " There is another thing which I think I
had better mention. After the first time of feeding
me, the doctor seemed very irritated and, before
leaving, he slapped me on the cheek; he did not
hurt me, but seemed to wish to show his contempt;
about this, too, I do not wish to complain as of an
insult to me personally. He no doubt was irritated
by his repulsive job, but this is hardly the right
mood for an official, and what he could do to one
woman he might possibly do to another. I think
such things should not be done. I asked him the
next morning, unless he thought it part of his duty,
not to do such a thing again, and he never has."
I made further complaints about too much food at
a time being poured in through the tube, and about
the one occasion when the tube was left in for some
considerable time and the feeding repeated again
and again, in spite of my continuous vomiting. I
did not, however, complain of these things in any
detail to the Governor, since they seemed to be
matters chiefly suitable for the medical officer. I

think I added, as I certainly did on one occasion to
the doctor himself, what a mercy it was that at
least the doctor was skilled in adjusting the tube
into the throat. The Governor made no reply but
listened to all I said.

It was on the afternoon of this day, Friday, that
the door of my cell was suddenly thrown open, and
the man who stood outside was announced to me
as the Government inspector. I asked, had he
come from London ? " Yes." He inquired in a
hurried way, as if he had a train to catch, had I any
complaint ? " Yes," I replied, " first of all about
being fed by force." He said, in a hurried and
insolent manner, all in one breath, so that it was
scarcely intelligible, " Are you refusing to take
your food—If so, the remedy is in your hands, you
have no reason to complain—Any further complaints ? " I hesitated for a moment, then, as it
seemed to me my complaints against the doctor
would certainly in this man's estimation come
under the head of grievances easily remediable by
the surrender of the hunger-strike, I answered, " No,
I suppose not," upon which he abruptly left me.

On this day, Friday, the Governor before he left
me had suggested that under certain conditions he
would allow me to write a letter. " For instance,"
he said, " if you had a mother you were anxious
about, perhaps I could give you leave to write to
her." I had so arranged matters before being
arrested that I knew my people, if they had traced
me, would conclude that by this time my hunger-
strike had been superseded by forcible feeding ;
that those most dear to me had implicit faith in the

reasonableness of all officials, that if at any moment
they chose to take advantages of the privileges
available to them, they could hear all about me ; and,
finally, that if they were anxious to the point of
disregard for those of my principles which they did
not share, they could pay my fine ; but hastily on
these reflections there followed the panic fear that
it was my mother who was ill, and the Governor was
breaking the news to me. He, however, reassured
me on this point and he left me. The permission
reeled in my brain. My mother would by this time
certainly suspect something. If I could write to
her and yet not let her know where I was ! The
prison paper would alone make this impossible. I
thought about it all night. The next day, Saturday,
January 22, I determined to eat my breakfast so
that I might be in a fit state to write, otherwise my
hands trembled and I could not steady my mind to a
letter. I told the wardress very early that morning
that I would eat my breakfast, and that I should
like someone to witness it. The little woman,
whom the doctor had told me was a nurse, brought
me in a cup of milk and a piece of white bread and
butter. It was the most delicious food I have ever
tasted ; the " nurse " was very kind to me and
stayed till I had finished. Then I wrote my letter ;
it was only on the slate, of course ; I must ask the
Governor's leave before I was allowed writing-paper.
I asked to see the Governor, by letter written on
another slate. I said that, if it were the same to
him, might I go to his room to see him, as there I
could stand near the hot pipes, which was a great
luxury. He came to my cell, and I told him I

would gladly avail myself of the privilege to
write to my mother, provided he would grant the
same privilege to my fellow Suffrage prisoners.   I
assumed, too, that he had done the same in the case
of Elsie Howey as in mine, omitted to punish her
for glass-breaking—I believed, from the sound, that
someone besides myself had broken glass—and I
reminded him of a remark he had made as to the law
being no respecter of persons.   By this time I had
an almost certain conviction that he knew who I was.
But he would not give me any assurance as to
like favours being granted to other prisoners, so I
refused to avail myself of the letter-writing privilege.
In the afternoon, however, I had decided that I
could convey news to my mother without revealing
my identity to the officials, supposing that they were
not yet fully aware of the truth, and that I had
better use every available privilege offered, since I
was in the dark as to the grounds on which it was
made.   I determined to write to the nurse of my
sister's children, who lived in Bloomsbury Square,
telling her to forward my letter at once to my mother.
I asked to see the Governor again, but he had left.
I was taken before the Matron, who told me the
privilege would anyhow be conditional, dependent
upon to whom my letter was addressed and the
urgency of the motive for writing it.   I said there
was no extreme urgency ;   she answered I must
await the Governor's return on Monday morning.

I wrote in my letter on the slate that the forcible
feeding was " only pain," and that my mother would
think that good for me.   I made no other complaint,
but said the short sentence would soon let me be

with her. My only object was to conceal all that I endured. In the evening I was again fed by force.

On Sunday morning, January 23, the cold was intense. I asked for some hearthstone to polish my tins—they had taken everything of the kind away and the tins were dull and spotted. I hoped to keep some sense of life in my hands and arms by trying to scrub with them. But it did not come. Presently the door opened and the Governor appeared ; I could not think why he came so early. Then I saw the doctor behind him, and the thought of the forcible feeding blocked my mind. I supposed the Governor had come to see it. He was nervous about startling me, I suppose, for he told me the great news twice before I understood. He told me of my release and that my youngest sister, Emily Lutyens, had come to fetch me away. I felt stunned with the quite unexpected shock of joy, it was too good to be true. After ascertaining that my fine had not been paid, but that I had been released on medical grounds, and that it had nothing to do with my mother's health, the chief aim for which I tried to pull myself together was to obtain what news I could of my fellow-prisoners. The Governor and doctor, however, left me without giving me any information. Again I was brought white bread and butter and milk for my breakfast, and the " nurse " stayed with me while I ate it. They brought me my clothes, but the more I realised the news the slower my movements became ; all strength seemed to have ebbed from my body. The wardresses knew nothing of the other Suffragette prisoners, whether they were released or not. When dressed I was taken out far

away to what was called " the Governor's room," but
it was not the same one that I had seen before. The
doctor came and talked to me, then after a little while
my sister came.   We greeted each other, of course, by
a tremendously warm embrace.   The doctor looked
away like a witness in a melodrama.   I sat there as
in a dream talking to him and to the Governor, who
presently came in.   The doctor said, " I have been
kind to you ? "   " Latterly you were," I answered,
" if you had not fed me.   At first you were angry
and not kind."   I told the Governor that the one
thing I wanted to know about was the other Suffragette prisoners, were they fed—were they released ?
He answered that they were not released, that one of
them was in hospital, that they were all quite well.
I said that was a curious answer ; if they were all
quite well, why was one in hospital ?   He said that
he could tell me nothing more.   The doctor said
they were none of them as bad as I was over the
feeding.   That was all that I could get from them
about the other prisoners.   I did not go over again
with them the points about which I had protested,
while still a prisoner, as to my own treatment.   The
Governor and doctor were courteous to me after my
release and to my sister, and the Governor's wife
had been very kind to her on her arrival in the
early morning.

Why we waited I do not know, but in about half
an hour we drove away in a four-wheeler.   The
Chaplain was just coming in to the prison as we
drove out through the gates ; he bowed to me.   I
went to the station first and got my trunk, or rather
my sister got it for me, then we went to the hotel.

We telephoned to Dr. Kerr that I was released and going with my sister to London. She sent her young daughter and man-servant to see us at the hotel, and we left word with them for Miss Flatman, who was not on the telephone and whose Sunday address we did not know.

I had a long bath, which was a tremendous luxury, although my legs were so thin I could not sit down without pain. My dear sister stayed with me the whole time ; my voice shook and I could not speak properly. We had a meal before we left.

CHAPTER XIV

THE HOME OFFICE

WE got into the train for London and I had a long sleep. During the last part of the journey my sister, Emily Lutyens, told how she had heard of me in Walton Gaol. She had a telephone message forwarded to her on Saturday night, January 15, from the Press Association. It was addressed to my eldest brother, who was abroad, saying it was rumoured that I was imprisoned in Liverpool—was it true? She rang up our friend, Mr. Arthur Chapman, who after an infinity of trouble got into communication with Mr. Thompson, one of the Prison Commissioners from the Home Office. In answering the telephone, he welcomed Mr. Chapman gleefully, as having news they had wanted much. "There is a prisoner at Walton Gaol, Liverpool," he said, "whom they have for some days suspected of being other than her declaration. We have wanted to release her, but have not been able to find out who her people were." This was a most extraordinary thing for a Home Office official to say. Why had they not released me to the W.S.P.U. organiser in Liverpool, or asked me with whom they should communicate? And why were they more anxious to set me free than the other Suffragettes? They had signed an order for my release,

The reason given was loss of weight; they did not mention my heart, since they knew nothing about it ! Mr. Thompson recommended that my sister should telephone to the doctor at Walton and he would arrange with the Governor to release me. With this news Mr. Chapman went to my sister Emily, who was dining out. They rang up Dr. Price, of Walton, and after communicating with him my sister felt almost sure the prisoner was myself. Without a moment's hesitation, and dressed just as she was, she caught the midnight train to Liverpool, where she arrived at about six in the morning. She reached the doctor's house at about seven and still was uncertain whether she would find me in the prison. Dr. Price, after some talk, took her to the Governor's house. The Governor's wife was very kind at that early hour and gave her breakfast. She said she thought it was inhuman to dress the prisoners in such frightfully ugly clothes, she felt only horror when she looked at them ; she would have different clothing for them if she had anything to do with it.

Dr. Price told my sister that he had written the report of me to the Home Office. " I said she was spare, very spare, and that she had a nose—I did not say aquiline, but of a somewhat Wellingtonian bend." We roared with laughter at this description of me.

The following is my sister's statement of a conversation which she had with the doctor on arriving at Walton : " After a preliminary conversation with Dr. Price in regard to what had taken place in connection with our telephonic communication with

him the previous night, I asked him whether he
could tell me anything with regard to my sister's
behaviour in gaol and the treatment she had been
obliged to undergo. In reply, he stated that she
had fasted for four days, that he had begged her to
take her food, and explained that if she refused he
would be obliged to forcibly feed her. As she had
persisted in her refusal, he had been obliged to feed
her through the mouth up to the date of her release,
with the exception of one meal, which she took of
her own accord on Saturday morning. He further
stated that, unlike some other Suffragettes, she had
shown no violence beyond refusing to take her food,
but that, in all his experience, he had never seen
such a bad case of forcible feeding. I asked him
what he meant by a ' bad case,' and he said ' *She
was practically asphyxiated every time.*' I then told
him that the medical officers at Holloway and Newcastle reported to us that my sister was suffering
from serious valvular disease of the heart, and I
asked him if his examination had led him to the
same conclusion. He replied ' Certainly not. My
subordinate ' (or some such word), ' who is a very
clever doctor, thoroughly examined her heart and
found no trace of disease whatever,' and I need
hardly say that this was a great relief to my mind,
as the reports of the other prison doctors had caused
us so much anxiety. He further stated that, in
spite of the forcible feeding, my sister had lost
weight at the rate of 2 lbs. a day, and that, consequently, he had been obliged to advise her being
released.

" Dr. Price several times repeated how much

my sister had suffered from the treatment, and, after I had told him about her heart, said that it might possibly have been due to her heart condition, though he had not been able to detect it."

My sister took me to their house in Bloomsbury Square, which we reached at about 8.30 p.m. There was our friend, Mr. Chapman, to whom I gave a brief account of my imprisonment. He went off with it the next day to the Home Office Prison Department, and returned with the news that the officials would be grateful to me if I would make a statement on paper, whereupon they would have it investigated. There were reasons why they would be very glad to have an open inquiry at Walton Gaol.

All that night I woke off and on with cold, and also with terror at the forcible feeding. My sister was most kind to me ; she reheated my hot-bottles and at last came and slept with me. I stayed in bed the next morning (Monday, January 24). In the afternoon I saw some of my friends—Mrs. Pethick Lawrence and Christabel Pankhurst. Some days after, when she returned to London, I saw Mrs. Pankhurst. They were all of them content with what I had done and the way I had done it. This was a most tremendous joy and relief to me.

I managed to write a letter to the *Times* and an article for *Votes for Women*. I could only do everything so slowly that I had not finished these until eight o'clock the next morning, after writing all night. I stayed in bed the whole of that day,

Tuesday. On Wednesday and Thursday (26th and 27th) I stayed in bed in the morning, but led a more or less normal life after. These days I could hardly sit in a chair, because my emaciated condition rendered it very painful; I ate my meals, very often, kneeling down at the table on a cushion.

On Tuesday, January 25, I wrote to Mr. Gladstone, the Home Secretary, to explain that it was not as the newspapers said, to play a practical joke upon him, that I had gone to prison in disguise. It was because of the totally different category of treatment meted out to one set of people from another, and the object of my disguise was to expose this for the sake of bringing such a state of things to an end.

On Monday, January 31, I woke with a blistered heel. I spoke at the meeting at the Queen's Hall, and it was heart-filling to meet all my friends again ; the whole audience seemed to understand. I stood for an hour on one foot. On coming home I had to wait about to get a statement finished and type-written. I had written very carefully for the Home Office of what happened to me in prison. After that I went to bed and stopped there for six weeks. The next day, Tuesday, February 1, the blister on my heel was much worse and my sister wished to send for a doctor. I had always been ill in the country and did not know of one. My sister called in Dr. Marion Vaughan, who from that moment was my doctor, and after she had been to see me I had a nurse. This is her report :—

"Report of Physical Condition of Lady
Constance Lytton.

"Tuesday, February 1, 1910.
"21, Thurloe Square, S.W.
"February 4, 1910.

"I was called in to see Lady Constance Lytton,
staying at 29, Bloomsbury Square, W.C., on account
of pain, swelling and reddening of right leg and heel;
with enlarged tender glands behind the knee,
associated with an inflamed blister on the heel.*
There was cellulitis of the right leg, extending to
the knee. Both legs were considerably swollen
(evidently due to failing heart), though the patient
and her sister, Lady Emily Lutyens, said this was
much less marked than on the previous day. The
patient's look of extreme illness, malnutrition, and
bad colour led me to examine her heart carefully.
This I found to be in a serious condition, considerably larger than normal, with its apex beat in 6th
intercostal space, $1\frac{1}{2}$ inches beyond the nipple line;
extremely irregular in force and frequency, a marked
difference between heart and pulse rate, due to
feeble transmission to terminal vessels. The heart
sounds were 'trembling' in character. The pulse
then (February 1, 1910, at 10.30 a.m.) and now is
slow, small in volume and irregular; its rate
varying from 48 to 52 per minute. (There is

* The shoes in Walton Gaol were exceptionally stiff, even,
as it seemed to me, for prison footwear. They hurt my
feet badly and made the heel of my right foot very sore.
As I have told, after I broke my gas-jet, the shoes were
changed to comfortable slippers, but I think this accounted
for the blister after my release, when my foot came to life
again.

perfectly clear evidence of mitral disease of the heart, with præsystolic murmur.) The most superficial examination of the heart cannot fail to reveal the grave risk to health and life to which the patient was exposed during the forcible methods of feeding recently adopted in Walton Gaol."

> Report by Dr. Marion Hunter (Mrs. Vaughan), Plague Medical Officer to Government of India, 1897—1898; Plague Medical Officer to British Government in Egypt, 1899; Assistant Medical Officer to London County Council (Education) 4½ years.

On Monday, January 31, Mr. Arthur Chapman wrote to Mr. Gladstone, enclosing the statement which I had made, and begging for an interview, in which he could explain matters to the full; this was refused. On February 4 Mr. Chapman wrote again, appealing for a full and impartial investigation. The following letter was received :—

" Please quote 187, 986/10,
    " and address to the Under-Secretary of State,
        " Home Office, London, S.W.

        " Home Office, Whitehall,
                " 9th February, 1910.

" Sir,—With reference to your letter of the 31st ultimo, forwarding statement made by Lady Constance Lytton, as to her treatment in H.M. Prison, Liverpool, and your further letter of the 4th inst., I am directed by the Secretary of State to say that he has caused careful and detailed

inquiry to be made by the Prison Commissioners
into the truth of the charges brought by Lady
Constance Lytton against the officers of the prison,
and as the result of that inquiry he is satisfied that
those charges are without foundation and that there
is no justification for Lady Constance Lytton's
account of her experience while she was in the prison.

" The Secretary of State cannot discuss her statements in detail. A single instance must suffice.
Lady Constance, with a view to showing that her
treatment as ' Jane Warton ' differed from her
treatment when her identity was known, asserts
that, whereas she was thoroughly examined at
Holloway and Newcastle Prisons and was found to
be suffering from heart disease, no attempt was
made to examine her at Liverpool before she was
forcibly fed. On reception at Liverpool Prison on
the 15th ultimo, Lady Constance refused to allow
herself to be examined and told the deputy medical
officer, who was on duty, that she was quite well.
He asked her a second time to allow him to examine
her and she again refused. His evidence on this
point is corroborated by that of the wardress who
was present, and the matter is placed beyond doubt
by the entry ' refused examination ' which was made
at the time in the medical reception register at
the prison. Before artificially feeding her for the
first time, the senior medical officer applied his ear
to the chest wall and satisfied himself that the
condition of her heart was such that the operation
of artificial feeding could, in the absence of active
resistance by the patient, be performed without any
immediate risk of injury to her health. In this

connection you will observe that the diagnosis
of the medical officers at Holloway and Newcastle,
arrived at after thorough examination, is fully
confirmed by the report of Lady Constance Lytton's
own medical attendant, which you have been good
enough to forward. 'Jane Warton's' foolish conduct in refusing to allow herself to be examined and
the deception which deprived the medical officers
of all knowledge of the medical history of her case,
must be held responsible for the fact that the true
condition of her heart remained undiscovered while
she was in Liverpool Prison. When it was found
that the injury to her health caused by her per-
sistent refusal to take food could not be prevented
by artificial feeding, her discharge was recommended by the medical officer and was authorised
by the Secretary of State, and this was done before
anyone at the Home Office or at the prison was
aware of her identity. The statement that the
medical officer was guilty of slapping his patient's
face is utterly devoid of truth, and can only be the
outcome of the imagination.

" In these circumstances the Secretary of State
does not consider that any further inquiry as to the
truth of the statements made and published by
Lady Constance Lytton is called for, and he must
therefore decline to accede to your request for
further investigation.

                         " I am, sir,
                               " Your obedient servant,
                                     " (Signed)   EDWARD TROUP."
" ARTHUR W. CHAPMAN, ESQ.,
          " 33, Whitehall Court, S.W."

In this letter it seems to be thought that it does not matter mis-stating things, provided the mis-statement is a small one, then the small things can be added together. Even supposing everything to be true in this letter, no mention is made of calling in the other doctor five days before I was released, on purpose to test my heart. He did so with a stethoscope on the heart itself, though anything but carefully, and pronounced it quite sound.

Eighteen days after my release I called in Dr. Anders Ryman, of 4, Wetherby Place, to give me Swedish treatment. He found that my heart had regained its normal size, but he thought my condition too critical for any but the very mildest form of treatment ; insisted on my being kept entirely in bed, absolutely quiet, and forbade all visitors or letters being brought to me. He would not let me be moved to the country for another four weeks, and, even after that, urged me to exert myself as little as possible and only walk upstairs backwards. He seemed to be alarmed at the great fluctuations between the heart beat when still and when I moved or spoke.

During my imprisonment, the side of the jaw on which the gag was used became painful and the whole mouth very sensitive, but five or six days after release all swelling had subsided and pain was only occasional and mild. About ten days after my release, the crown of my artificial tooth broke away entirely. Owing to this and to sensitiveness in the upper tooth affected, I did not use that side of my mouth in eating, but I was unable to leave my bed to visit the dentist. Some time after I was up the

doctors urged upon me that I was still unfit to
undergo dental treatment.   I went in March, but
my dentist thought I could not undergo any but a
temporary treatment of the harmfully exposed
surfaces.   It was not till April that full treatment
was finally given ; that is why the date of the
report made by the dentist is so long after the
release from prison :—

> " 10, Park Crescent,
> " Portland Place, W.,
> " April 14, 1910.
> " Lady Constance Lytton.
>
> " In order to restore the masticatory efficiency of
> the left side of the lower jaw, a bridge consisting
> of one gold crown and two porcelain crowns was
> constructed.   This was attached in May, 1896, and
> has continued in satisfactory condition until the
> application of a gag, recently employed in forcible
> feeding, cracked and broke away the face of the
> crown of the bicuspid on the lower jaw, also breaking
> the enamel of the upper natural tooth.
>
> " Sufficient force having been employed to
> occasion this damage, it was feared that the root of
> the tooth which forms the front anchorage of the
> bridge was split, but this is not the case, and the
> inflammatory symptoms have now subsided.
>
> " H. Uren Olver."

On February 3 came the news that Selina Martin
and Elsie Howey were released from Walton Gaol.
I was by this time in bed and received no news and
no letters ; when the information was brought to

me, I felt quite overwhelmed with joy. This release was more than three weeks before their sentence had expired.

By the time the last letter had been received from the Home Office, February 9, my eldest brother had returned from abroad, and he took up the case. All his attempts to have a public inquiry failed. Mr. Gladstone was relieved of the Home Office preparatory to taking up the work of High Commissioner in South Africa, and my brother pleaded in vain with everyone that had to do with the matter. In the meantime, the W.S.P.U. was asked not to take up my case in any way for fear that the authorities would thereupon refuse to listen, and a letter from Sir Edward Troup to the *Times*, in which he said there was no foundation for the declarations against the officials, remained unanswered.

On March 30, my brother had the following letter in the *Times* :—

" SIR,—On February 10 a letter was sent to the Press by Sir Edward Troup, relative to a statement made by my sister, Lady Constance Lytton, regarding her treatment in Liverpool Prison, in which he declared on behalf of the Home Secretary that there was no foundation for any of the charges which she had made. I am anxious to explain why this official imputation of untruthfulness has hitherto remained unanswered.

" Lady Constance was seriously ill at the time as the result of her prison experiences, and unable to defend herself. I therefore undertook the task of vindicating her veracity. Before making any public

statement on her behalf I was anxious to find out
what steps had been taken by the Home Office to
investigate the matters referred to in her statement,
and I hoped by a friendly intervention to secure a
full and impartial inquiry into all the circumstances
of her treatment by the prison officials.

"I have had several communications with the
Home Office on the subject, and owing to the retire-
ment of Mr. Gladstone and the appointment of a
new Home Secretary, they have necessarily been
protracted over a considerable period. My attitude
throughout has been entirely conciliatory, and the
only claim which I have made was that in the
interests of justice, charges of this nature should be
submitted to a full and impartial inquiry which
would, of course, involve a separate examination of
both the parties concerned. This claim has been
refused by the Home Office on the grounds that the
prison officials have been closely interrogated, and
that as they deny entirely every one of the charges
made, 'no useful purpose would be served' by
granting my request.

"In the absence of such an inquiry as I asked for,
the matter must be left to the opinion of unbiassed
minds. I desire, however, to say that nothing
which I have been able to learn has in any way
shaken my belief in the substantial accuracy of
my sister's account. The idea that her charges can
be disposed of by the bare denial of the persons
against whom they are made, is not likely to com-
mend itself to anyone outside the Home Office,
and no amount of denial can get over the following
facts :—

" 1. Lady Constance Lytton, when imprisoned in Newcastle, after refusing to answer the medical questions put to her and adopting the hunger-strike, received a careful and thorough medical examination, which disclosed symptoms of ' serious heart disease,' and on these grounds she was released as unfit to submit to forcible feeding.

" 2. Three months later ' Jane Warton,' when imprisoned at Liverpool, also refused to answer medical questions or to take prison food. On this occasion she was entered in the prison books as having refused medical examination, and was forcibly fed eight times. Such medical examination as took place during the forcible feeding failed, according to the medical officer's report, to disclose any symptoms of heart disease, and she was eventually released on the grounds of loss of weight and general physical weakness.

" These facts are incontrovertible, and though the Home Office is quite satisfied that in both cases the prison officals performed their duty in the most exemplary fashion, your readers will form their own opinions of the justice of a Government Department which brings accusations of untruthfulness against an individual whilst refusing the only means by which the truth can be established.

" I am, your obedient servant,

" LYTTON."

My brother did not give up his efforts till in April Mr. Winston Churchill, the new Home Secretary, who was well known to him, came to stay at Kneb-

worth, his country place.   Mr. Churchill read through
the whole case, until he came to the report of the
letter to my mother written on the slate.   " 'Twould
be hopeless," he said, " to bring forward any complaint with this letter in the background."   I don't
know, of course, what they had made of it, as it had
been rubbed out long ago, but I know that I had
not told my mother anything of the treatment.   I
had said that the forcible feeding was " only pain "
—so it was.

In the autumn of this year, 1910, I had a slight
heart-seizure.   I got out of bed in the morning, and
was taken with paralysis down one side.   I could
not move for about an hour, when I managed to
crawl back to bed.   I had a nurse for six weeks and
then it was over.

CHAPTER XV

THE CONCILIATION BILL

On June 12, 1910, I received a letter from Mrs. Pethick Lawrence, in which she told me that I had been made a paid organizer to the Union, at £2 a week, and that the committee wished to make this appointment retrospective for the past six months from January, 1910. I felt very much honoured and pleased. It enabled me to take a small flat in London near the Euston Road, so that I was not far from the office at Clement's Inn and close, too, to a good many railway stations. It was quicker for me than having to go home to the country when I was on speaking tours, and also far more convenient for the London work.

In February, 1910, a truce was called after the elections. Mr. Gladstone, made Lord Gladstone, went to South Africa as Governor-General, and he was succeeded by Mr. Winston Churchill at the Home Office. Mr. Brailsford had spent much time and effort negotiating between all the Suffrage parties in the House of Commons, and he as secretary, and my brother, Lord Lytton, as president, negotiated a committee for the "Conciliation Bill." This is the Bill in full :—

"THE CONCILIATION BILL FOR WOMAN SUFFRAGE.

"A Bill to confer the Parliamentary Franchise on Women.

"1. Every woman possessed of a household qualification within the meaning of the Representation of the People Act (1884) shall be entitled to be registered as a voter, and when registered to vote for the county or borough in which the qualifying premises are situated.

"2. For the purposes of this Act a woman shall not be disqualified by marriage from being registered as a voter, provided that a husband and wife shall not both be registered as voters in the same Parliamentary borough or county division."

That is the Bill which was slightly modified in 1911, so as to remove any reasonable fear of plural or faggot voting. It looked as if the Conciliation Bill had everything in its favour and that it would pass. Ninety city, town and county councils, and thirty district councils petitioned or passed resolutions that the Bill should become law. These included the city councils of Birmingham, Bradford, Cardiff, Dublin, Edinburgh, Glasgow, Leeds, Liverpool, Manchester, Newcastle, Nottingham, Sheffield. In 1910 the Bill was carried on second reading by a majority of 110. In 1911 it was again read a second time and secured a majority of 167. Among those who voted for it were Mr. Birrell, Mr. John Burns, Sir Edward Grey, Mr. Runciman; Mr. Balfour, Mr. Bonar Law, Mr. Lyttelton, Mr. Wyndham; Mr. Barnes, Mr. Keir Hardie, Mr.

Ramsay Macdonald, Mr. Snowden ; Mr. Devlin,
Mr. Healy, Mr. Swift MacNeill, Mr. W. Redmond.
All parties made friends over it.

On Friday, November 18, 1910, Mr. Asquith made
a statement in the House of Commons omitting all
reference to Woman Suffrage, but announcing the
Dissolution for Monday, November 28. On learning
that Mr. Asquith had definitely decided to shelve
the Conciliation Bill, it was determined to send a
Deputation to him forthwith. At the head were
Mrs. Pankhurst, the founder of the W.S.P.U. and
Mrs. Garatt Anderson, twice Mayor of Aldeburgh,
who is one of the pioneer women doctors and sister
of Mrs. Fawcett. Among other well-known women
were Mrs. Hertha Ayrton, the distinguished scien-
tist, Mrs. Cobden Sanderson, Mrs. Saul Solomon,
Mrs. Brackenbury, widow of General Brackenbury,
over seventy years of age, Miss Neligan, who is
seventy-eight years of age, the Hon. Mrs. Haverfield,
and the Princess Sophia Dhuleep Singh. The Deputation was composed of 300 women, but was divided
into detachments of twelve each. They were not
received and were treated worse than any since the
conflict between women and the Government began.
The orders of the Home Secretary were, it appears,
that the police were to be present, both in uniform
and in plain clothes among the crowd, and that the
women were to be thrown from one to the other.
The police were guilty both of torture and of
indecency. The women were accused of violence
and mendacity. Reports were afterwards made by
Lord Robert Cecil, K.C., and Mr. Ellis J. Griffith,
K.C., M.P., on the women whom they had examined

Lord Robert Cecil writes in his letter to the *Times* :—

" All that can be said at present is that the women strenuously deny that they were guilty of any such violence. If they were, it is at least curious that they were not immediately arrested, and that, as I understand, no evidence of any serious assault was offered against any of those who were ultimately brought before the Court. . . .

" Mr. Churchill accuses them of mendacity. Such an accusation requires more than the *ipse dixit* of a Minister to support it. Nor is it in accordance with the principles of British justice to reject without investigation the evidence of scores of apparently respectable women.

" In conclusion, may I ask whether anyone thinks that if the Deputation had consisted of unarmed men of the same character, their demand for an inquiry would have been refused ? Who can doubt that the Home Secretary and the other Ministers would have tumbled over one another in their eagerness to grant anything that was asked ? Are we then to take it as officially admitted that in this country there is one law for male electors and another for voteless women ?

" Yours obediently,
" ROBERT CECIL."

Mr. Ellis Griffith wrote at the end of his letter to the *Times* :—

" It is certainly difficult, under the circumstances, to bring responsibility home to individuals, but I am amply satisfied that there was unnecessary and excessive violence used against the women who took part in the Deputation, and that they were assaulted in a way that cannot be justified.

" Under these circumstances, I strongly support a searching and impartial inquiry. . . .

" Yours faithfully,

" ELLIS J. GRIFFITH."

The Home Secretary refused all idea of a public inquiry.

The morning after the Deputation, Saturday, November 19, 1910, those who had been arrested the night before were all dismissed ; it was thought bad election tactics to be responsible for the imprison- ment of women of good reputation who were merely fighting for their freedom.

Mr. Asquith on Friday, November 18, promised that he would make a statement about the Women's Bill on the following Tuesday. On Tuesday, November 22, accordingly, it was made : " The Government will, if they are still in power, give facilities in the next Parliament for effectively pro- ceeding with a Bill which is so framed as to admit of free amendment." The statement fulfilled none of the conditions which had been made by the W.S.P.U We held that the pledge must be to give full facilities for a Woman Suffrage Bill next Session—next Parlia- ment was a mockery of a pledge. The Bill in question must be no more extended in scope than the Bill introduced by Mr. Shackleton or the Women's Enfranchisement Bill introduced two years ago by Mr. Stanger. A pledge to give facilities to a Bill on a so-called democratic basis would be worthless, it would not have a chance of passing through either House of Parliament.

The House rose immediately when Mr. Asquith had made his statements. The women waited this pronouncement in the Caxton Hall, and on receipt of it marched to Downing Street, Mrs. Pankhurst at their head, to see Mr. Asquith. Here the detachment of police at first was small and the line was broken by the onrush of the women. But reinforcements of police rapidly arrived and a severe struggle ensued. Many women were hurt who were thrown about the street or crushed, and there were 150 to 160 charged at the police court the next day. In the evening parties of women visited the houses of the Cabinet and threw stones, breaking some of their windows. Mr. Muskett, who prosecuted the next day, withdrew all the cases of " simple obstruction," and only allowed the cases of " stone-throwing and assault." From the day of " Black Friday," as November 18, 1910, was called, stone-throwing became easy to the women—it ensured arrest instead of being assaulted and injured.

This was the eve of the election. The policy of the W.S.P.U. was to oppose all Liberal candidates unless they could get a definite pledge from the Prime Minister that, if in power, he would allow the Conciliation Bill to be taken through all its stages next Session. The Liberals were returned, still commanding a Parliamentary majority in the House of Commons, and the House of Commons contained an even larger majority of members prepared to vote for a practicable scheme of Woman Suffrage, on the lines of the Conciliation Bill. In May, 1911, this Bill was brought in by Sir Alfred Mond; it triumphantly passed the second reading by a majority of 167.

In June Lord Lytton had written to Mr. Asquith asking for assurances (1) that the facilities offered for next Session were intended as an effective opportunity for carrying the Bill, and not merely for academic discussion; (2) that the week offered would not be construed rigidly, and also that provided the Committee stage were got through in the time, additional days for report and third reading would be forthcoming; and (3) that there would be reasonable opportunities for making use of the closure. To this Mr. Asquith replied (on Friday, June 16, 1911) :—

" MY DEAR LYTTON,—In reply to your letter on the subject of facilities for the Women's Enfranchisement Bill, I would refer you to some observations recently made in a speech at the National Liberal Club by Sir Edward Grey, which accurately express the intentions of the Government.

" It follows (to answer your specific inquiries) that 'the week' offered will be interpreted with reasonable elasticity, that the Government will interpose no obstacle to a proper use of the closure, and that if (as you suggest) the Bill gets through Committee in the time proposed, the extra days required for report and third reading would not be refused.

" The Government, though divided in opinion on the merits of the Bill, are unanimous in their deter-

mination to give effect not only in the letter but in
the spirit to the promise in regard to facilities
which I made on their behalf before the last General
Election.

"Yours, etc.,

"H. H. ASQUITH."

This letter was further certified in August :—

"MY DEAR LYTTON,—I have no hesitation in
saying that the promises made by, and on behalf of,
the Government, in regard to giving facilities for
the 'Conciliation Bill,' will be strictly adhered to,
both in letter and spirit.

"Yours sincerely,

"H. H. ASQUITH.

"August 23, 1911."

This promise, after the phenomenal majority in
the House of Commons, was a solemn pledge made
by Mr. Asquith to be fulfilled in the next year. It
was a pledge which the friends of women took
absolutely in good faith. On the strength of it,
the truce was prolonged in 1911 with belief in the
guarantee for the following year.

On November 7, 1911, Mr. Asquith announced to
a deputation of the People's Suffrage Federation
that he was going to bring in a Manhood Suffrage
Bill next Session. There was no agitation or
demand for more votes for men ; this was in answer
to the widespread demand of votes for women. The
majority already recorded for Woman Suffrage in
the House of Commons was composed of members

of all political parties. The Government's present policy destroyed this composite majority by alienating Unionists and moderate Liberals. In other words, it rendered impossible the non-party solution of the Woman Suffrage question, towards which we had been working for months. We consented to the Conciliation Bill because it gave virtual equality to women with men, and because it made inevitable the equality of the sexes under any subsequent franchise measure. But we absolutely refused to accept the Conciliation Bill as the accompaniment of Manhood Suffrage Bill.

We and many other of the Suffrage Societies were received in deputation by Mr. Asquith, only to be told the case over again. He had not changed his opinion since 1908. The Manhood Suffrage Bill would make no difference to us, who could bring in an amendment!

The leaders of the W.S.P.U. determined to go on a deputation to the House of Commons on Tuesday, November 21, with Mrs. Pethick Lawrence to lead them. I intended to accompany them as a stone-thrower; the police on Black Friday (1910) had made the other way—that of going on a deputation—impossible for me, unless I were to see death, and this seemed useless. It was an understood thing that this time, if we were imprisoned, we should not hunger-strike.

CHAPTER XVI

I DETERMINED that I would do my work alone. I was afraid that, if I combined with others, I might fail them, through illness, when they counted on me. Some days later Miss Lawless said she would come too, and, as she kindly chose to do the job with me, all was well. I selected a post office window in Victoria Street, on the left-hand side, facing Westminster. I went to buy some stamps there the day before to make sure of my bearings. I studied all the windows where it would be safe, and where not safe, to do the work of smashing without hurting anyone inside.

A friend, Mrs. MacLeod, came to see me the evening before, November 20, 1911. She brought me flowers, lovely lilies-of-the-valley and two bunches of violets. She told me she had bought them in Piccadilly from a girl that was sitting round the fountain. " They are for a friend of mine who is going to fight for the women to-morrow " ; she wasn't sure she had said it in a way the girl could understand. " Oh ! May God bless her, God bless them all ! Here, lady, take this extra bunch of violets for her." She called this out enthusiastically, as she collected the flowers.

This time I had a small hammer as well as three stones wrapped in paper. The hammer, of course, was

the safest as well as the most efficient of my tools,
but one had to be quite near to the window in order
to use it.   Another dear friend, Dr. Alice Ker, came
to me from Liverpool on the day, Tuesday,
November 21.   She was coming to the fray in
Westminster, but she did not wish to get arrested.
Towards six o'clock we took a taxi and went together
to the beginning of Victoria Street.   Then we got
out and each went our own way.   I walked up and
down the street, first along one side, then along the
other, and I inspected the side parallel streets.
Victoria Street I had always supposed was rather a
long one, but on this occasion it was infinitely short,
and I seemed to pass the same people over and over
again.   Once I jumped into a 'bus to go up again
towards Westminster, and there I came across
many of my friends, who doubtless were going to the
preliminary meeting at Caxton Hall.   At last when
standing, as it seemed to me, for the fiftieth time in
front of a door with pillars, which was our trysting
place, I met Miss Lawless and soon after Miss
Douglas Smith, who had said she would join us for a
little, as she had to go to all who were " active " in
Victoria Street.   We turned into a " Lyons " for
some tea, the whole place was full of our friends and
a detective or two.   A cat was there ; she came to
lie on my lap and I had to turn her off when we
left.

The time was getting near ; we were to wait until
the clock struck 8 ; we were none of us to move
before and not much later.   At last there was a
noise of many people coming round the corner of a
street ; it was Mrs. Pethick Lawrence walking at the

head of her Deputation. A large crowd surrounded
them and cheered them on their way to Westminster.
Miss Lawless and I had taken up our position
already on the steps leading to the post office we
had selected. As soon as the Deputation had
passed, the clock of Big Ben began striking eight.
I said, " I can wait no longer," and I turned and
smashed the glass of two doors and one window. I
raised my arms and did it deliberately, so that
every one in the street could see. Miss Lawless
smashed the windows to my right. We were going
down the steps and I was afraid no policemen had
been near, when two came from over the way. All
was peaceable and friendly. My policeman said to
me with a smile, " I'll take you this way, lady, see ?
And that won't inconvenience you." With that he
adjusted his grasp at my elbow. I said to him :
" Unless you are obliged, don't hurry your pace
more than you can help," and he walked at my pace
through Westminster to Cannon Row. He also
disarmed me, taking my hammer. In Westminster
the crowd was immense and at the bottom of
Whitehall, but we got through all right, and Miss
Lawless kept close behind me.

Cannon Row was already crowded with women.
We stood in a closely packed ring to give our names,
and afterwards our names were called out before we
went upstairs. To my surprise and great delight
Lady Sybil Smith was there. I knew she herself
had been wishing to go on a deputation for some
time. We were taken into the cells to be searched,
but this was not the grim business that it sounds.
We were left to walk quite by ourselves ; a policeman

showed us in and we were put four or five together
in a cell. The door was left open, and a wardress
asked respectfully if she might search us. We said,
" Yes, most certainly," and began to deliver up our
stones. The wardress's face was all kindness, and
no sooner had the policeman gone away from the
door than she burst out with : " Oh ! you ladies,
I'd be with you to-morrow if it weren't for my
child. I am a widow with one child. If only these
politicians knew what that meant ! They can talk
fine about the widow, but when it comes to her
earning a livelihood they don't help her." It
seemed wonderful, she understood. Meanwhile she
was picking out the stones from our pockets. We
were allowed to go back to the central room as soon
as it was finished, we left a friend behind us in
the wardress. Upstairs, in the policemen's billiard
room, we sat in crowds, and everything was notice-
ably different from last time. All was joy and
triumph, and there seemed the echo of these from
the street. I felt quite an old hand, and was going
about the room collecting telegrams ; I had bought a
packet of forms on the chance. A policeman was
singled out and stood waiting for them in a meek and
respectful attitude. One woman, who looked about
sixty or sixty-five, had written a telegram but had put
no signature ; I asked if there was to be none. She
hesitated for a moment and then added : " Well—
put Mother." I thought it must be rather trying
when it was a " daughter," but much more when it
was a " mother," and she getting on in years. There
was a girl lying down in the window recess where I
had gone with my cough last time ; she was ashy

pale. I went up to her and asked her if she felt ill.
Her face immediately lit up with a radiant smile—
"I'm not ill now, but I have been for three months."
I said how wonderful was the feeling of the movement, as one realised the difference which a year
had made it was impossible that one should feel
depressed, though one might be depressed for oneself. "No," she said, "I am never depressed now."
Had she a mother ? "Oh ! mother would be here
too, only she is a cripple."

Mrs. Pethick Lawrence had come and was given
a great cheer. She looked well and beamingly
happy. The Deputation had been much more
hustled about than we who had done damage, but
still, there was no real roughness that I could hear of,
and they had been arrested comparatively quickly.
Mr. Lawrence's welcome face came and he bailed us
out, though it was a long business this time. When
we drove away, every window in Whitehall bore the
mark of the women upon it, with the unmistakable
smashing, till it looked, as I passed, as though
every window smiled.

On Wednesday, November 22, I sent off a telegram, saying that I was arrested, to our organiser
at Liverpool for a meeting at which I was going to
speak. It was a joint meeting of W.S.P.U., National
Unionist and Conservative Suffragists ; Lord Sel-
borne was to speak for the Conservatives. It had
been arranged when we were at peace with the
Government ; that peace was now at an end. I
then went to Bow Street. There were crowds of
women ; we each took luggage and wraps, for
under Mr. Winston Churchill's new rule we were

allowed to wear our own day and night clothes,
and not obliged to have prison food. There was no
difference in being allowed to see visitors or have
letters. Books not dealing with current events
were allowed, but one could not take them out of
prison. At Bow Street we were put into the
big room upstairs ; again a policemen's billiard
room. Large as it was, it was very crowded, and I
kept my seat on my luggage in the passage outside.
Amongst others, there was a little American woman,
whose husband stuck by her like a man till he should
be separated by imprisonment. They had been in
India, had heard much there about the Suffragettes,
and one lady with whom they had dined had warned
him against his wife becoming one of them. I saw
there two Hertfordshire members, which did my
heart good, when I remembered that a little time
ago the whole county was asleep. Whenever I was
able, I sat back on my luggage and wrote letters ;
it was the only way I could escape from talking to
everyone, which was most delightful but I was very
tired. We waited all day to learn in the evening
that we must return to-morrow. I went to my
mother from Bow Street who was staying in London
at that time.

Three times this autumn, after making a speech,
I had been taken with heart-seizure and incapacitated for about a quarter of an hour. On Thursday
morning, November 23, I was ill, on waking, with a
heart collapse. In spite of my best efforts, I could
scarcely hold up my head or speak. Mrs. Francis
Smith, one of my dearest friends, had come to my
rooms to see how I was, and she determined to call

at Bow Street and find out for me if I could not put off going there till the afternoon. She came back, saying that she had had an interview with Inspector A——, who had already shown great kindness to me, and he had said I was not to trouble about the morning, that it would do quite well if I came in the afternoon. I lay down on my bed till nearly 2 o'clock, when I felt much better. Then I went to Bow Street. The woman who did my room came with me and carried my luggage ; she also fetched me milk into the police station. She knew several of the policeman personally, so she managed everything very easily. I went on a deputation with Mrs. Haverfield and Mrs. Mansell-Moulin to Inspector A——, to say that unless the women could be told on leaving whether they would be wanted the next day, they would not go away. As this meant finding cells for all of us—we were 220 women in all—probably we should have to be put four or five in a cell together ; it was speedily arranged and we were told that night when we should be wanted ; I was one of those who came the following day. I went again that evening to my mother.

The next morning, Friday, November 24, I woke all right and went to Bow Street quite happily. Before our trial we were taken down into the passage next the police court, and put *vis-à-vis* to the policemen who had arrested us, as at my first trial. The magistrate was Sir Albert de Rutzen, who was too old for his work. Miss Lawless was accused with me. The hammers and stones were shown in witness against us, and the damage estimated at £3 15*s.* Mr. Muskett, the prosecutor, in totalling up my record, mentioned that I had been to Holloway after a deputation to the House of Commons, and in Newcastle I was imprisoned for throwing a stone at a motor car, but he did not mention " Jane Warton " at Liverpool. When I reminded him that he had left her out, he said testily, " Well, I'm very glad if I have." I said it was quite true that I used a hammer and stones to break windows. I realised that this was the only effective means of protest left to us by a Government which boasts of Liberalism and representation where men are concerned, but ignores the elementary principles of representation where women are concerned. Votes and riot are the only form of appeal to which this Government will respond. They refuse us votes, we fall back on riot. The wrongs they inflict on women are intolerable, and we will no longer tolerate them—— Here the magistrate interrupted me ; he could not enter into a discussion on the subject, and referred to the fact that Mr. Asquith had received a deputation last Friday. I said, " I heard Mr. Asquith say he would do nothing in regard to women." The magistrate then advocated peaceful agitation. I answered that this Government have said they will do absolutely nothing as a Government, and Mr. Asquith is exactly where he was in 1908; all our peaceful agitation has been valueless in his eyes. I said that although we committed the acts alleged, we were not guilty of crime, our conduct being fully justified by the circumstances of the case. " I appeal to you, Sir, to vindicate the fundamental laws of liberty which our country has revered for generations," and with that

I concluded. Miss Leslie Lawless said that if to
fight for one's liberty was a crime, she was guilty,
but she pleaded not guilty, as that was the only
protest that this Government understood. Our
sentence was one of a fine of 40s. and 37s. 6d.
damage each, or fourteen days' imprisonment—half
the sentence that I had received when I went to
the House of Commons, doing absolutely nothing
and being mauled by the police.

We were not put into the cells, but again taken
upstairs to a room close to the larger one. There
was my friend, Adela Smith, with Olive Schreiner's
friend, Mrs. Purcell, and Mrs. Tudor, of St. Albans.
All these were not among the condemned, but had
been let in to see their friends. Towards half-past
five Inspector A—— came and told me that
presently a taxi would be round to take me to
Holloway, that there would be a policeman inside,
but that the other two could be any " fellow criminals " I liked. I at once chose Mrs. Leigh, who had
been condemned to two months' imprisonment,
though she was said only to have struck a policeman
in defence of another woman. I was immensely
proud to take her with me. I also chose Miss
Lawless. The policeman was in plain clothes and
very amiable. Miss Lawless discovered that she
had left her purse behind. We went back for it,
and, on arriving at Bow Street, I decided that the
constable should get out with Miss Lawless, put her
in charge of another policeman, then return and
mount guard on us. He was delighted to do this.
From the point of view of our safety, of course,
nothing could have been more absurd ; we were not

in the courtyard of the police-station, and nothing would have been easier than to open the door the other side of the pavement and, with the noise of the street, Mrs. Leigh or I could have escaped. But it was understood all round that this was not the game, and we waited quietly for the policeman to return and, finally, Miss Lawless and the purse.

At Holloway all was civility ; it was unrecognisable from the first time I had been there. There were no reception cells for us, but we were taken at once to our separate cells in D X, where, after a time the Matron, and afterwards the doctor came to see us. Nothing could have been more charming than the Matron—another woman than had been there before. She asked me at once after Miss Davison ; was she coming this time ? The Matron had been at Manchester when the hose-pipe had been played on her. This she asked before two wardresses, and in a voice of sympathetic intonation. I said I did not think she was coming this time, but it would not be long probably before she was in prison again. Then came Dr. Sullivan. His manner was kind, as it had always been, but I no longer felt the same towards him since he had fed some of the prisoners by force. He said at once, after testing my heart, that I could not stay there, but must go at once to hospital. I said I was much more comfortable where I was than in the general ward, and that I could not sleep there. He said he meant to put me in a cell apart. I was then moved over to the hospital side. There on the ground floor was the superintendent officer I had known before. I smiled, but she looked as if she did not recognise me. She went with me

upstairs. " I believe," I said, as she opened a door,
" it is the very same cell I had before." " No," she
answered, " the one next door," and her reserve, to
my great delight, broke down. I unpacked my
flannel sheets, my flannel nightgown, and my long
bed-socks, and made myself ready for the night.
It was almost unbelievable to have so much comfort
in a place which before had been the very acme of
discomfort. They brought me a pint mug of milk
and a small white loaf before the night. It was
about eight o'clock by the time I got to bed, but the
hours, I supposed, were the same as they had been
in Holloway before, and besides, I was dead tired.

The next day, Saturday, November 25, I felt ill
in the morning. The prison was scarce of food—at
least, there were no vegetables ; they gave me bread
and butter and a pudding for luncheon. The
Governor came, Dr. Scott, and he was amiability
itself, I was only to take care of myself. Since all
was made easy, I stayed in bed that day.

The girl who was let in to wash my floor was fair-
haired, with a most pleasant and intelligent face. I
longed to know about her, but a wardress stood at the
door looking on at her work all the time, and I did
not once catch her eye. On Sunday, November 26, I
felt no better and again stayed in bed. The second
doctor, a new man, who was pleasant in his manner,
came to see me. In the morning when I had been
let out to the sink, the little prisoner who washed
my floor met me coming out. My back was turned
for a moment ; she patted my shoulder and said, in
a tone of voice of utmost comfort, " Cheer up ! "
By the time I looked round she was off somewhere

else and no one would have supposed that she had communicated with me. After that I was determined to get some snatch conversation with her when she was in my cell. When she washed out that morning, I said to her—it was always the first thing—" How long have you got ? " " Three years," was the answer. This greatly surprised me, for Holloway was not the place for long sentences, but I could not ask her then, there was not time to tell, only time for bare questions and answers. I asked, " What was it for ? " " Stealing my mother's skirt," she said. This was more startling than ever. Where was the mother's skirt one could " steal " ? But the wardress looked in and we were obliged to stop. On another occasion she told me that she had been very ill on first coming to Holloway, and that was why she had been kept there. Another time she slipped this notice under the door, and signalled to me by opening the gas-jet glass from the passage. On one side of the little torn bit of paper was written, " Z— A—, Boardstil Institution, Hails-bray " ; on the other side, " I shall be glad to hear from you because I have no friends at all and it will cheer me up." I longed to speak to her, but I did not see her again after this. It was my last morning in prison when she put this paper under the door. After I came out I, of course, wrote to her, thanked her for her cheering words to me, asked if I might go and see her, and sent her a little 3*d.* book of extracts from my father's poems. I sent these to the chaplain at Aylesbury and asked him if he would deliver them. He sent my letter back, saying that he would not be allowed to give it, for she

had already chosen as her correspondent her grand-
mother or some old lady. I do not know anything
of her, of her failings or virtues ; I only know that
there was no loosening the net that clung round her
so tightly for three years.

On Sunday, November 26, in the afternoon I
went out to exercise. This was indeed a changed
world. All of us assembled were walking about
arm in arm, as we liked, in rows facing each other,
or round the ground ; some of us went apart in a little
side-walk, all talking to one another, and all, of
course, wearing our own clothes. One or two
wardresses were there, but they were smiling all the
time and chatted with us. One of them asked me
why I had not come to visit Holloway. I told her
that they would not allow " criminals " to come
back except as prisoners, that I had tried in vain.
She said I could come as someone who visited the
cooking places, or something of that kind. I was
afraid I was too well known in Holloway, as I had
paid rather frequent visits to the Governor. I saw
and walked with Mrs. Pethick Lawrence, arm in
arm, and nothing that we did caused any disturbance.

On Monday, November 27, I stayed in bed again,
and at about 11 o'clock the doctor came and
offered me vegetable soup from outside, and massage
from my masseur-doctor, Mr. May. I said surely
that would not be allowed ! He told me that of
course in the ordinary course of things it was not
allowed, but, if I wished for it, he would see what
he could do. I refused all these offers, which were
not, so far as I knew, offered to the others. I heard

after my release, how my dear friends had put themselves about to get me all these things, and how my
servant had brought soup to the prison every day,
which she had made.   I had a tin of biscuits sent in
to me and some orange sweets.   As I was not feeling
well, I was unable to eat these, but I managed to
give a good many to the girls who washed my cell.
I only once got a look into the general ward.   I saw
Mrs. Mansell-Moullin, Mrs. Mansel and others, but
it did not seem to be the thing for the prisoners from
the cells to go into the general ward.   That night
Mrs. Mansel came in to see me from there.   She and
some others were to be released the next day.   She
had suffered from influenza and had a bad time of
it while she was in prison.   We had a long talk, and
she gave me *The Man-made World*, by Charlotte
Perkins Gilman, to read, as a wonderful book
that had just come out.   She was not allowed to
take it out with her.   The publisher, Mr. Fisher
Unwin, had kindly sent me the book, but I had not
yet had time to read it.   I read it that night and
found it all that she had said—a most remarkable
book.   It is dedicated to a man, showing that the
woman's movement has in it nothing, as is sometimes supposed, against men, but only against the
vices of some men.   In a chapter called " Crime and
Punishment," this passage struck me with intense
truth :   " Does a child offend ?   Punish it !   Does a
woman offend ?   Punish her !   Does a man offend ?
Punish him !   Does a group offend ?   Punish them !
' What for ? '   someone suddenly asks.   ' To make
them stop doing it ! '   ' But they have done it.'
To make them not do it again, then.'   ' But they

do it again and worse.' ' To prevent other people's doing it, then.' But it does not prevent them—the crime keeps on. What good is your punishment to crime ? Its base, its prehistoric base, is simply retaliation."

On Tuesday, November 28, I felt much better and went out to exercise in the morning. While there I was summoned to see the Governor. He told me that my fine had been paid anonymously and that I was free. Among my friends there is none that I can think of who would have paid my fine ; my state of health, I suppose, after the forcible feeding, was " dangerous," and it was thought safest to pay the fine " officially." To my great surprise, the super-intendent came with me to my flat. She was very dear but quite " official." As I had packed up my things rather quickly, I felt ill and not inclined to talk much. She told me how very overworked the superintendent officers had been with the 220 Suffragette prisoners there were this time, she her-self sometimes not getting to bed till one or two in the morning. She looked very tired and I felt very sorry for her. It seemed hard that, when they made us prisoners, so much extra work should fall upon the wardresses. When we reached the Duke's Road, I did not like to ask her into my rooms, not knowing who would be there, so I said good-bye to her, kissed her, and begged her to take back the taxi at my expense. This, however, she refused to do ; she pre-ferred to go home by omnibus, and we parted at the front door. I went upstairs and found three of my friends. We were delighted to see each other, but they soon went away, and I rolled wearily into bed.

I frequently had to lie up during the winter and spring months that followed. On May 5, 1912, I had a stroke and my right arm was paralysed ; also, slightly, my right foot and leg. I was taken from my flat to my sister Emily Lutyen's house, and for many long months she and my mother and Dr. Marion Vaughan were kindness itself to me. From that day to this I have been incapacited for working for the Women's Social and Political Union, but I am with them still with my whole soul.

And what is this which yet comes to us from the prisons ? The torture of the " Cat-and-Mouse " Act and of forcible feeding ! Oh ! if only people could know what these things signify ! But surely they must understand that they are barbarous practices such as we have not tolerated for long in our prisons. " Cat-and-Mouse " Act—what does it mean ? The prisoner does not eat or drink, nothing to pass the lips ; it may be three days, it may be a week, it may be nine days. Then the prisoner is let out, watched day and night, and taken back to prison, back to hunger and thirst, till she is again at death's door. This they do twice, three times, four times, five times, till life is all but out. Not yet have the Government admitted that they will stop the " Cat-and-Mouse " torture short of death itself. And the forcible feeding—what is that ? The only possible excuse for it is that it prolongs the prisoner's sentence by so many days, so many weeks, and that is all. But heed what it is. I have described it exactly as it was done to me. See what it has meant in the recent case of Mary Richardson. It took eight wardresses and one man to overcome her.

On two occasions it was said: "Twist her arms—the only way to unlock them." They held her feet by pressing in the hollow of her ankles. Occasionally the doctor pressed her in the chest to hold her down. He announced that he was going to use the stomach tube. As he could not get through her teeth, he put his fingers to the extremity of her jaw, and with his finger-nail deliberately cut her gum and cheek until her mouth was bleeding badly. He then inserted the gag and stomach tube, but she was so choked by the process that he stopped the feeding, and said he would return to the nasal tube. This is inhuman, like the feeding of a beast—no, of an insentient thing. Where is the gain? A week or several weeks more of imprisonment, and you have let in torture to our form of punishment; yes, and repeated torture, for these prisoners are let out by the "Cat-and-Mouse" Act, and, on those ghastly terms, the police will mount guard on them to seize them again if, according to their judgment, they have regained sufficient fitness.

And why are these women imprisoned? Because they and many thousands, or rather several millions, of women with them, have asked for the vote, but the Government would not give it to them. For forty-five years women have supported their demand in Parliament for enfranchisement with ever increasing vigour. Petitions, processions, meetings and resolutions all over the country were infinitely greater in number than have been achieved for any other reform. When the Conciliation Bill was framed, women waited to see what the Government would do for them; the vote on the second reading

of the Bill, for the second time, was immense.
Women listened to the pledges of the Government
and they seemed to hold out a certainty of the vote.
Now, when these promises have all been broken,
women have taken to burning empty houses, railway
stations and stacks, though they have respected
life and refrained from wounding, as men would
do for far less a cause. Yes, and they will burn
buildings until they are treated rationally as an
equal part of the human race.

I hear the cry go up from all parts of the country,
" How long ? How long ? " The time is fully ripe,
when will women be represented in Parliament by
the vote, equally with men ?